PASSAGE TO A HUMAN WORLD

How immense resources are being created now that people and societies are learning to change to become more productive—with the unrecognized result that the whole world is rapidly becoming wealthy.

PASSAGE TO A HUMAN WORLD

Max Singer

HUDSON INSTITUTE
INDIANAPOLIS, INDIANA

Designed by Robert Sugar, AURAS Design, Washington, D.C.
Manufactured in the United States of America

ISBN 1-55813-000-4
Library of Congress Catalog Card No. 87-82068

This book may be ordered by

Writing to:
Hudson Institute
P.O. Box 26-919
Indianapolis, Ind., 46226

or

Calling 1-800-962-2962

To my father, Sumer Wolf Singer,
who died before I studied these things;
and to Herman Kahn,
who died before I published them.

"Resources"—tangible and intangible—are what we use to meet our needs and protect ourselves from nature, and to learn and to educate ourselves.

●

Most resources are created by people and societies, primarily by learning how to produce more effectively.

●

From the beginning of human life until about a century ago all human societies were poor—they had so few resources that most peoples' lives were dominated by nature.

●

What is happening in history now is that we are in the middle of the few centuries during which we began to learn how to be more productive and during which that understanding is spreading throughout the world.

●

During our time people are creating enough resources to make the world wealthy. That is, we are making a world that has enough resources so that most people can live fully human lives—the way the world will be for the rest of history.

The finiteness of the Earth does not doom us to a scarcity of essential raw materials or to a polluted environment. The "spaceship Earth" and "limits to growth" visions come from a misunderstanding of the facts of the physical world.

●

These visions are part of an "edifice of error" that diverts us from the real challenges we face as we complete the "passage to a human world"—to make the human worlds of the future good worlds.

●

The apparent public consensus supporting this edifice of error, despite clear evidence and expert opinion to the contrary, shows that this edifice is a symptom of something wrong.

●

I hypothesize that the edifice of error about the physical condition of the world is the result of low national morale among those Americans responsible for ideas and public discussion—people whose jobs put them in the category of "university-oriented Americans"—a category which includes ten per cent of our population who see the world very differently than other Americans.

List of Tables

Text-Tables

End-Tables

ACKNOWLEDGEMENTS

T HIS PROJECT STARTED, with a grant to me from the Sloan Foundation more years ago than either of us would like to remember—when I was still at the Hudson Institute. The project originally concerned work on how public policy should respond to both the reality and the public perception of subtle environmental risks. I have followed this issue in unexpected directions. What was originally intended to be the focus now appears as part of chapter thirteen and Appendix E, but the whole work can be seen as addressing some of the original issues. In any event I am grateful to the Sloan Foundation, both for its generosity and for its patience.

The first draft of the book, with its current scope, was written during the pleasant year that I spent as a Visiting Scholar at the Russell Sage Foundation in New York. I very much appreciate both the financial and intellectual support given to me by that stimulating institution.

My debts to Hudson Institute and to my many friends who have worked there recently and in the past are too numerous and complex to spell out. Of course I have to mention Herman Kahn—although, like practically everybody who knew him, I always think of him as "Herman" and have a hard time using his full name. Many of the ideas here were his, or grew out of our years of glorious talks together at Hudson. (Conversation with Herman was always such fun that it was hard to get to the business at hand.) Also I learned more from Frank Armbruster than I know, especially about the great majority of people in this country who are not "university-oriented Americans."

The main thing about Hudson I learned only years later, that it was not like other places. What seemed ordinary and natural there was in fact very rare and valuable, and I am very grateful to have been a part of it.

Without the encouragement and confidence of my editor, Herbert E. Meyer, this book would not be out now, so I am very grateful to him. And also to Robert Sugar, the book's designer, who contributed more than designers usually do—and pleasantly.

The final acknowledgement must be to my wife Suzanne and to my sons, Saul, Alexander, Daniel, and Benjamin, whose loyalty and love have sustained me, and each one of whom has given me comments that have improved the book.

F O R E W O R D

ONE OF THE EXTRAORDINARY ironies of post-World War II American history is the simultaneous occurrence of rapid economic growth and rampant economic pessimism. Just why this should have happened, future cultural historians may (or may not) understand better than we do. Perhaps they will be able to see through what Max Singer calls "the edifice of error" more penetratingly than we now can. On the other hand, it could remain one of those teasing paradoxes that history not infrequently offers up to us. What is beyond doubt, as Max Singer convincingly demonstrates, is that there is a paradox here, an anomaly that may yet turn out to be of great political importance.

The reality of economic growth over the past four decades is as substantial as it was surprising. Those of us of a certain age can still vividly remember the deluge of books—by liberals, socialists, Marxists of various kinds—in the 1930s, all explaining that the Great Depression could only be overcome by some version of a "planned economy," and that such a radical reorientation of the American economy (and the American polity as well) would then "unleash the productive forces" held in check by "capitalism." The end of World War II witnessed a continuation of this intellectual trend, as it was generally anticipated by almost everyone that the "war boom" could necessarily be followed by a resurgence of the Depression. It didn't happen—and it has continued not to happen. Instead, economic growth has brought the American people a standard of living that once would have been regarded as beyond human reach. If one goes back to the "progressive" literature of the 1930s, and looks at their most optimistic scenarios for a "planned economy," one finds that our economic reality far surpasses their most extreme expectations.

One could understand if our satisfaction with this remarkable economic performance was tempered with concern for some of the more disagreeable social changes that have accompanied it. The world is a complex place, and all changes for the better inevitably give rise to some unanticipated changes for the worse. No one in the late 1940s, having been provided with advance, "inside" information on the course of the American economy in the future, would have dreamed that increasing affluence would be accompanied by a massive increase in crime, drug addiction, teenage pregnancy, etc. Economic prosperity, in and of itself, has only an oblique relation to that rather vague thing we call "happiness"—as Max Singer well knows. It would not be astonishing, then, if a certain measure of skepticism with regard to the unqualified merits of economic growth were to emerge. There has been some of that, mainly from traditional conservatives who have never been enthusiastic about economic growth in the first place. What *is* astonishing, however, are the waves of skepticism and pessimism about the very possibility of continuing economic growth itself. Even as this growth (however unevenly and irregularly) takes place before our very eyes, we are swamped by apocalyptic forecasts that explain why it couldn't have happened and, since it did, why it is but a transient illusion. The United States today is populated by a large, educated class—often, though inappropriately, called "elites"—that takes comfort in predictions of disaster.

Since these people speak with the authority of "scientists" or "social scientists," they are bound to make an impression on public opinion—to make the American people feel unnecessarily uneasy. It is important, therefore, to get the facts right, to set the record straight, and to demonstrate that there are many good reasons for thinking that our human future, at least in material terms, is more likely to be better than worse—around the world, not just here in the United States.

Getting the facts straight is the task Max Singer has set for himself. It is a double task: first the destruction of long-held myths, then presentation of a realistic alternative. I think he has accomplished this double task with distinction—especially because he gives a common sense basis for understanding why his picture of what is happening in the world is realistic, and what is producing the world he describes.

There is much in our future we can reasonably be worried about. Mr. Singer shows us why there is much in our future we have good reason to be confident about—and provides real benchmarks for telling what it is that we can be confident about in our "passage to a human world."

—Irving Kristol

PART I

The Passage

What Is Happening in History

There are three kinds of optimist. First there is the fan who boldly predicts at the beginning of the season that the home team will win the pennant—a predicting optimist.

Second there is the small child who says happily, "life will be wonderful when I have a puppy"—a defining optimist.

Finally there is the girl lost in the woods at night with her small brother who consoles him by saying, "don't worry, morning will come and it will be light again"—a recognizing optimist.

I plead guilty of being a "recognizing optimist."

WHEN YOU ARE WALKING through woods where you have never been before, sometimes it is good to climb to the top of a tall tree so that you can see where you are in the landscape—where you came from and where you are going. In this book we will do the same thing, not in space but in time. Fortunately, once we climb above the woods of current controversies, the lay of the land is so clear and dramatic that we will be able to see where we are in history.

Human history is quite long. But we can cover it in a brief space if we omit the usual gossip about the doings of famous people and only look at news about the life of the millions and millions of ordinary people. Let's look at how few changes there have been in the important features of the lives of most people during the many thousands of years from when the first few of them picked fruit and hunted game on the Earth until the United States declared its independence in 1776.

If you want to know what people's lives are like, the important questions are: Do they have enough to eat? Do they have their health? How are their families? How do they get their living? What are they afraid of? What do they know? What kinds of things concern them most of the time?

Until recently, asking such questions about human life on Earth always produced the same answer: there was surprisingly little news. If an intelligence agent from a distant galaxy visited Earth shortly after people began roaming Africa, and came back for a second visit in 1776, she would have few changes to report after her second trip. Most important, she would note that life expectancy had scarcely changed. It was still everywhere less than thirty years (having risen only a few years).

This single grim statistic tells much about the fundamental nature of people's life experience. It says that few children grew up with two parents, that most adolescents had more brothers and sisters dead than alive, that the person who got to know his grandchildren was rare indeed. So human life was always full of the death of loved ones, and the likelihood of dying young.

After her first visit to Earth—in the time of cavewomen—our intergalactic intelligence agent could have described the basic features of people's lives very briefly. Most people produced what they consumed by monotonous, arduous, outdoor work, and lived in cramped and dirty surroundings. Most of them spent their entire lives not far from where they were born and spoke to no more than a few hundred people before they died—even the rare ones who lived a long life. They were at the mercy of powerful forces which they did not understand. Violence was part of their daily life, and most of the time their thoughts were about the unpleasant side of nature: dirt, disease, and death.

After her second visit, two centuries ago, our intergalactic intelligence agent would have had a few important changes to report—but only a few: there were many more people; they had learned to create large complex societies; a small minority had learned to read and write (an accomplishment that affected many others); and many people had come to believe in God.

The crucial point here is that, when confronted with a realistic description of the nasty details of the way all the ordinary people actually lived until the last century, most of us would exclaim: They lived like animals!

To be sure, our modern judgment that the lives of most people were animal-like is too extreme. People have always been significantly different from other animals; and during our long history we have produced great human creations and achievements which justify pride. But, compared to the human life we experience here today, the human life of the past—or of parts of the poorest countries today, indeed of almost everyone who has ever been born—seems so different that one can easily think of it as more like the lives of animals than like the human life we know.

IF AT THE END of her eighteenth-century visit our intergalactic intelligence agent decided to take one more spin around Earth before going home to report, but first turned away for an instant to sneeze, so that three or four hundred years passed before her final look, suddenly everything would be different. When she[1] looked again—one or two centuries from right now—she would see great contrasts with all her earlier views. For example, she would see that people are plentiful and that many of them are mature or even old. After this "wink in time" most people live nearly their full life span. Life is very precious because few people experience much death in their own family, and most people know both their grandparents and their grandchildren.

And after this "wink," people are doing completely different things than they used to do. They spend a lot of time at what they call work (although most people from human history wouldn't understand how reading and writing and talking to people in comfortable buildings could be compared to the kind of work they had had to do). Most of their thoughts no longer are about the unpleasant aspects of nature, but about man's creations: science, art, politics, commerce, bureaucracy, entertainment, and, sadly, crime and war. Nature is primarily something to protect and enjoy. Sometimes it is a disturbance, but very rarely is it a serious threat.

Ordinary people, after the brief period in which almost everything changed, know something of their own and the world's history. They know something of the other people who share the Earth with them. Sometime during their lives they can go to see almost any place they want. They have a reasonable degree of knowledge of the basic facts about nature. The character and quality of most people's lives depend on the choices they make. Their lives are filled with choices: Where should they live? What kind of work should they do?

In brief, most people live the kinds of lives we are familiar with.

A Human World

No other word as aptly describes the character of the new world into which we are passing as the word "human." The new features of this world are being created by people. In this new world the most basic fact of life—how much of it each person will have—will be determined by the genes of our human species, not by external natural forces that cut human life short. Humans will be plentiful, and their lives will be the kind of lives that we think of as normal human lives—concerned mostly with human creations, not with a constant struggle against nature. Formerly nature dominated man (but not completely); after we finish our current brief passage man will dominate nature (but not completely).

We must still use the future tense to speak of the "human world," because it is not yet true that almost all people in the world live in what we call "human conditions." But we are well on our way to a human world and, since many people have already arrived, there are samples of this world that we can see now. We can get a feel for what a human world might be like by looking at the lives of the people in countries that have already crossed the threshold from poverty to wealth.

Despite the inevitable uncertainties about the future, already we can see that in the "wink of an eye" the world is being changed more drastically than it had been changed in all previous human history. We are living in the middle of that wink. We live today just

4

about at the middle of a period of only a few hundred years, during which mankind is changing the world as it has never been changed before into the way it will probably be from now on.

AMONG OTHER THINGS this perspective tells us to beware of the normal inclination to think of the current situation as permanent. Naturally we think that the world is the way we see it. But the most fundamental thing about the world is that it is changing.

We are now in the middle of a passage from one "place" to another. If you ask a man on a train where he is, he might answer, speaking of the moment, "on the fifth car of the train" or "just East of Pittsburgh." But if he answers with a broader perspective he would say "I am on my way from New York to Chicago." (If you ask him where his family is, he might say "we are moving to Chicago," even though some of the family is already in Chicago and other members haven't yet left New York.)

This perspective can help us to balance the normal static, snapshot view of the world with a broader understanding. For example, we are often told that the world is divided into rich countries and poor countries. This is a little like describing a family as being divided into little people who have no money and have to go to bed at nine o'clock and big people who are allowed to drive the car and stay out as late as they like. The big people were once little, and the little ones will become big.

In a family the current arrangements don't mean nearly as much as a sense of the process that the family group is going through. And since adults are so familiar with the pattern of development and family life, most of us don't usually see families as snapshots, we see them in relation to the pattern of the generations. We compare the ten-year-old daughter not to her fifteen-year-old sister or to her mother, but to ourselves as ten-year-olds, or to other ten-year-olds. We don't look only at where she is, but we see her in relation to where she has been and where she is going. (Of course the ten-year-old, lacking the perspective that comes from experience, sees things differently. She is much more aware of the "injustice" of the moment, and the moment seems much longer.)

If we look at the world with the kind of dynamic, historic perspective with which we look at a family, we would give a more realistic description by saying: "The world is passing from poor to rich. All countries were poor, some countries are already rich, others are nearly there, and others still have farther to go." Because we are now in the middle of the development process that is responsible for our passage from poor to rich, some countries are now widely separated from others. And since we are barely conscious of the process, the current distance between countries seems permanent, and therefore highly unfair and immoral. But to have a reasonable perspective on the moral question, the world, like a family, should be seen as a dynamic process in which today is only a long moment.

"Richer" Not "Better"

The confident statement that we are creating a human world sounds optimistic and arrogant. To see why it isn't, two points need to be emphasized. The first point to emphasize is that the word "human" is not used here in the sense of being the opposite of God. God created people as much as He created the rest of nature. While man is special, man is also part of that nature. There is no reason not to think of man's creations as part of the work of God. There is no reason one has to think that people, by changing the world from nature-dominated to human-dominated, are denying or challenging God—rather than carrying out God's will—or hope.

Second, although we can be confident that the world will be human, we cannot know whether it will be better. This book makes no claim that the future will be better than the past. We humans have amply demonstrated our power to do evil and create unhappiness. Human domination of the world is a challenge, not a seal of success. Change is not necessarily progress.

Richer is definitely useful, it is widely desired, but it is not necessarily better. This book only talks about "richer" and "more human." It leaves the question of "better" to the future.

The future will bring to the world—as has already come to our society—widespread wealth, power, knowledge, and freedom. Our actions in the future will determine whether these much desired qualities will have desirable results. So the future may teach us that what we thought were ultimate values are really only means that can produce either good or bad ends.

The prediction that we are making a human world is a realistic description, not an optimistic hope. (And some people will feel that it is a profoundly pessimistic prediction.) Since no claim is made that everything will be wonderful, or even better than before, obviously the point of the argument is not to make people feel good.

That we are in the middle of the passage from a natural to a human world is the basic fact about what is happening in the world now. The recognition of this fact will produce different feelings in different people. The purpose of the book is not to make people feel one way or the other. It is only to help people to see the facts. The only conclusion intended is that anyone who wants to be concerned with the great problems of the future should worry less about the physical limits of "Spaceship Earth," and pay more attention to the problems that human beings create for themselves and for each other. In a human world the main dangers, also, are human creations.

Dangers of Modernity

In a natural world the primary dangers were to our bodies. The four horsemen the Bible listed as threats to mankind were famine, plague, pestilence, and war. In the more human world we are bringing, only one of these—war—will be left. And perhaps the primary dangers we will face will be to our character.

The four horsemen we have to fear in the future will be wealth, power, knowledge, and freedom. These are all desirable— therefore they are goals we work to achieve. Nevertheless they also undermine important traditional influences that strengthen human character. Therefore our success in achieving these goals creates an important problem.

The child doesn't know about the world, and the adolescent doesn't believe it. It is in the nature of things, and inevitable, that growing up means learning to accept reality—which is that each of us is vulnerable, has only limited power, and must share the world and attention with many others.

In the traditional, natural, poor world these lessons came early and were never far away. Everybody was either harshly buffeted by the reality of nature—hunger, cold, and dangerous animals—or keenly aware of how lucky they were to escape. And death was everywhere. Nature's harshness was inexorable—and whining or cajoling brought no relief.

The protection that clothes and buildings provide against cold is a metaphor for the protection that money gives us from reality. Millions of children can't imagine a refrigerator that is not full of food. ("Starving" is how you feel after playing football before having dinner.) And the world is full of salesman who work hard to make people who have money feel that they are important and cared for.

Strength and character come from the experience of overcoming adversity—directly or vicariously. Throughout history two important forces that helped to shape people's character were (1) personal experience with nature and adversity, and (2) cultural responses to poverty and danger. But affluence largely destroys nature's opportunity to discipline our character, and to teach us a number of harsh but useful lessons. It eliminates many kinds of adversity. And in the modern world many of the specific sayings and stories through which we receive the teachings of religion, philosophy, and literature increasingly seem anachronistic and irrelevant, and are therefore much less potent teachers.

Other aspects of a modern, human world—such as its cosmopolitan economy and its reliance on computers and other machines—can also threaten traditional bases of shaping healthy characters. Therefore one of our greatest tasks is going to be finding new bases for helping people to develop good characters.

Perhaps the characteristic dangers in a human world are decadence and arrogance. Decadence is the unhappiness that is caused by weak character and inability to resist temptation. The other danger that wealth seems to produce is an unrealistic and undisciplined idealism that seeks to make the world over without regard for consequences. What most of us will have to fear the most in a human world will be lack of enough strength of character to discipline our minds and bodies so that we can have the joy which comes only from knowing we are using ourselves as best we can to discharge our responsibilities as human beings.

Trends vs. Patterns

Some people may ask: What kind of tree has this fellow climbed that lets him see the future? The general answer is that if we can see that a powerful process has been shaping events, and if that process is still working and has no reason to stop now, then it is not very bold to predict that the process will be completed. It is as if a thrown ball were in mid-flight; no one would hesitate to predict where the ball is going. This book describes a process now dominating history that is almost as clear as the path of a thrown ball.

Of course there can be no guarantees of the future. Just as a ball can be knocked off-course, so the process now bearing us towards a human world could come to an abrupt end. For example, it could not continue if a meteor hit the Earth with enough energy to destroy human life or the Earth itself. But barring some extraordinary and unforeseeable development we can confidently expect the completion of the current process.

I should emphasize that this approach of predicting the future by trying to understand the processes now at work is very different from a crude extrapolation of trends. If I were merely extrapolating trends I would have to say that a ball that is thrown upwards would continue upward forever. But if I understand the forces working on the ball as it flies through the air I can use its path in the past to predict its path in the future, even though the direction will change. This is only possible to do by understanding the process at work well enough to ask the right questions to judge whether it will continue.

THE PROCESS that is working now to build a human world is the spread of understanding of how to create wealth. The word "wealth" refers to economic resources. It carries no implications either of happiness or of caviar and polo ponies.

Throughout this book we will use words like "poor" or "wealthy" in relation to all people, not just to the people of a particular time or place. And we will define as "wealthy" any society which has enough resources so that its people live in what we now think of as human conditions. And we will call "poor" any society that does not have enough resources to provide such decent human living conditions—and this includes all past societies.

The first purpose of the book is to describe this process of creating and spreading wealth which is driving history today. A summary follows; and the next three chapters give a more thorough description and explanation.

Creating Wealth

About two centuries ago some societies began to learn how to increase the productivity of human work and thus to become wealthier and wealthier. Since then the first societies to learn have continued to apply what they had learned, and continued to learn more, so that their productivity has continued to grow and their wealth has continued to accumulate. Also, one after the other, other nations have begun to learn how to steadily increase productivity. Some are doing it fast and catching up; others are going more slowly. Some haven't started yet and others have started and then fallen back. But all nations are going along essentially the same path, starting from poverty, learning gradually to make the changes necessary to be more productive, accumulating wealth, and adjusting painfully to the changes.

Until about a hundred years ago there were no wealthy societies. Today almost one quarter of the people of the world live in wealthy societies. Because one can understand the process by which this tremendous amount of wealth was produced, one can have great confidence that the much greater amount of wealth required in the future will also be produced.

In about a century—or perhaps two—the great majority of people will live in countries that have crossed the threshold from traditional poverty to wealth that is sufficient to provide human lives for their people. No one can know how much further the wealth accumulation process will go after that, or what patterns it will follow.

In the long run, after the next century or so, the main problems of the world will be the problems of a wealthy world. Our national experience teaches us that such problems can be very difficult and cause much suffering, but they are very different from the problems we are used to thinking about—those that come from the fact that there are not nearly enough resources to go around.

Most briefly, one can say that about two centuries ago the people of some countries learned how to use human effort to create wealth with increasing efficiency. Today we are in the period during which that understanding, and the social change it produces and needs, is spreading gradually and unevenly from country to country, and being applied, so that more and more countries have begun the process of increasing their productivity and of creating more wealth.

THE PROCESS that is now creating and spreading wealth is important for understanding the present as well as predicting the future. For this process of economic change explains much that concerns us. The basic thing that happens in economic development is that people become more valuable. As a society becomes modern and wealthy, people and ideas multiply, but the output of field and factory multiplies faster.

So, compared to physical things people become scarcer, therefore more important, and more valuable. High productivity, the basis of wealth, means that our time becomes more valuable when we sell it, just as other people's time becomes more expensive when we buy it. Productivity requires integration into larger, more complex economies, as well as constant change. One result is that it is no longer possible to use the fixed ideas and traditions of many different cultures to shape our lives.

A few simple forces—more people and longer life, increasing wealth making so many things widely affordable, higher value of people's time, constant change, greater integration—drive most of the social changes we are concerned with. A large share of social commentary is removed from reality by a failure to recognize the source and power of these few forces.

Does the Earth Have Enough Room?

Does all this confident talk of a wealthy world ignore the widely voiced concerns about population growth, about the future scarcity of raw materials as we consume more and more nonrenewable resources, about the danger of pollution ruining the natural environment, or about increasing risks to human life from modern science? It does not. The bulk of this book is devoted to these issues. The conclusions here are based on an examination of these concerns, and are consistent with almost all the particular pessimistic estimates which have any basis in reality. But they are put into a more complete perspective.

For example, Lester Brown, head of Worldwatch, a leading doom-sayer, has frightened people with the specter of a disastrous erosion of the topsoil essential to the growth of our food. One who has heard about Lester Brown's works might think that the statements below about the feasibility of feeding vastly larger populations are much too optimistic because they fail to take into account the problem of topsoil loss. But in fact Brown's pessimistic estimates of topsoil loss don't contradict the confidence expressed here about having plenty of food in the future. Brown himself agrees that, even if his predictions come true, soil erosion would not be enough to noticeably increase the long-term cost of food.*

Later chapters are in effect a nontechnical review of long-term raw material and environmental protection problems. This review is based on the best academic studies and analyses, and it takes into account the arguments and concerns of the leading pessimists. We will see in common-sense terms the basis for claiming that the real problems for people in the future will be human problems.

It is always easy to point to statistics, and even facts, that can be made to seem very frightening—when taken out of context. But we will also see why the vast public discussion implying that the Earth's resources and environment will be inadequate unless people

---

* Actually the biggest cost of soil erosion probably comes not from the harm to the land the soil leaves but from the harm caused where the soil goes. But these costs, while worth doing something to prevent, are not dangerous.

become radically wiser and better behaved, is in fact a diversion from the real problems of the future.[2]

THIS DESCRIPTION of what is happening in history may, at first, seem bold and controversial. But if you step back and think about it for a moment, you'll realize that it isn't bold and controversial at all— in fact it is rather obvious. Certainly it is obvious that in the last two hundred years the world has become much richer than it ever was before. That is history; there is no way to deny it. (And the life expectancy numbers are an objective measure.)

What seems to be the hard question is whether the second half of the process I describe will happen. Will we have another few centuries of rapid growth of wealth, enough so that most of the world will be wealthy in historic terms? Looking at today's problems the task of making the whole world rich seems extraordinarily difficult, and success may seem very doubtful. But if you compare

TABLE 1
Some Catchy Numbers to Describe the Passage to a Human World

	Before the Passage (1780)	Now (1980)	After the Passage (2180?)
Gross World Product (billions of 1980 $)	$200	$10,000	$250,000
World Population (millions)	800	4,000	10,000
Average Income (GWP/person, 1980 $)	$250	$ 2,500	$ 25,000
Life Expectancy (worldwide)	30 years	60 years	80 years

the difficulties of this second half of the job with those of the first half, they don't seem so formidable. After all, for two hundred thousand years people weren't able to begin the first half of the job. Then it was done in two hundred years. Why isn't it reasonable to think that we will do the second half of the job about as quickly as the first half? Are we much worse than we used to be? Table 1 shows why it is not unreasonable to say that "the first half" of the job has been done.*

Of course the second half of the job of moving from a poor, natural world to a rich, human world may go more slowly. But if it takes twice as long as the first half it wouldn't change the picture painted here.

TABLE 2
Comparison of the Amounts of Change

	1780 to 1980	1980 to 2180(?)
Gross World Product grows: *that is, overall it:*	2% per year *multiplies by 50*	1.6% per year(?) *multiplies by 25*
World Population grows: *that is, overall it:*	.8% per year *multiplies by 5*	.5% per year(?) *multiplies by 2.5*
Average Income grows: *that is, overall it:*	1.2% per year *multiplies by 10*	1.2% per year(?) *multiplies by 10*
Life Expectancy grows: *that is, overall it:*	.35% per year *doubles*	.14% per year(?) *grows by 30%*

So it is not bold and controversial to think that most countries will achieve wealth—by historic standards—within a few more centuries. That achievement is less demanding than what was done in the past.

All I am doing is pointing to two simple facts: (1) for a very long time the world was poor, and pretty soon it will be rich;** and (2) there is a big difference between being rich and being poor. These facts lead to the conclusion that the short period we are living in now is a passage between the kind of life people lived throughout the past and the very different kinds of lives that many people are

---

* Of course there are other ways of counting which could lead someone to say that only a much smaller fraction has been done so far. But I think a better case can be made that we are more than halfway there.

** I think in about a century; but even if it takes two or three more centuries it would still be "pretty soon" compared to how long it took before we started.

living today, and that most people will live in the future.

In other words, when you think about them, some obvious points lead to a very dramatic conclusion.

THIS PERSPECTIVE—which sees our time as dominated by the dramatic passage to a human world—raises another question: Why haven't we noticed? There is a mountain outside our window and practically nobody has seen it. Certainly our children are not being taught the basic fact about the world today: that we are in the middle of a passage from a natural world to a human world. What prevents us from seeing the main thing happening in the world? Why do we not have any understanding of the basic nature of the process of growing and spreading wealth that is now driving history and changing our lives?

The answer is that what I call an "edifice of error" blocks our view. This book will examine this huge structure of popular misunderstanding, to show that the view of the future given here is not a boldly optimistic prediction, but a straightforward description of what is happening in the world—based on standard, noncontroversial data and on high quality, well-reviewed scholarship.

The book presents only a few new ideas; it is not a controversial new theory, but an integration and presentation in common-sense terms of the solid work of leading experts.

But just as colors such as red and black have become associated with political points of view, so have some ideas about the physical world. As a result it is hard to talk about some things, like resources and pollution, for example, without seeming to be making political points. Recognition of the real facts is resisted by some because of possible political implications.

In Part IV—after having described the edifice of error by showing why many "facts" or ideas that are widely accepted are not really true, or don't have the significance usually given them—I will present an hypothesis that may help to explain why this book is necessary (that is, why everybody doesn't already know what it says).

T W O

The Nature and Sources of Wealth

**Modern wealth comes mostly from intangibles;
"ideas" are more important than any kind of "rocks."**

P EOPLE ARE AMBIVALENT ABOUT WEALTH. Almost everybody has a
prejudice against it but wants more of it. Even most
millionaires don't call themselves wealthy.

You often hear things like: Millionaire X is "not really
wealthy" because he is not happy. Or, "the Joneses are not really
poor because they have a fine happy family." People think that
somehow wealth and happiness should go together, but they
recognize that in fact they often do not. These usages express the
wisdom that wealth is a means to other ends, not an end in itself.

In this book the words "rich" and "poor," or "wealth" and
"poverty," will be used factually without emotional connotations.
"Wealth" refers to economic resources, which can be physical, like
machines or houses, or financial, like stocks and bonds, or even less
tangible, like education or leisure.

The idea of economic resources (or wealth) is so broad that
it is hard to realize how much is covered by such a simple phrase,
everything from a gigantic steam shovel to a computer program,
from an hour of time to a house at the beach. They are all linked
together because they are measured the same way, by their price
in money. One kind of resource can be converted to the other by
selling it and using the money to buy another.

"Poverty" means only "the lack of things that could be bought with money." "Wealth" does not include "the love of a good woman" or "the peace that passeth all understanding," or other things that should be more important to people than wealth. Nor do the words as used here have any moral connotation either way. To say that a country is poor is not a criticism but a description—one that we will shortly make precise. To say that a country is wealthy is not to praise it.

A determination not to think of wealth as an end in itself produces a tendency not to notice how useful wealth is. So people are often reluctant to appreciate how many good things that we normally do not associate with wealth—like health and education—actually depend on wealth (although they do not require nearly as much wealth as we have in the United States). And, partly because we have quickly become used to wealth and take it for granted, we don't give full credit to the power and usefulness of wealth.

A Wealthy World

The word "wealthy" is one of the most relative words in our vocabulary. Now it suggests champagne and racing cars. At other times and places it would have brought to mind a warm place to live. So we must be precise about what we mean by saying a country is wealthy. To do so we will define a wealthy society in relation to the historic passage we are describing.

The "passage perspective" is that human life always used to be one way and after a short "passage" is completed it will always be another way. Life before the passage was *traditional, poor, and natural.* After the passage, life is *modern, wealthy, and human.* These adjectives aren't used to praise or blame. They are chosen because they describe the fundamental and interrelated features of the passage we are making.

Throughout history, when people lived in traditional ways, they had few economic resources and therefore did not have the power to escape from the domination of nature. When societies become modern they can produce enough economic resources to overcome many of the traditional effects of nature on them, and so people can live human lives.

Of course things are too complicated for three words to explain everything. And words have too many meanings to fit perfectly with such broad statements. So it is easy to poke holes in this kind of summary.

TO SEE HOW THIS IDEA is put together, start at the end, the idea of human lives. Although we are using "natural" and "human" lives as opposites, any life must contain elements of both, and there must be a grey area in between. But to make the contrast clear we can use a precise definition of a "human society," and say that all societies that *don't* fit the definition are "natural societies."

The distinction between "human societies" and "natural societies" is given an unchanging meaning by saying that a group of people have a less than truly human life unless:

(1) Their food, living conditions, and medical care are sufficient to keep them reasonably healthy throughout almost the whole human life span.*

(2) Virtually all children receive elementary school education, and most, including almost all the intellectually talented, can obtain a high school education. (This requirement assures that the group is literate and has access to world technology and culture.)

(3) Post-high school education is available for the most talented and industrious, not just for the well-off.

(4) Most people earn their living by working in reasonably comfortable conditions; can take vacations from time to time, can visit or communicate beyond their local area, and can occasionally travel to foreign countries; and have cultural opportunities beyond those which can be created in the local community.

(5) Finally, the economy gives most people some choice about where they live and how they earn their living.

Since all of these requirements can only be provided if a society has sufficient economic resources, we say that a society is

---

* See Chapter 13 for a discussion of human life span.

"wealthy" if it has enough resources to provide a decent human life for most of its people, and it is "poor" if it does not.

It is shocking to realize that none of the great societies of the past were truly wealthy. But when we use our modern understanding of what is possible, in order to say what a wealthy country is like, we see that no society was wealthy before this century. Until about a century ago there was no society where most people lived what we would now call human lives.

Of course a society can be great even though it is not wealthy. Ancient Athens or Rome, the China of the Mings and other successful dynasties, the Mayans, Incas and Aztecs of this hemisphere, and others, were great societies. They had substantial wealth and dazzling accomplishments. But they were not *wealthy societies* if you focus, as we do, on the ordinary people of the society. The great societies of the past had enough wealth to build temples, pyramids, and other monuments to the creativity of man. But before this century no society was wealthy enough to provide a decent human life, such as we have come to expect, for the majority of its members.

It seems peculiar, if not perverse, to say that present-day Ireland and Bulgaria are wealthy, whereas the societies of the past that created so much of our cultural heritage were all poor. The paradox comes from the fact that we are used to thinking of societies in terms of their upper classes, of their special people, of their achievements and contributions to history; we do not usually think about the ordinary people of history.

The proof that all previous societies did not even come close to being wealthy is that the people of no society before this century ever had a life expectancy as high as thirty, while people of all countries as wealthy as Ireland or Bulgaria have life expectancies of over seventy-two (except special cases like Saudi Arabia and Libya). Since life expectancy statistics are calculated by looking at how long *all* the people in a given country actually live, they show a lot about people's living conditions. Although a small number of rich people can have enough money to raise the average income in a country far above what the average person has, nobody can live long enough to raise average length of life much. It is not possible for half of the people of a country to live in traditionally poor conditions and for the country to have a life expectancy of sixty-five.*

So the words "wealthy" and "human" go together to describe the world after the passage because it is wealth that makes it possible for us to live human lives. The word "modern" goes with them partly to refer to time, and partly to refer to the new ways in which a society must operate to be able to produce the wealth to make human lives possible. The use of these words with their favorable connotations is not intended to deny or conceal in any way the pain and horror that may afflict a modern, wealthy human world.

Since we are interested in the passage to a wealthy world we need to keep track of when a society has crossed over the threshold to wealth so that we can know when most of the world's population is in wealthy societies. The only importance of the sharp distinction between poor countries and wealthy countries is to keep track of how far the process has gone toward making all countries wealthy. (And to keep the measure from moving as we change.)

Our point of view is doubly populist. We measure the wealth of each society by the condition of the great majority of the people in it. And we judge whether the world is wealthy by the condition of the societies that have the great majority of people in them.

When we ask: How soon will the passage to a wealthy world be completed? we are not concerned with total wealth or average wealth. We are concerned with the conditions of most people's lives. We are asking: When will most people live in countries where almost everybody lives a human life?

---

* If societies were to stay long at the border between poor and wealthy the sharp distinction we are using would be too arbitrary. It would be necessary to pay a lot of attention to borderline cases, for example where a society may have enough resources to provide a human life for its people but not use the resources in the right way or distribute them fairly. Or where a society has begun to have enough income so recently that all the effects are not yet spread through the society. Or where a borderline percentage of the population—two thirds or three quarters— has decent living conditions, but a large share does not.

But we don't have to pay much attention to dilemmas about the borderline because most societies don't stay there very long; they keep getting richer until there is no doubt that they are "wealthy." The only question about the borderline is exactly when it was crossed—which, of course, is not critical to the idea of the passage.

ON THE OTHER HAND, this book does not address the question of how to be sure that everyone shares. There are poor people in many rich countries. The problem of poverty in a wealthy society is a special problem of great importance, but it is not the subject of this book. Neither is the possibility that even after almost all the world is wealthy there will be twenty or thirty or forty countries, with 10% or 20% of the world's population, that continue to be poor for generations. There is no way of knowing whether that will happen, or if so, what the reason will be. But even if there is so much poverty left, the world will have completed the passage to being a wealthy world. It will have to confront the problem of poverty in a wealthy world, just as we have to confront the problem of poverty in a wealthy country.

Some things about the future are easy to predict, but most are impossible. This book only describes the major, obvious development of the future; everything else is unknown. The main development is that the world will be wealthy. We can't know much about the wealthy world, and one of the things we can't know about it is the amount of poverty it will have.

Ideas vs. Things

Two different perceptions about the nature of productive wealth are possible. One perception is the old-fashioned and obvious one: things like fertile land, rich oil deposits, and large stocks of gold are what comprise real wealth. The alternative perception, which is the modern view of productive wealth, is that wealth is mostly intangibles, for example, the characteristics of a people—such as their culture and their education—that enable them to create wealth gradually from whatever things they have. In a word, *the modern view is that most productive wealth is not "rocks" but "ideas."*

Much of the edifice of error which blocks our view of the real world is built on the unexamined, old-fashioned perception of wealth as "things." This out-dated perception has many important implications. If wealth is things it is natural to wonder whether more can be created. Where can the things people need come from except from other things? Any particular thing can only belong to one country at a time. If wealth comes from things it is natural to think that the poor can only get wealthy if they get things from rich countries. And the suspicion is very easy that rich countries' wealth came from taking things that somehow belonged to, or should have gone to, poor countries. (After all, the countries of the world used to be much more equal.)

All in all, the old-fashioned perception of the nature of wealth leads easily to a paranoid view of the world, full of fears and pessimism. For people in rich countries the old-fashioned perception can also easily lead to feelings of guilt because our things seem to be what others need.

Of course seeing wealth as primarily coming from things also leads to the fear that resource scarcity will prevent wealth from spreading to the rest of the world. Part II will show why this fear is unrealistic.

The modern perception of wealth, which sees it as mostly coming from ideas, has a number of happy implications; that wealth is unlimited, that it can be created everywhere at the same time, and that our wealth doesn't conflict with others' wealth but is more likely to add to it.

This perception about the nature of wealth also fits naturally with a positive and creative response to the world, and with good and optimistic general feelings; but it does not preclude realistic pessimism about specific problems or dangers, or realistic appreciation of the human costs involved.

The most significant implication of seeing that wealth comes from ideas is the theme of this chapter: *A nation's path to wealth is primarily a "national learning experience."* (Of course words like "ideas" and "learning" are intended as metaphors standing for a very broad range of activities.)

What I call "national learning" is not primarily a matter of technical information. Social and cultural change are a much more critical part of the national learning experience than acquiring information and technology. Economic growth comes from people learning to work better; but many people are not really free to work better without gradual and often subtle changes in their society. The culture that admires truth and effectiveness, at least at work, will produce more than the culture that prefers observance of traditional forms and cares little about truth and effectiveness. Most work is done in organizations—particularly after the beginning stages of economic development; so the way people work and relate to each other in organizations is a key to improved productivity. Obviously this reflects the culture.

Social and cultural change are inevitable results of increasing wealth, and they are also necessary for a society to be able to become more productive and thus wealthier. Such change is the most painful part of the process.

Compound Interest and the Accumulation of Wealth

Two links are necessary to connect learning and wealth: the accumulation of capital, and compound interest. While wealth is not limited by any shortage, the speed with which a nation can become wealthy is limited. Questions about the future of wealth are not: How much is possible? but: How fast? What rate of income growth is possible for each nation at any time?

The accumulation of capital includes both things and ideas. "Capital" means both money and nonmonetary resources that are useful for production. Experience, learning, and machinery are all capital. They embody work done in the past that is adaptable to do work in the future. Capital is created when a country doesn't consume all it produces, but saves some of that production to produce more in the future.

Saving isn't easy. It requires giving up things that people want. It is especially hard for poor countries to save, but even in very rich countries like the United States most people find it hard to reduce their consumption to save more. In fact the United States has one of the world's lowest saving rates.

Saving is easier if your income is going up, so that you can increase your savings while continuing to increase your consumption. But whether it is easy or hard, accumulation of capital is necessary, and each country must decide for itself how fast it will accumulate capital by deciding how much of production will be consumed and how much will be invested. This decision, which is only partly governmental, is a major influence on how fast the country becomes wealthy.

The fact that according to financial accounts a nation must save to increase its capital is only part of the story. Since wealth comes in part from changing attitudes and values in the society, there are crucial gains in productive power that are not the result of saving. One can think of economic development as two parallel processes—the process measured in financial reports, involving saving and the accumulation of capital, and the intangible process of community development toward a social environment that supports increased productivity.*

The awesome power of compound interest is not generally appreciated. Throughout almost all of human history there was no broad, sustained growth. So a sustained (that is, average) rate of growth of 2% per year over a long period of time is rapid growth—and a tremendous force for change. 2% per year means doubling every thirty-five years and multiplying nearly eight times in only a century. Therefore, although growing at 2% per year sounds almost like standing still—especially for a country whose average income is only $400 a year while the average income in the rest of the world is $3,000—a 2% growth rate is powerful force for change.

TABLE 3
Evaluating Long-Term
National Growth Rates

(all growth rates are average per person rates)

Rate of Growth	Evaluation	Result in 50 years
2%	"good"	multiplying 2.7 times
4%	"rapid"	multiplying 7 times
6%	"extraordinary"	multiplying 18 times

Table 3 is one standard for evaluating long-term rates of economic growth.

* While the second is not measured it too can be thought of as a rate-limited accumulation of intangible "capital"; it may well be more important than the first.

25

A country that starts with an annual per capita income of only $500 and grows at 6% per year will have an average income of $9,000 in only fifty years (not counting any inflationary change).*

Few countries are able to maintain 6% per year for fifty years, maybe only Japan and South Korea, and they haven't yet done it for that length of time. But even 2% is revolutionary. The British were the leaders of the world for many years largely because of their economic growth, and they never exceeded about 2% for long. Long-term U.S. growth rates, per capita, before this century were not nearly that high. The great growth of U.S. economic power came not because of extraordinarily rapid growth of per capita income, but because immigration made our population increase rapidly.

THERE ARE MANY DIFFERENT kinds of evidence that ideas and other intangibles are more important than things for producing wealth. The simplest is to notice that a couple of centuries ago the world had many fewer people and their income was equivalent to less than $400 per year. That is, the average person lived the way someone would live today spending $400 per year. (Yes, it really was as bad as that—or worse.) The world hasn't acquired any new physical resources since those days, but now there are about five times as many people, with an average income nearly ten times as high. The world is now wealthy enough to make possible fifty times as much consumption each year as there was two centuries ago. Since the physical resources available are the same (and some people would erroneously say they are less because of what has been used) it must be intangibles that enable us to produce so much more.

Another way to get the same message is to look at which countries have been most economically successful since World War II. The outstanding performers have included Japan, South Korea, and Singapore; a large, a medium, and a small country each

---

* There is a convenient way of estimating the results of long-term growth rates. The time it takes for something that is growing, to grow until it is double its original size, is approximately 72 divided by the average rate at which it is growing. So with an average growth rate of 4% a country's per capita income will double in 72 divided by 4 years (18 years).

relatively poor in natural resources, each with large numbers of people compared to its arable land. None of these countries has done well because of their natural resources; neither has Denmark, Switzerland, The Netherlands nor many countries.

On the other hand, countries with great natural wealth, such as the Sudan, Zaire, or Argentina, have not grown at all well and are relatively poor. (Argentina was one of the richest countries in the world fifty-odd years ago, but then its politics changed and its economic growth largely stopped.) Of course some countries with small populations like Libya and Saudi Arabia, have become wealthy only because of their great oil resources. (And the Pacific island of Nauru has so few people that they are wealthy because of their huge stock of bird-droppings, which they sell for fertilizer.) But overall it is apparent that natural resources are not the principal factors determining which countries are rich and which are economically poor.

I am trying to show that wealth comes mostly from ideas and not from things, but so far my evidence has been only that wealth doesn't come mostly from natural resources. What about other kinds of things? Does our wealth come from tools and machinery, from steel mills, bridges, and dams, and things like that? Yes and no. Obviously these things are important for producing wealth, and are themselves forms of wealth. They are capital. But where did they come from? They resulted from ideas in the form of technology and social organization. The important thing about a dam or a bridge or a steel mill is not the iron or sand and concrete that it is composed of. The important thing is the ideas that people use to put those things together.

Capital embodies work. It is an intermediate step. People use work (mostly ideas) to produce capital and use the capital to produce more wealth.

Resources, people, and ideas are all that exist; so some combination of them must be the source of wealth. At least one of them must change if we are to get more wealth. Which of these has been changing to increase our wealth? Not the original resources; they are fixed. Not the people; their fundamental characteristics are largely what they have been for forty thousand years. (The total number of people has increased, but obviously not the average number of people per person. That is, the increase in the number of people doesn't explain the fact that each of them is richer.) The big change is ideas. Since wealth is multiplying and the only potential source of wealth that is changing is ideas, it must be the ideas that are responsible for the increase in average wealth. New ideas are being created all the time and useful old ideas are spreading. More and more people are learning how to create wealth.

The point that most wealth comes from ideas not from things needs to be belabored because it is so absolutely fundamental, and because the opposite idea is so insidiously natural and common.

We have the same experience domestically as we do internationally. How do people make fortunes in the United States? Occasionally someone discovers gold or oil on his property and gets rich because he has or gets some things. Much more often, the great fortunes result from one or more ideas, from a new way of doing something, or of organizing, or a piece of new technology. Ray Kroc's McDonald's fortune of over $100 million came from a few simple ideas about how to organize to provide fast food (and about how franchising could be used for rapid expansion). Even little ideas, small improvements in the way things are done, can produce large fortunes because ideas make the difference.

Sources of Wealth

Let's think a minute about why the United States is so wealthy. One hundred fifty years ago, when Abraham Lincoln was a young man, this was a poor country. Of course, the land had more gold and coal and iron and oil and topsoil and trees than it does now, and there were fewer people to share this great wealth of resources. But the people were poor. They could not afford to live what we think of as decent human lives.

You might say: The country was poor because it did not have all the roads and dams and factories and power lines that now make our country rich. But why hadn't the Americans of that time built that equipment if they needed it to be wealthy? There are two reasons—which reflect the two driving forces behind the spread of wealth. One is that they did not know how. The other is that accumulating capital takes time. Each year you have to produce more than you consume, year after year.

Since, as I was told by a taxi-driver in Mexico City, "poverty is the result of people not knowing how to do anything," the way to get rich is to learn. Basically, a nation gets wealthy by learning how to be more productive, and then by accumulating capital.

"Productivity" is the key concept; it is the amount of value that an hour's work produces. We are wealthy because an hour of work today produces more than ten times as much as an hour of work in Lincoln's time. Normally, a country can only be wealthy if its people have high productivity.

Obviously the reason we are more productive than Lincoln's friends is not that we are born stronger or smarter than they were. We are more productive because our society has learned things that theirs didn't know. Some of what we have learned is built into equipment like power plants and computers, but most of what we know that makes us so productive is expressed in the overall system that keeps producing new techniques and solving problems.

T H R E E

The Spread of Wealth Around the World

There is an epidemic of wealth. To study it we have to see how one country after another is infected with new ideas, until eventually the whole world becomes wealthy.

THIS CHAPTER SHOWS why we can expect that the three-quarters of the world that is not yet wealthy will become so in the next few centuries. It describes the process by which nations become wealthy—one of the most dynamic and decisive forces moving the world. And it will become apparent why there is nothing about this process that makes it likely to stop before the passage to a wealthy world is completed. In Part II we will deal with one of the potential obstacles that many people are afraid will prevent the rest of the world from becoming wealthy—lack of natural resources. The chapters of Part II explain why we can be confident that sufficient raw materials will be available for the poor nations to become rich.

WHAT IS THE DIFFERENCE between the United States and India that causes one to be so much richer than the other? Let's do a mental experiment. Suppose that there were a miracle and when everybody woke up tomorrow morning all Americans were in India and all Indians in the United States, and there were notices on bulletin boards that the transfer was permanent and everybody had better get used to it. The Indians would have all of our machines and roads and we would have theirs. (And we had also exchanged population size.) What would happen?

Such a thought experiment should not be taken literally. (Nor should anyone think that it reflects smug national or racial superiority.) The point is simply that the Indians would find that they did not know—as a society and, in most cases, as individuals—how to do what is necessary to make our system work. As a result the income of this country would drop sharply.

Even though we may feel that our system doesn't work very well, it is producing at a very high level. It would be many years before the Indians were able to make it produce as much as it does today. The proof that much of the learning is in our society, rather than in individuals, is that if an individual Indian comes to the United States she can quickly learn how to do well, and how to attain high productivity in our system. But when she goes back to India she will not produce as much. The skills learned in the United States may not be appropriate at home, and she can't be as effective without the rest of our system.

It is hard to think of our country as fabulously efficient and productive. Most of us don't think of ourselves as working terribly hard or using wonderfully productive skills. It's clear that most of those around us aren't straining themselves. Many of us are working in jobs that don't seem to produce anything at all. How do all those public relations advisers, foundation executives, stock brokers, and the armies of salesmen and promoters contribute to the national wealth? Much of the success we see richly rewarded seems like just one rip-off after another. Everybody has his game for making money—but how many people produce anything that is useful for people, or for the country?

But we are doing something right. People buy what we produce, much of it in world markets where nobody does us any favors. Hard as it is to believe from what we usually see, our country is productive and efficient. If we can get a feel for why our economy works as well as it does, it will be easier to understand what is required for other countries to grow.

For the Country to be Richer Somebody Has to be Smarter

At the root of increased productivity is continuously improving technology, and improved methods of production. Generally this requires dividing work in new ways or into smaller pieces, and using special tools or specialized labor.* This, in turn, creates a need for better ways to coordinate the specialized work.

The key to understanding what's going on is to realize that the complexity we need to be efficient requires a tremendous amount of coordination and delicate decision making. By analogy this could be called "thinking." We have to buy the efficiencies of specialization by spending a lot on some kind of "thinking" that is necessary to make these efficiencies possible.

But where is that "thinking" being done? Does anyone know who is thinking about how the farmer in Georgia and the fashion consultant in Los Angeles should cooperate to make America rich? It is certainly not the government that coordinates all of our efforts. Instead each of us, whether privately or in the government, thinks about how to get his own job done and how to get ahead, taking into account the situation he faces. In effect, the system that we are all part of is the substitute for the "thinking" we need. "The system" is what does the job of coordinating all of our specialized efforts. And it works automatically, in the sense that we didn't design it and don't pay attention to it (but like our automatic system of digestion it sometimes produces a lot of rumbling, gas, and pain). The increases in efficiency resulting from specialization are so great that we can afford a very expensive system to provide the necessary coordination.

How does nature decide where to plant seeds? It doesn't. It produces ten thousand or ten million seeds to get one adult. It wastes production to save thinking. The amount of nature's waste gives an idea of the value of thinking.

If you ask yourself how you would do the job of assigning

---

* These statements use the language of physical production because that is easier to visualize, but essentially similar factors work in the service sector and in the production of intangible products.

each person, every piece of equipment, all the materials we use each day and deciding exactly how they should all be used, and motivating everybody to do what they should—you will realize how much of a job it is.

We use a system of telling everybody to pursue their own goals more or less. Basically this means that people are guided by the prices of all kinds that they have to pay and the prices they can sell their effort or product for (and by many customs and other values). This technique, which requires all kinds of special gimmicks and controls to operate satisfactorily, produces a complex system that provides the coordination we need. But the system has the side effect that lots of people are doing things that don't seem to be very useful. A better system would have just as good decision making and less decadent silliness and time wasting. But nobody has ever seen a system that was better. (Maybe we should tell nature to stop wasting so many seeds.) Nature pays to be able to avoid thinking by using wasteful production; we pay for our thinking by having a social system that involves a great deal of waste.

In addition to learning things like how to program computers or how to weld plates efficiently, each of us has had to learn how to operate effectively in our system. We can't do well unless we understand how to use the system. Because technology and economic conditions keep changing, the system must keep changing to be efficient. Therefore we have to learn to keep up with the changes in the system. We have to learn to live with change itself. These are demanding tasks. But unless we are skilled at them, we don't do well. And unless many people have these skills, the system that coordinates all the productively specialized labor would not work as well.

The point of the thought experiment about our changing places with the Indians is to show that the primary reason the United States is richer than India is simply that we have already learned to do a lot of things that India has not yet learned. Our society is well adapted to high productivity. The main thing we have learned that adapts us to high productivity is a social system that lets us work together in constantly changing ways.

Can a Country Learn?

The countries that are still poor have had centuries of experience accommodating to mostly static local conditions. In many cases these countries have attitudes, values, and behavior patterns finely tuned to their own conditions. A tremendous amount of difficult "learning" is required for a traditional society to develop the different skills needed in a modern economy.

Of course when India learns how to be more productive it won't learn to do things exactly as we or others do them. The Indians will learn their own way which will be about as difficult for them to learn as our way was for us.

The word "learn" is misleading because it is a single word standing for many processes. Also "learn" suggests that there are clear right answers, which is not always true. *"Learning" is a metaphor to sum up many changes in the thinking and feeling and behavior of individuals and communities.*

But make no mistake about it, the economic development process now shaping our world is best understood as a learning experience—using that phrase in the broad metaphorical way I have described. If you want to understand the spread of wealth around the world, or to predict whether economic development will happen in a country, or how fast; or if you want to understand the obstacles, or what to do to make the wealth spread faster, you need to think about how to predict or influence a *learning process.*

OF COURSE CAPITAL ACCUMULATION is also required for wealth. The need for capital is another reason countries cannot become wealthy in a few years.

Reducing barriers to trade, controlling foreign exploiters, and other financial measures can be useful, but they are not the center of the problem. Certainly natural resources or their lack are not the key to development (except that very large natural resources can make a valuable contribution, especially for a country with a small population). These traditional subjects of the economic development literature may provide practical tasks to work on at the margin, but that agenda should not be allowed to confuse us when we try to get a strategic perspective on the overall task of development.

When we try to understand how a learning process can be responsible for the creation and spread of wealth we see that there are three kinds of learning: (1) discovering, like a scientist; (2) copying or studying, like someone starting a new job; and (3) maturing, like a child:

(1) Nobody built an electric generating station to give young Lincoln light to read by because electricity hadn't been invented. That is, some increases in productivity result from inventions that are new to the whole world.

(2) When an Indian company wants to solve a problem it often doesn't have to invent what it needs. The company can learn from others. That is, some increases in productivity come from changes that are new only to the country making the change. Much wealth comes from the spreading of ideas.

(3) What I call maturing, or development, is the most important and complex form of learning. Why don't we tell children everything they need to know right away? Why does each one have to learn for himself and make his own mistakes? Similarly, if we are rich and India is poor because we know how to be productive and India doesn't, why don't we just tell India what we know, all at once?

It is not possible to jump to the end. Each country, like each person—although for different reasons—has to go through a learning process, step by step. At each point one can only learn to take the next step, not how to jump up to the final level.

(Of course there are many special cases where it is possible to jump ahead to advanced forms without first going through the experimental stages. This is one of the things that make it easier for countries to become wealthy today.)

"Community learning" is the key part of the learning process that enables a country to become wealthy. We are wealthy because we work in a society that has developed (learned) a culture and a system that supports high and growing productivity.

To review. The main difference between rich countries and poor countries is that the rich countries know how to do things that the poor countries don't know how to do. From this it follows that the way a country becomes rich is by learning.

36

Change, Growth, and Pain

People like to see decisions as black-and-white. If something is the right thing to do, it produces only benefits. Looking back it is hard to remember or understand the costs that resulted from making the changes in our society that were necessary to produce the wealth and productivity that we now have. But people should not kid themselves that because a change is necessary it is good for everyone and harms no innocent victims. Even if there were no malice or greed, immense amounts of suffering and sacrifice would be required to achieve economic growth.[3]

The main reason that learning is as slow as it is, is that learning means giving up ideas, habits, and values. Some of the old "learning" that has to be given up or "unlearned" was useful in the past, and is still useful to some of the people in the society. Some of the things that people have to unlearn are traditions that are dear to people, and that may be part of their personal character development. Some of what needs to be are forgotten ways of living that still have important values to people.

Learning means changing. In any society changing means hurting somebody. Sometimes the hurt is small or affects only few people, sometimes not. Sometimes the hurt can be lessened if care is taken, but often that is not possible. So change is often avoided either out of consideration for the potential victims of the change or because those who will be hurt have the power to prevent the change.

The reason that the poor countries haven't learned how to be efficient producers is not that there is something wrong with them. The things that they need to learn are hard to learn because there are resistances that interfere with learning.*

Since even we who live in a modern economy do not really comprehend either the fundamental forces that make our economy work or how to do what economists call "fine tuning," it is not

---

* The reason why an adolescent is slow to learn not to do foolish things is not that he isn't smart enough or hasn't been given the necessary information. The reason is that something in his experience or his mind prevents him from learning until he goes further in his development.

surprising that people from a very different society will have great difficulty when they try to learn from us, mistaking superficial characteristics for the driving forces. Thus a second reason why they don't learn faster is that it is hard to know how to copy.

In science it is said that important old ideas are never defeated by argument; a new idea triumphs only when a new generation that was never attached to the old idea becomes dominant. If that is true in science, where the superiority of better ideas is relatively easy to demonstrate and where there is a moral commitment to truth and to objective thinking, how much more true it is about the values and ideas that guide our personal lives. These ideas and values must be changed for economic development to succeed but it is in the nature of things that there is a limit to how fast such ideas can be changed.

Implications of Thinking about Economic Development as a Learning Process

The first implication is that we can expect that wealth will spread to the rest of the world. If wealth comes from learning, and all countries want to be wealthy and can learn, then all countries will learn and become wealthy. Why not?

The second implication of the learning metaphor is that a country will fail to become wealthy only if it can't learn. Happily there is no reason whatsoever why any country should not be able to learn what all the other countries have learned.

The third implication of thinking about economic development primarily as a learning process is that economic development can not be achieved in only one or two generations. You can give a student the answers to all the questions on all the tests, but that won't mean that he has learned. Learning is a process that has to be gone through, each person and each society in its own way and at its own pace. It takes time. (And, of course, the need for capital accumulation is a second reason why there is a limit to the pace of economic growth.)

Therefore the right question (as with other kinds of learning) is: What speed is possible? What speed is so slow that it implies something is wrong, and perhaps can be fixed? It seems trivial to get bogged down in discussions of interest rates or growth rates, as if we were deciding in which bank to deposit our money. But, since it is change we are trying to produce, the measure by which we must judge ourselves is a measure of change, that is, a rate of growth.

Unrealistic expectations can make people throw success away. If you want people to work harder it is fine to say, You aren't going fast enough. But dissatisfaction that leads to unwise pursuit of faster growth can be dangerous. Unless people understand what rates of progress can be expected, sympathy for the people who are doomed to finish their lives in poverty—because their country is developing so "slowly"—can produce reactions that will turn out to make growth even slower. Unpleasant as it may be to acknowledge a nation may, at least for a while, only be capable of growing at 1%-2% per year (per capita).

The fourth implication of understanding that economic development is primarily a learning process is that outside help must be less important than what a country does itself. We need to handle this implication carefully. It is not an excuse for rich countries to leave poor countries to their own devices.

We have to divide this idea into several sub-propositions:

(1) All poor countries learn a lot from rich countries without any effort to teach them.

(2) Most, if not all, poor countries can develop without any deliberate help from other countries.

(3) Rich country programs designed to help poor countries grow faster can speed the process—but can also slow it down.

(4) The markets and sources of supply that exist in rich countries make it easier for poor countries to grow faster. The more and wealthier rich countries there are, the more benefit there is for the poor countries. (The fact that a statement is self-serving doesn't mean that it is false.)

(5) Rich countries, by trade practices and other measures, can increase or reduce the extent to which their economies are helpful to poor countries.

(6) Economic growth requires not only learning but also physical capital. Rich countries can usefully provide some capital—taking care to avoid causing distortions. But ultimately, most of the capital has to come from internal savings.

The conclusion of all this is that the relation between how much the rich countries can do to help and how much the poor countries have to do for themselves, is a complicated one indeed. But even if it is clear that the rich countries can and should do more, the most important actions are those that the poor countries must take for themselves.*

The fifth and final implication is that for overall thinking about the problem other views of economic development should be rejected or subordinated to the "learning process perspective." People must have one or a few simple metaphors in mind when thinking about how to do something complicated like helping another country to develop more quickly. One might have in mind the idea that growth comes from transferring money or technical information. Or one might think that what growth requires is that poorer countries be given the modern techniques or ways of organizing that are used in modern countries. But, at least occasionally, both of these ways of thinking about the task will be misleading, or will miss an important issue that would be seen by someone who thought of the basic job as helping a society to learn; that is, to change and develop.

that might stop world growth. The fact that there are many complexities, special cases, and uncertainties shouldn't be allowed to prevent us from recognizing how much is reasonably summarized by the simple, metaphoric syllogism: Wealth comes from learning, all countries can learn, therefore all countries will be wealthy.

---

* My personal view is that the United States ought to do more to help the poor countries by reducing trade barriers and by giving more money. I doubt that this does much for our narrow national interest, but I believe it is important—for our broad national interest and beyond it—that we act to express the best parts of our national character, such as our generosity. The main limit on my enthusiasm for increased US efforts to help the poor countries is that too often such efforts hurt rather than help. There is no reason in principle why a large program designed and intended in good faith to speed the economic development of poor countries can not have the effect of slowing that development—in addition to other unnecessary bad effects, and to the waste of the money that we taxpayers could make good use of. In fact, I believe, a substantial part of US foreign economic aid programs have had substantial harmful effects in addition to the benefits they produced. The edifice of error and the low national morale described in this book are responsible for much of the harmfulness of US aid.

Will Wealth Really Spread All Over?

It seems hard to be confident that the whole world will be wealthy soon. Transforming the lives of the vast masses of humanity in Southern Asia, where tens of millions of new children are being born each year, seems like such an immense requirement. Where can all the capital come from? And some of the African countries seem far from being able to build and operate a modern economy. Some are moving backward and are even less able to feed themselves than they were.*

It is hard to believe that in a couple of centuries this will all be behind us, difficult even to remember; just as we have no real memory of how our ancestors lived even a century ago. But the fact that such a change is hard to visualize doesn't mean that it won't happen. To get beyond the stage of wonder—like that of a new father at the idea that the tiny ten pounds he holds in one hand will in only sixteen years become as big as he is—and to think rationally requires a deliberate search for perspective.

First, we should remember what has happened in the twenty-five years from 1955 to 1980. All developing countries together averaged over 5% growth per year for the whole twenty-five years. The GNP of those developing countries more than tripled during that time. Because of population growth, average incomes "only" doubled to $730 per capita. (These figures don't count the high-income oil exporters like Saudi Arabia.) This is an astounding record. No one in 1955 believed that such a long period of sustained worldwide growth was possible.

Second, there are many reasons for thinking the first part of the growth process is the hardest. Recent experience is generally consistent with this idea; the more advanced of the developing countries grew faster than the poorer—on average. Now many of

---

* When I talk to people about prospects for economic development, it seems that often their pessimism comes from being dominated by their very bleak view of Sub-Saharan Africa. But this region is only 10% of the world. Even if its prospects are so bleak, it represents an exception—a special problem—it is not the basic case to have in mind when thinking about economic development. (And there is evidence that at least some countries in Sub-Saharan Africa will be able to develop at quite a respectable rate.)

the poorer countries are almost where the faster growing group was twenty-five years ago, and many are ahead of where they were.

Also, population growth rates are slowing. This means that even if the national growth rates of the developing countries slow down in the next generation, average incomes in those countries can still grow as fast as they have been.

IN THE END THERE CAN BE NO PROOF. Each person finds confidence in his own way. Perhaps we should close this attempt to decide whether the expectation of continued growth is realistic, not with data, but with personal observation of specific examples. In 1980 Richard Critchfield,* a reporter who for many years had been systematically visiting villages in poor countries all over the world, made a tour of twelve of the villages that he had come to know in previous years in Africa, South America, and Asia. To his surprise they all seemed to have turned a corner. Physically and economically they were distinctly better off than they had been—although still agonizingly poor. But more exciting to Critchfield, in all of the villages there was a fundamental change in attitude. Peasants no longer believed that the future had to be like the past. They understood that their efforts could change their lives. As a result they were willing to make the efforts necessary for economic advance.

* See Critchfield's book, *Villages*, published by Doubleday in 1983.

F O U R

The Distribution of Wealth in the World Today

A score-card for seeing how far through the passsage we have come up to now and some comments on how to go faster.

I N DISCUSSING THE PASSAGE TO A WEALTHY WORLD we define a country as wealthy when its people have decent living conditions. (Life expectancy and infant mortality are convenient objective indicators of decent living conditions, although they don't cover everything.) But in this chapter we will mostly put aside that fundamental definition of wealth. Instead, in order to use statistics and arithmetic, we will talk in terms of money. We will put the dividing line between poor countries and wealthy countries at $3,000 income per year per person. (Of course this doesn't mean that each person in the wealthy countries actually has $3,000 per year; it means that the country's income—its GNP divided by its population—is $3,000. Endnote 4 discusses some of the weaknesses of this measure.)

There are over 150 countries and five billion people in the world today. To get some feel for the size of the problem of completing the passage from general poverty to general wealth—and to indicate the general shape of the current world situation—these countries can be divided as follows:

TABLE 4
The Distribution of Wealth
in the World, 1984

Category of Country	Number of Countries	Total Population (millions)
1. Already Wealthy *(over $3,000)*	32	1,100
A. *Very Wealthy:*	23	700
B. *Mid. Class Wealthy:*	9	400
2. Nearly Wealthy *($1500-$3000)*	22	600
3. Well Begun *($600-$1500)*	30	500
4. Barely Started *(less than $600)*	45	2,500
A. *China and India*		
China		1,000
India		700
B. *Growing Nicely*	11	400
C. *Problems*	32	400
World Total	**129**	**4,700**

How Far Along to the Spread of Wealth?

Group 1: The Already Wealthy Countries

The almost one-quarter of the world's people living in the Already Wealthy countries have four-fifths of the world's income. This group includes both countries that have only recently passed the threshold of $3,000 per capita income per year and a top group whose members are three times as wealthy. The former, called here "Middle Class Wealthy" are nine countries with average incomes in the range $3,000-$6,000. Three communist countries have most of the population of this sub-group. (East Germany is the only Very Wealthy communist country.)

While 24% of the people of the world now live in thirty-two countries which are already wealthy, the populations of these countries are growing slowly, so that in two hundred years these thirty-two countries will have only about 13% of the world's population.*

If we decided which countries were Already Wealthy only on the basis of money, three other countries—Saudi Arabia, Libya, and Oman—would be included in Group 1. But since "wealthy" as we define it has more to do with the conditions in which most of the people live—which are shown by evidence like high life expectancy and low infant mortality—these three countries, all of which have high per capita incomes only because they are large oil producers, have been put with the Nearly Wealthy countries. (Since their combined population is only about thirteen million, the overall picture is not affected much by which list they are put on.)

Almost all of the people in the Already Wealthy countries have life expectancies of seventy-two or more, and infant mortality below twenty.** (The numbers for the United States are: Life expectancy seventy-four, infant mortality thirteen.) No country in the other groups has such good health, although several poorer countries are already quite close.†

---

* Country by country population projections for 200 years into the future are mere hypotheses. But the World Bank goes through the exercise of estimating the hypothetical stationary population of every country. (*World Development Report,* 1986, Table 25.) That is, they make assumptions for each country, on the basis of recent trends in that country, about its declining birth and death rates. On the basis of these assumptions and the current age structure of the population, they calculate when that country's population is likely to stop growing, and at what level. These numbers are as good a way as any to estimate the distribution of people among countries in 200 years—by which time, according to the Bank, populations of all countries will have leveled off.

** There are two exceptions. One is the Soviet Union, the only developed country where life expectancy is falling (now only 67 according to the World Bank). The other is Venezuela, whose life expectancy of 69 is not yet quite as high as that of the group of wealthy countries which it has recently joined.

† In fact almost all life expectancy numbers are unrealistically pessimistic because they are calculated as if current medical conditions will continue. In fact, throughout the world life expectancy is still increasing and infant mortality falling. So a baby's real life expectancy is higher than the official number.

Group 2: Nearly Wealthy Countries

The economies of the twenty-two Nearly Wealthy countries have been growing rapidly; averaging 3.6% per capita per year, which means doubling every twenty years (with the exceptions of Libya, Chile, and Argentina which have had growth rates below 1.8%). The group includes middle-size powers from all over the world like Brazil, Mexico, and South Korea, and four of the European communist countries.

It seems reasonably likely that most of this group will move into the Wealthy category within the next generation. Undoubtedly some will run into or create trouble of some kind, delaying their growth perhaps a generation, perhaps even longer for others.

Group 3: Countries Where Economic Development is Well Begun

This group is now composed of thirty countries and 480 million people spread all over the world. Sixty percent of the people are in five large countries: Nigeria, with nearly 100 million people, and Turkey, the Philippines, Egypt and Thailand—each with about half as many people as Nigeria.

In this group the range of income is from about $600 to $1,500, but all of the countries are growing well, almost all above 2% per year, and together they average nearly 3%.* If the experience of the last generation is a basis for predicting, most of these countries will be wealthy in another two generations. (At a growth rate of 3% it takes less than sixty years to go from $600 to $3,000 per capita income.)

To recapitulate. It is likely that the countries where over 40% of all people now live will be wealthy before the middle of the next century. However, since the populations of these countries are growing more slowly than the rest of the world, a conservative estimate is that only a little over a third of the world's people will be living in wealthy countries by the year 2050.

---

* An adjustment which would raise some of these income figures is discussed in the next subsection.

Group 4: Countries Barely Started on the Passage to Wealth

This group of forty-five countries with 2.6 billion people, located principally in Asia, is dominated by China and India. Together these two countries have more than two-thirds of the total population of the group. The other big countries are Indonesia, Pakistan, Bangladesh, and Vietnam, which together have over half of the rest of the group's population.

The regular GNP per capita estimates for the countries in this group are mostly in the range of $200-$600, but GNP figures at this level of income are not readily comparable to those of the advanced countries.

The World Bank has supported a major research program to estimate the real income of the ordinary person in the poorer countries. To be realistic they tried to figure out how to express that income in units that measure practical purchasing power. In other words, the studies asked the question, "How many dollars would the ordinary poor person of a country like India need in order to live in America the way he lives at home?"

The results of the studies indicated, for example, that it would cost about three times the income of the typical poor Indian to pay for an equal standard of living if he lived in the United States. In other words, an Indian family with an income in rupees, which the official exchange rate would say is equal to $200-$400 per year, has a living standard that they would need $600-$1200 to buy in the United States.

In other words, although India's GNP per capita, for example, is only $240, and so the typical poor family in India spends only $200-$400 year, the things that that family actually buys in India with their income are more like what they could buy in the United States with $600-$1,200.

This means that for comparisons of personal expenditures the income of poor Indians is about three times as large as the standard estimate (made by converting Indian incomes from rupees to dollars with normal exchange rates).

Of course it is very hard to compare realistically the full

practical effect of different incomes in different countries. Many things that affect people's lives are not purchased and don't get taken into account in a simple economic comparison. It is probably reasonable, for purposes of comparison with the Already Wealthy countries, to think of the average incomes in most of the Barely Started countries as having a purchasing power that is in a range from $300 to perhaps $1,000. (Incomes in the Well Begun group of countries should also be increased for comparability, but not as sharply.) For a list of World Bank estimates of some Purchasing Power Parities for 1975 see End-Table 5.

The group of Barely Started Countries is very large and heterogeneous. While some of its members seem to have started on the path of economic development, others, because of their political situation or for other reasons, have had very little or no economic growth over the last twenty years. And some show few signs of being able to achieve sustained increases in average income. The following line of reasoning seems to me to be a sensible way of estimating the prospects of this diverse set of forty-five countries.

First, we should separate India and China from the group and think about their prospects individually, because these two countries are over two-thirds of the population of Group 4. For the rest of the countries in the group we can say: (1) probably some of them will succeed in achieving sustained growth for a few generations, but (2) we must assume that others will fail to do so. That is, some countries in the group may not begin to achieve economic development during the next fifty or one hundred years.

If we follow this line of thought how can we guess how many people will be in the countries which, for one reason or another, are not able to learn to grow for a very long time? One way to answer the question is to look at the experience of the twenty years from 1965 through 1984, and to say that it is probably a reasonable guess that as large a fraction of the group will be able to grow in the future as were successful from 1965 to 1984.

If we think that there will be countries that won't grow or will grow very slowly, but we don't know which ones, how can our calculations take the problem cases into account? The following may be a reasonable first approximation. We will take the present group of problem cases as an estimate of how big the problem will be in the future. This assumes that the countries that become problem cases in the future will be more or less matched by the countries that stop being problem cases. Table 4 uses India's annual growth rate (per capita) during 1965-1984 as an artificial dividing line. The "B" group of eleven countries, with a total population of 370 million, did better than India during those twenty years. The "C" group of thirty-two countries with 440 million people were less successful.*

On this basis I think that it is reasonable to say that about half of the smaller countries of Group 4 will probably do as well as—or better than—India, and half will do worse in the future. This means that when India and China cross the threshold only about one-sixth of the group will be left behind, less than 10% of the world's population at that time. (And, of course, we can expect that by then a good share of this group will be fairly close to the threshold of wealth.)

Now let's look at Group 4 more carefully, dividing this diverse group into three parts.

Group 4 (A): China and India

Completing the passage to a wealthy world depends principally on India with its nearly 750 million people—and on China which already has over a billion people but whose population is growing more slowly than India's.

Although India's economy grew at a rate of 1.6% per capita from 1965 through 1984, India had reached an income level of only $260 per person by 1984. (However, as was noted above, most of India's people bought three times as much with their dollars as we could if we were trying to live as they do. Therefore for some purposes it is more reasonable to think of India as starting from a base of somewhere between $500 and $700 of GNP per capita.)

---

* A number of countries in the "C" group, including Burma, had growth rates nearly as high as India's. It is clear that the distinction between better and worse than India can not really have very much significance. So I would not give much credence to the fact that a particular country is in sub-group "B" rather than in "C," or vice versa.

49

Taking into account the purchasing power of its money, let's say that India must become five times as rich as it is now before it becomes wealthy. How long will this take? Some arbitrary scenarios are shown in Table 5.*

TABLE 5
Alternative Scenarios for Future Growth Rates of India

	Growth rates	Time Required to Become 5 Times Wealthier
Scen. #1:	Continued Growth at 1.6%	*101 years*
Scen. #2	10 years at 0%, *and then* next 10 years at 1.6%, next 10 years at 2.8%, next 10 years at 0%, next 20 years at 0.9%, next 20 years at 1.6%, *and* next 35 years at 2%	*115 years*
Scen. #3	10 years at 1%, *and then* next 10 years at 2%, next 10 years at 1.5%, next 10 years at 2.5%, next 10 years at 2%, next 10 years at 3%, next 10 years at 1%, *and* next 11 years at 3%	*81 years*
Scen. #4	Average 1%	*162 years*
Scen. #5	Average 2%	*81 years*
Scen. #6	Average 2.8%	*58 years*

* If it is a mistake to take into account the difference in purchasing powers when estimating how long before India becomes "wealthy," India will have to double its income one more time than I assume before it crosses the threshold to historic wealth; this might take another forty years—or it might take less than another twenty years.

None of these scenarios is implausible. In all except Scenario Number 4, India becomes wealthy by the end of the next century (the year 2099).

Of course, it would not be impossible for India to grow more slowly than the slowest of these scenarios, or faster than the fastest. If I had to bet personally, I would bet that India will average 2% or more until reaching $3,000 per capita. In other words, I think that the chances are better than even that India will become wealthy by the third quarter of the next century—one lifetime from now— unless there is some kind of cataclysm before then. On the basis of our general experience of economic growth and my sense of the nature of the process, it seems to me that there is less than one chance in four that India will need more than another 120 years to become wealthy.

Of course, there is no proof that these predictions are correct. But no team of experts, with any amount of study, could reach a conclusion which would be entitled to more confidence. In short, there is just no way of knowing about India's future growth rates. But if you need as good a guess as can be made, to get a general perspective on how long it will take before India is wealthy in historic terms, it is hard to argue against a range of 60-120 years.

Creating hopes or expectations that India can multiply its per capita income five times in less than sixty years is dangerous. (But specific goals, especially health ones, can be accomplished much more quickly.) On the other hand, if it starts to look as if India will take more than 120 years to become wealthy, it probably makes sense to consider drastic changes.

THE QUESTIONS about China's economic development are different than those about India. The effects of Chinese communist ideology, of the Party's desire for total control, and of the extreme changes in policy which such totalitarian systems can produce, have been very costly for China since 1949. For most of that time there were virtually no gains in productivity. (That is, increases in production were the result of increasing the amount of labor and other resources used.) Until recently there were chronic problems with hunger, and for thirty years the country may have had half of all the famine deaths in the world.

China's poor economic performance contrasts sharply with that of the other countries populated by Chinese people—especially the Republic of China on Taiwan, which was one of the poorer parts of China when it was separated in 1949, and which has grown at least five times faster than the mainland. Singapore and Hong Kong have also done outstandingly well, as have the large Chinese populations of Indonesia and Thailand.

Recently, of course the Chinese communist government has been changing its policies. There has already been a radical change in farm policy, giving farmers greater control over their own work and a chance to keep more of what they earn. The new policy has already greatly increased food production. (This is strong evidence that a good share of the thirty million Chinese who died in famines since the communists gained control of Chinese agriculture were victims of communist ideology. As soon as the Party changed that part of its ideology there was ample food.)

It seems clear that the current communist leadership wants also to make much of the rest of the Chinese economy more free. If they succeed in doing so it seems quite possible that China can grow fairly rapidly, perhaps 4% or even 5% per year per capita. There are two questions: First, how much will the leadership succeed in making the economy more flexible and efficient— against the demands of ideology and of the political system (and the interests of the huge Party apparatus and membership)? Second, will there be another radical shift in policy, like those that have come every decade or two since the Communist Party came to power? If so, periods of good growth may well be at least partly offset by periods of standing still or going backwards.

So long as the communists are in power, Chinese growth depends principally on such practical effects of Chinese communism. Of course, if the Communist Party loses power such questions will no longer dominate, and then the questions of Chinese growth would become more like the questions of economic growth in other countries. (And even with the communists in power there are many parallels between China and other developing counties.)

I don't want to get into the question of whether communism

or Marxist-Leninism is a good system. Most of the questions this book focuses on will have the same answers whether or not one thinks well of Marxist-Leninist analysis or principles.

Personally, I oppose communism because of the human rights record of communist countries; because of the Soviet Union's need, as a totalitarian imperial power, to try to protect itself by working to eliminate the power of the United States; and because of Soviet anti-Semitism. As far as I am concerned, communism is a system for getting and keeping political power—not primarily an economic system. But those are issues for another book.

Group 4 (B): Growing Nicely (although still poor)

Growth rates in this Group have averaged about 3.6% per year (measured in GNP per person—without adjustment for purchasing power equivalent). At this rate it would take about seventy-five years for all of these countries to become wealthy.

About the same amount of time would be required if you adjusted the countries' starting point to reflect real purchasing power instead of official exchange rates, but also assumed that their growth rate slowed down to a little over 2% per year. On the other hand, if some of these countries begin to grow at the faster rates that are more common among the Well Begun countries, most of them could be wealthy by the middle of the next century, sixty-five years from now. (And, of course, if growth rates slowed these countries could require another century, or even longer, to become wealthy.)

Group 4 (C) Problems

The fact that a country is listed here in Group C, means only that its growth rate during 1965-1984 was less than 1.6%, and certainly is not a prediction that it will have slow growth in the future. In fact, I believe that at least several of the countries in Group C will have splendid growth records in the next century and will pass some of the countries in Group 4 (B), and may even pass some countries from Group 3.

The reason to have a Problems Group is not to predict which countries will grow slowly, but to remind ourselves that probably *some* countries will grow very slowly, or possibly not at all. The 4 (C) group stands for the slow-growing countries, whichever they turn out to be, and gives a basis for estimating how large a share of the world's population might still live in poor countries at the end of the next century—about 10%.

The big countries in Group C are Bangladesh with nearly 100 million people, and Zaire with thirty million. But the Group also includes the Sudan, Nepal, Ghana, and Madagascar, each of which has over ten million people.

Summary

It was not until the 20th century that the world first saw a wealthy country. By the end of the 21st century there is a good chance that over four-fifths of the people of the world will live in wealthy countries. Although in 1900 no one lived in a wealthy country, by the year 2100 the great bulk of the people of the world may be wealthy enough to live the more human life of the future rather than the more natural life of most of human history. After ten thousand generations of poverty, humankind is requiring ten generations to straggle through the passage to a human world and across the line to wealth. (And there is much dismay that we cannot keep better order and all move more nearly together.)

How Can We Speed Passage to a Wealthy World?

It is not enough to say that it is likely that most of the world will have crossed the threshold to wealth by no less than sixty and no more than 120 years from now. Even though in the long sweep of history it doesn't make any difference whether the passage to a human world is completed in 60 or 120 more years; it will make a great deal of difference to the quality of life of hundreds of millions of people—indeed, it will determine how long many of them will live.

Many of the people in countries that are not yet wealthy are necessarily living lives that can be called less than fully human. A decent concern for these people requires us to do what we can to speed the day when all countries are wealthy. This is a task of great subtlety because it involves helping others to do what mostly they have to do for themselves. Nevertheless outside help can be of great value.

Probably the most important thing that we can do to help is to reduce the extent to which we hurt poor countries. Even though, presently we are helping much more than we are hurting, there is no reason why we shouldn't stop hurting and exploiting them.

There are three principal ways in which we hurt poor countries. One is by trade barriers of one form or another. These are usually created because of the political pressure of interest groups here, such as the steel industry, labor unions or beet sugar growers. While our country as a whole doesn't gain much by such trade barriers—and may well even lose by them—they are important to the particular groups they protect, who put substantial effort into them.

The second way we sometimes hurt poor countries is when American individuals or companies exploit those they do business with in the poor countries. "Exploitation" can be defined as what happens when the benefits of a relationship are unfairly divided between the parties because one of them has greater strength or understanding. It is important to note that the one who is exploited may still gain from the relationship, even if "by rights" he should gain more.

While there is a great deal of talk about such exploitation, my impression is that it does less harm to most poor countries than the other two ways in which we hurt them. Nevertheless, it is worthwhile to work at the task of preventing individuals and companies in the United States from exploiting people in the poor countries—so long as we can do so without reducing the benefits that poor countries get from their relationships with US businesses. But if we concentrate too hard on protecting poor countries from being exploited, the result could be that we reduce the benefits they get from relationships with US companies—which would be one of the ways of hurting them.* (We also have to protect ourselves from being exploited by them, but that is a different problem.)

The third, and perhaps greatest, way in which we sometimes

* See the last section of Chapter 13.

hurt poor countries is by giving them wrong advice and by doing the wrong things when we try to help them. Our good motives don't guarantee that our efforts work in the direction that we intend. This is especially so because countries—including our own—always have mixed motives. Even if Congress and the Director of the U.S. Agency for International Development are primarily motivated by a desire to speed economic development, the bureaucrats, business firms, and "do-good organizations" that become involved in the program, may have other motives. And those with selfish or crusading motives often spend more time and more intense effort to achieve their own ends than the people with good motives.

Here are some of the ways in which we have hurt countries while trying to help them.

Often we haven't understood the nature of the development process and have led countries to do things that might make sense for us but don't make sense for them. We sometimes get them to buy something, like a railroad, by paying part of the cost, or by lending the money for it at very low interest rates, when they cannot really afford the railroad even on a subsidized basis.

When our government gives development assistance to a poor country we usually give it to or through the government of that country. This often strengthens the position of the government vis-a-vis the people and businesses, and this may be just the opposite of what is needed.

Also, when we give help to a government and ask for economic plans to make sure that the help isn't wasted, too large a share of the few people who are capable of writing plans, and of looking competent to our aid-givers, may be diverted from productive work within the country to the job of maximizing aid from outside.

Perhaps the greatest way in which we have harmed the poor countries has been psychological—and therefore difficult to quantify. Their job is to learn and to change. One of the principal obstacles to learning is that some people who are reluctant to change try to sell the tempting message that change isn't necessary, that their lack of wealth is the result of foreign "devils." Many well-motivated people from the rich countries have been helping to sell various tempting easy-way-out theories, thus delaying the necessary changes and tough decisions required for economic development.

This agenda of big problems facing the world is not only for governments. Americans who want to use their lives to work on important tasks, such as speeding the spread of wealth to poorer countries, don't have to do it by getting our government involved. People can work on any of these problems in a variety of ways; as professional experts, as businessmen, or working for foreign governments or firms.

Helping the countries that are moving more slowly on the passage to wealth is a big and demanding job. It can use the creativity and devotion of as many people as are challenged by the task and willing to learn the skills and understanding necessary to be truly helpful.

Note on Poverty in the World

Our discussion of wealth focuses on countries rather than individuals. We have set our definition of a wealthy country high enough so that most of the people of wealthy countries will have enough money to be able to live modern, human lives even if their country has the kind of unequal distribution of income that is seen in many countries today.

The pessimistic assumption, that income distribution patterns in the poorer countries will not become more even, is not a prediction. And it certainly is not a recommendation. It is just a conservative way to estimate. If income distribution in poorer countries becomes more even, then more of the world will become wealthy more rapidly than estimated here.

But many people will want to know something about people as well as countries. How many people live in poverty today, and how quickly will the spread of wealth among countries reduce the number of people in poverty?

I can't provide a full analysis of this issue, but the next few paragraphs provide some orienting numbers. They are from a World Bank study which estimated the number of people living in poverty in the poorer countries in 1960, in 1975, and the number "expected" for 2000.

The study was trying to show how slowly the number of people living in poverty was being reduced. The discouraging starting point was that even though national incomes had been rising fairly rapidly, and were expected to continue doing so, two factors prevented the number of people in poverty from declining. One factor was population growth. When there are more people it means that the number of people in poverty can grow even if they are a smaller percent of the population.

The second factor was the uneven distribution of income, and its tendency to get more uneven. The study reported evidence that when most very poor countries get a little richer, their lowest income groups get smaller shares of the new wealth. In other words, the income of the poorest people rises more slowly than the income of their countries. (Usually this trend to more inequality is reversed when a country's income rises further.)

This set of World Bank studies used a definition of poverty much lower than the standard we are using in this book for the historic distinction between poverty and wealth. They defined absolute poverty roughly as the level of income below which people in India eat less than about 2,300 calories a day. By this definition, 45% of the Indian population was in poverty in 1975. (By the definition of this book, of course, all of India is still a poor country.)

With this definition the World Bank estimated that the number of people living in poverty was 750 million in 1960, about 800 million in 1975, and expected to be down to 600 million in 2,000. (These numbers don't include China and other centrally planned economies, and don't include the small percent of people living in such severe poverty in the industrialized countries.)

In percentage terms the numbers look quite different. The number of people in poverty declined from over 50% in 1960, to 38% in 1975, and according to the standard expectation will drop to about 16% in the next fifteen years.

The World Bank hopes that extreme poverty will be reduced faster, by the lowest income groups moving more quickly toward an even share of their country's income. But, it will be difficult even to reduce the percent of people in poverty to 16%.

In summary, if you take the World Bank definition of poverty, perhaps 30% of the people of the world are living in poverty today, and a reasonable expectation is that in the year 2000 it will be between 15% and 20%.

(Remember that this World Bank line between poverty and wealth is above the level of severe hunger, so there are many fewer hungry people than there are "World Bank poor." But the World Bank poverty line is much below the line we use to distinguish between traditional poverty and modern wealth. Of course all of these definitions are arbitrary, and the current and historical data are almost as uncertain as the estimates for the future. Therefore, these numbers should not be thought of as precise or reliable, although they are the best available and are estimated with enough care to give a reasonable feeling for reality.)

P A R T   I I

The Earth Has Plenty

Many young couples about to have their first child become overwhelmed with worries. There are so many things that can happen to the baby, so much to do to bring it up right.

You want to reassure such a couple, but you can't tell them: Don't worry, your baby will grow up to be a fine person. They need to worry about their baby—and to do the things that their worrying leads to. Some of the main and best uses of their time result from this worrying.

On the other hand, as a statistical matter, they don't have to worry. There is a very high chance—better than 95%—that the child will grow up alright. Of course no one can be sure. The child may be hit by a bus when he is sixteen. So you can't give a guarantee.

This part will show why we don't have to worry about running out of raw materials—about the finite limits of the Earth. What this means is, "We can expect, with high confidence, that things will work out alright; but it will take a lot of effort, and skill, and worry to make it happen—and there is no absolute guarantee of success."

In raising our children we should have confidence and work on the assumption that we will succeed—while working very hard to make it come true. Part II says that in thinking about getting the resources we need from the Earth, our expectation should be of success. We have a sound basis to assume that the Earth will provide plenty of what we need—although some of us have to work hard to make sure.

THE SEEMINGLY OPTIMISTIC description of the future outlined in Part I naturally raises two kinds of questions. The first question: Will there really be enough money for so many people to become wealthy? was discussed in Part I. In this part we will discuss the answer to the second question: Is the Earth big enough? or will there be enough material?

When I say to people that I'm going to talk about the question of whether mankind will always have all the raw materials it needs, people look at me as if I'm crazy. Sometimes they say something like: You mean enough for hundreds of years? I say: No. Thousands or tens of thousands of years. That doesn't help my credibility.

Anyone who still takes me seriously enough to continue the conversation, is likely to say that the question of very long-term resources will be determined by the nature of a future technology which we can't imagine. But to respond to people's feelings and concerns I want to do better than say: Don't worry about the distant future, people will figure out how to solve the problem. That is probably true but it isn't convincing enough.

What is the human concern I want to address? It is the widespread view that modern society is riding for a fall; that our way of life uses so much material, and that population is growing so fast, that sooner or later we have to run into dangerous shortages; that, after all, the world is finite.

Another form of this concern is the common idea that, somehow, the question of whether the rapidly increasing billions of people in the Third World can catch up depends on whether there are enough raw materials left for them at reasonable prices.

Yet another form of the scarcity perspective is the feeling that it is somehow unfair that the United States should be using a quarter of all the raw materials taken out of the Earth, that we are taking more than our share. This feeling that somehow it is imprudent or unfair for us to be using so much stuff can relate either to poor people or to future generations.

What I want to say is that all of these forms of the scarcity perspective are absolutely wrong. They are as wrong as Gary Cooper was when, in one of his early movie comedies, he was worried because the new baby he was taking care of increased its weight by 20% in three weeks and he figured that this meant the baby would weigh over a hundred pounds within a year. (Of course he was right that the baby would continue to grow.)

It is hard to get at something as broad as the scarcity perspective because people just assume that the scarcity perspective is correct—without even realizing that it is a particular perspective, that it might be wrong, and that there are alternatives to it. They don't say: I think there will be a big scarcity problem in a hundred years because . . . . They don't think specifically about long-run scarcity because it is too difficult and doesn't seem relevant to any practical issues. Since the scarcity perspective seems as natural as breathing, people would say that they have never thought about long-run raw material supply problems. But, in effect, they have. Anyone who has any of the concerns I noted above is acting as if he thought about the question of whether there will be raw material scarcity problem in the future and reached the conclusion: Yes, sooner or later there will be a problem.

Of course, some people have a much stronger position. They say: There definitely will be a problem soon. Or: We are already feeling the first effects of the scarcity caused by the finiteness of the Earth. These people want to act now; they feel we are already late in mending our ways, slow in changing our attitudes to meet the new scarcity imperatives.

The official statement of the US government, *The Global 2000 Report* (GTR), said that the world could only avert drastic scarcity problems by the year 2000 (perhaps in the form of pollution) by drastically changing the way the world is organized. (This was not a routine bureaucratic document; it was strongly promoted at high levels and was the basis of one of the three themes of President Carter's Farewell Address.)

Of course, if people are specific enough to point to a particular problem and a particular date, they can be answered specifically and shown why that particular scarcity fear is unrealistic. This has happened repeatedly, and many specific predictions have come due and been proven wrong by events. The problem is that many people observing, for example, a debate about whether GTR is correct, have the following kind of reaction: (from a *Washington*

Post report on meetings where *The Global 2000 Report* was strongly criticized) "A consultant to Earthwatch acknowledged that the original Global 2000 projections may turn out to be wrong but said, 'that is not the point. The idea was to call attention to the fact that we are destroying out habitat. That is still true.' "*

That is the reaction that I want to address. It is not only that the particular argument in *GTR* or *Limits to Growth* or *The Population Bomb* is wrong. (Although the particular arguments and conclusions in these reports are wrong, as wrong as the book *Famine-1975* which was published in 1967 and sold tens of thousands of copies.)

The important thing is that the whole perspective is wrong. There isn't anything there. Of course, there are practical problems of how to grow more food, enable poor countries to get rich enough so that their people can live decent lives, and many other urgent tasks. But these problems have essentially no connection with long-run scarcity or with the finiteness of the Earth.

Now you can see what I am trying to do. I want to show that as a practical matter there is no reason to worry that mankind's safety or standard of living need ever be threatened by resource shortages or pollution problems. (Of course there are dangers, and problems, which I discuss in Part III, but they don't invalidate this statement.)

If I just show that we have enough for a thousand years people will say: How can he be sure? Maybe his calculations aren't exactly right and there is only enough for five hundred years, or even a hundred. And anyway, if we're going to get into trouble maybe we have a responsibility to begin to move at least a little way in the direction that will need to be taken eventually. It seems somehow shabby and second-class to be going against history, against the long-run imperative facing mankind. It seems selfish and shortsighted to try to get away with what we can take, and leave the

---

* Sometimes people get angry at you for criticizing studies like GTR or the Club of Rome's *"Limits to Growth."* They say, in effect: You are quibbling over details and preventing people from facing up to one of the world's greatest problems. By arguing about the specific numbers in these studies you are giving people an excuse for continuing their selfish and dangerous wasteful practices. You should not treat such studies like an academic exercise; if people don't recognize and do something quickly about the danger of exploding world population and the ecological limits of spaceship Earth we may pass a point of no return.

ultimate clean-up job to our remote descendants, just because they aren't here to complain or vote.

That is why this part will attempt the seemingly silly task of answering the question: Do we have enough, essentially, forever?* We might not have to worry even if I were not able to show you that the very likely answer to that question is yes. We might well be able to take care of long-run future problems with ideas or resources that will be found in the long-run future. But fortunately, it is possible to show that we can take care of at least the big problems, using what we know now. We may be able to do better with what we learn in the future. And the possibility of future discoveries and scientific breakthroughs gives us a margin of safety to cover problems that we haven't been able to think of, and to deal with the dangers discussed below. But I won't have to lean on the useful things coming in the unknown future very much.

* Of course I don't really mean "forever." For example, I don't deal with the question of geological changes, or the sun becoming a red giant. These are matters of millions or billions of years. I am only concerned with human history which so far has been measured in tens of thousands of years.

F I V E

Perspective on the World Population Explosion

The population of the world will double soon—whatever we do. But it probably will be a very long time before it doubles again—even if governments do nothing to stop it.

THE GENERAL SHAPE OF THE QUESTION of future world population is fairly straightforward and noncontroversial, although of course there are substantial uncertainties. The following broad picture of what has been happening would be accepted by just about any expert on population, and should clarify the seeming contradictions in some of the statements one hears.

By 1800, world population was still under one billion. It is now over five billion and it will reach about six billion by 2000. On the basis of current trends most demographers expect world population to become more or less stable in about a hundred years at a level of about ten billion people, although a few countries are expected to continue growing for a few additional decades. These general estimates are shared by the World Bank, the U.S. Census Bureau, the United Nations, the Soviet Union, Worldwatch, and the Population Reference Bureau, and there is no one who has made a careful estimate outside of this range. But all estimators could be wrong together; they have been in the past. To evaluate the professional consensus we should look at the facts and the theory behind the consensus.

Beginning in Europe in the seventeenth century, wealth and

technology began to reduce death rates, especially infant mortality. This produced a rapid increase in population. Then, in country after country, the reduction in death rates was followed, after various lengths of time, by a reduction in fertility rates (i.e., the number of children the average woman has during her lifetime). This, of course, eventually resulted in a slowing of population growth.

The process of moving from a stable low population with high birth and death rates to a stable high population with low birth and death rates, through an intervening period of rapid population growth, is called the "demographic transition."[5]

The key uncertainty in predicting future population is how far and how fast fertility and birth rates decline. It is not easy to find out exactly how these rates have been changing in recent years. In any case, even if we knew everything about the present and the past we would still be uncertain about the future.

The basic theory about why we can count on the second part of the transition (i.e., declining fertility and leveling of population) seems pretty sturdy. It rests on the idea that as countries become richer: raising children becomes more expensive, child labor becomes less valuable, and few children die before their parents. So people decide to have fewer children.

Demographers' confidence in their view of the overall pattern comes from: their confidence in the general theory of what is happening, the fact that many countries have definitely followed the expected pattern, that so far no country is clearly outside the pattern, plus the fact that virtually all of the reasonably good data are consistent with the theory.

There is not enough decent information available about a number of the African and Middle Eastern countries, including big ones such as Nigeria, to know about their trends. At least for some of them, fertility may not yet have started to fall, and in some cases may even be rising; which is sometimes an early effect of increased health and nutrition in extremely poor countries. But these countries do not have enough people to significantly change the worldwide picture.[6]

Birth rates, or population growth rates, are affected by the age of the population as well as its fertility. When the average age is young, as it is in countries which have been growing rapidly (e.g., Mexico 17, India 19), the population will continue to grow long after fertility has declined to the point where the average woman has only enough children to keep population constant in the long-run (the "net reproductive rate"). After a period of rapid growth it can take a century before age-specific birth and death rates are in balance, and the population becomes stable.*

The specific projections of future world population made by the demographers of the World Bank and other groups are based on estimates of the trends by country and region, of fertility rates and death rates. These trends are projected forward and combined with information about the current population in order to get future population. The details of the estimates should not be taken as more than illustrative. There is undoubtedly a large margin of error. But we do not depend on the estimates being even approximately correct.

Taking the world as a whole the results are quite dramatic. For millennia the average population growth rates were very low, about one-tenth of 1% per year.** But beginning in the seventeenth century the world population growth rate increased rapidly for about three hundred years. It probably reached its peak of about 2% per year (twenty times as high as "normal") for a few years in the early 1960s.

During the last two decades the world population growth rate has been going down. It is now probably about 1.7%. The current estimates are that the four hundred year "spike" of high population growth rates, up to 2% and back down again, will have increased

* For example, the World Bank estimates that in India fertility will fall to long-term replacement level by 2010, but because the population is so young it will continue to grow for another 130 years, when it is expected to be about 1.7 billion. The dates for Nigeria (estimated static population 528 million) are 2035 and 2130, and for Brazil (estimated static population 293 million) are 2010 and 2075.

** Some experts believe that earlier growth was not steady, that a major share of it came in perhaps two previous "bursts" of growth, and that there have been sizeable fluctuations. Certainly there have been dramatic rises and falls in the population of large areas such as Europe, China, and South America.

FIGURE 1
Population Growth Rate in Long-Term Historical Perspective

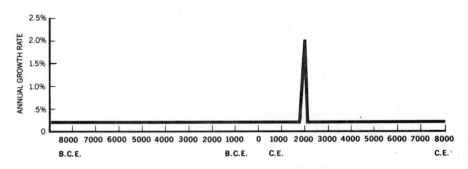

Based on Ronald Freeman and Bernard Berelson, "The Human Population," *Scientific American*, September, 1974, p. 36-37.

world population from under one billion people with average lives of less than thirty years to ten billion people with average lives of around eighty years.

In view of this dynamic history, it is easy to use the facts to make scary predictions. If population were to keep growing at today's rate, the world population two hundred years from now would be 128 billion. There is very little legitimacy or significance to such a calculation; it is like estimating a baby's weight on the basis of its growth rate at age three months. Any serious estimate must take into account more detailed trends, such as changing birth and death rates, and age structure.

The overall pattern has become increasingly clear in the last fifteen years. *The Scientific American,* September 1974 special issue on population described the situation as it is presented here. More and more evidence came in during the 1970s to support the idea of the demographic transition. The evidence from the late 1970s and 1980s seems to clinch the general validity of that idea, to confirm that world population growth rates peaked in the 1960s, and to accelerate estimates of how fast fertility is declining. By now there is no reason why anybody who looks at the matter at all seriously should get a wrong picture—although an ordinary citizen whose ideas were formed by information from the 1960s, or by recent but incompetent writers, could easily go wrong.[7]

National population issues

Current projections are that the population of some countries will multiply five times before stabilizing—unless something happens or is done to make their fertility fall faster. A faster decline of population growth rates probably would increase the speed with which some poor countries move out of poverty. This would be important to people in those countries. (Some population experts, such as Julian Simon, argue that moderate population growth helps economic development in most countries, but this argument does not necessarily go against the value of more quickly getting away from the very high population growth rates found in some countries today.)

Some scientists have performed experiments with rats that show how bad overcrowding is for the health of rats. And some deep thinkers have concluded from this that population growth may produce enough crowding to threaten human health or at least our psychological comfort.

The seemingly irrefutable point is made that population growth is certainly making the Earth more crowded. But that point is as meaningless as it is irrefutable. The population of Greenland is undoubtedly growing (it recently passed 50,000), but does that mean that Greenland, which is more than four times as big as France, is getting more crowded?

There is no recognized measure of crowding—if that word is used to mean harm or discomfort. Since there is no measure of crowding, no one can say whether crowding has been increasing or decreasing—or whether it will increase or decrease in the future. (We do know that the number of people living on Manhattan island in New York City is less than it was fifty years ago.)

Usually the amount of living space available to a person depends on her income—and her preferences. Therefore as

71

people's incomes rise in the future, any increases in crowding will be those preferred by people.[8]

While careful scientific study may show that the people who live in the most expensive sections of New York City are endangering their health because of overcrowding, such overcrowding must have some compensating advantages because people are paying a lot of money to get it. There may be subtle harms from such overcrowding, but I believe that generally the health and life expectancy of the people living on Park Avenue is not worse than the people who live in the Borough of Queens, which is a much less crowded part of New York City (also less expensive and less convenient to the theater).

At least until more definitive studies are done with rats, perhaps it is reasonable to assume that it is safe for people to live at population densities slightly less than that of Manhattan Island, 50,000 people per square mile. Indeed, while some people prefer much less crowding, other people will pay a lot of money to live in even more crowded conditions. (And in Chapter 7 we will learn, by using the powerful tools of multiplication and division, that there is plenty of land available in the world—even if most people choose to live ten times more spread out than this conservative "maximum safe density.")

Conclusion

World population will almost certainly more than double, and it is unlikely to double twice, before it more or less levels off. No population policy or program has much hope or fear of changing this broad conclusion. (But some people think that population programs might be able to significantly slow population growth in particular countries, which might help them to become wealthy sooner.)

Therefore population programs are not important to concerns about very long-term world resource/pollution issues. We need to be, and can be, so confident that we have enough space and raw materials for ten billion people that we do not need to fear twenty billion. If the difference between ten billion and twenty billion people were enough to justify fear of real resource shortage dangers, then we would have to be afraid of resource shortages now.

The fact that this discussion contradicts many of the arguments often used in favor of supporting international family planning programs does not mean that I am not in favor of such programs. It is not the programs with which I disagree, only some of the arguments often used to gain support for them. Voluntary family planning programs are amply justified by the value of enabling couples to have greater choice about the number and timing of their children—regardless of whether the result is good or bad for their nations' economies, which nobody will ever know.

Running Out of Raw Materials: The Scarcity Error

The short—and surprising—answer is that we won't run out of raw materials because we don't use much of them (except fuels—which can be replaced by sunshine if we have no better fuel).

"RAW MATERIAL" IS A SIMPLE CONCEPT that, like almost any familiar idea, gets somewhat less clear if you focus attention on it—as we need to in this chapter. After we look a little more sharply at what the concept "raw material" means, we can see why raw materials are what you need to think about to judge the scarcity perspective.

What's the Difference Between Raw Materials and Other Materials?

Economists and statisticians define raw materials in several ways, based on two different roots of the concept of "raw material." One idea is that a raw material is what you start with when you make something. This has the problem that you can keep pushing further and further back. A cow is the raw material for a steak. But the cow is not what you start with. You start with a mother cow and grain. But the grain is not what you start with either. Grain comes from fertilizer, seed, labor, farm equipment, land, etc. It is possible to work things out to make a reasonable definition following this approach. But the useful way to make the distinction depends on what you're interested in.

The other root of the concept of "raw material" is essentially the idea of extraction from nature. Raw materials are what we get from nature; everything else is what we make for ourself out of raw materials. The reason for the distinction is that some questions about what we get from nature may be different from questions about what we make ourselves. In fact much of this book is about one such question: Will the world ever run out of raw materials? Such a question doesn't make sense applied to anything other than raw materials. How could we run out of things that we make for ourselves?

The line of thought we want to examine says that what nature has given us is finite and fixed, so we need to ask: Will it be enough? To do that we have to ask: What in fact do we get from nature? Raw materials are the things we get from nature, so that is why we are looking at raw materials.

To see how this definition works, and why it is important, let's take an example. How can I say (below) that in 1980 food costs for the average American were only $500 per year (2,000 pounds at 25¢ per pound), when obviously we spend much more than $1.40 a day for our food? The answer is that $500 is the cost of the raw material part of the food we eat. And it is the raw materials that we are concerned with in this book.

Grain, for example, is produced by farmers and delivered to a mill. The price the mill pays for that grain is the raw material cost. The mill grinds the grain and makes flour; the flour is baked into bread; the bread is then packaged and sold at retail. Or the bread may be, in effect, packaged more expensively and sold at a restaurant or at a McDonald's. But no one is worrying about running out of bakeries or McDonald's or advertising.

The cost of the bread we buy is determined mostly by the cost of flour mills and bakeries and McDonald's. These costs will be influenced by many things and are unpredictable, but they are largely independent of the cost of the grain bought by the mill that makes flour. (Of course the cost of the mill will be affected by the cost of other raw materials, like the steel and concrete from which the mill is made.)

The difference between the dime that the grain costs and the dollar that the bread costs is not some arbitrary profit margin added to the "real" cost. All the profits—those of the miller, the baker, the advertiser, and of the store—come to less than a dime. The rest of the difference goes to pay for the people who work at all the jobs along the way, and to buy trucks and stores and mills and paper, etc. And there are eager businessmen looking for ways to make their fortune by finding a cheaper way to do any step in the long process from farm to table.

Why should the cost of all those things go up just because the cost of grain goes up? Many people are confused by the experience with inflation, which is different. Inflation is when the costs of things-in-general go up. Of course, if grain prices go up because of a general inflation, then the other costs of bread will go up too. But the other costs of bread aren't going up *because* the price of grain is rising; they are both rising because of inflation.

It is very important to keep in mind the difference between inflationary price changes and relative price changes, even though it is often hard to tell them apart. Regardless of inflation, the prices, of particular things in relationship to the prices of other things, keep changing. For example computers get cheaper. So does the cost of listening to good music at home; of baseball gloves. We take declining costs as our natural due and don't notice them (except spectacular ones like computers). Especially during an inflation we only notice the prices that are going up, although on a real, inflation-adjusted basis there are just as many prices going down.

If because of a long-term scarcity of grain the cost of grain went up, apart from general inflation, it would be different from an inflationary rise in grain prices; and would not have to be accompanied by a rise in the cost of other elements of the cost of bread. What would make the cost of selling bread go up just because a new grain disease, for example, increased the cost of grain? Why shouldn't the cost of selling bread just as well go down because the cost of computers and radios is going down? Generally the real cost of each part of the process is more nearly independent than it is tied to the cost of the raw material.

People are worried that the things they buy—or that their great-grandchildren will buy—will become very expensive, because so much of the necessary raw materials have been used up. Fortunately, there is no reason to think that in the long run the other costs of providing a loaf of bread to the consumer— transportation, storage, processing, advertising and marketing, research, etc.—bear a fixed ratio to the cost of the grain. Now, it takes a dime's worth of grain and ninety cents' worth of other things to make a dollar's worth of bread. If the grain cost rose to forty cents (without inflation), there is no reason to assume that the cost of the other things, processing, marketing, etc. would rise from ninety cents to $3.60. Therefore if the cost of grain went from ten cents to forty cents, and the cost of the other things stayed the same, the cost of bread would go from $1.00 to $1.30. (Actually things don't work out so neatly, but the general direction is correct.)

The grain/bread situation is an analogy for all raw materials. *When we see that only about fourteen cents of every dollar we spend goes to raw materials, it means that even if raw materials costs were to quadruple in the long run, the total cost of the things we buy need only increase by less than half.*

This is only part of the story. Actually things are both better and worse. Worse, because if you're worried about raw materials getting more expensive you may say: Why should rising raw material costs stop at four times the current level? Maybe they will go to four hundred times the present level, or four thousand times. If the grain for a loaf of bread cost $400, it won't be much help that the bakery and the supermarket and the advertising agency still only cost ninety cents. But the good news is that generally raw material costs are not rising at all, not even slowly. As we shall see shortly, they mostly are going down.

More important, we will show that for the big items, food and fuel, there are specific reasons to be confident that the raw material cost can't go up very much, not more than two or three or four times what it is now, and probably less. So the grain/bread analogy should be a powerful source of confidence.

IN SUMMARY, since in this book we are talking about the possibility that some day we will run short of raw materials—the materials that we get from nature—we need to look at what materials we now get from nature and how much they cost. So we will focus on the raw material part of the food we eat, rather than the larger part of the cost which comes from manufacturing and services. By looking at the raw materials we actually use we will be better able to judge whether we will always have enough of such materials, or of satisfactory substitutes for them, at affordable prices.

Why Long Term Raw Material Scarcity is a Myth—Overview

With this perspective and background we can now provide a summary statement of our thesis here in Part II. Then we will discuss some of its complexities.

1. In 1980, Americans used only $170 worth of raw materials per person, apart from fuels and foods.* Therefore the long term raw material scarcity question comes down to the question of food and energy.

2. Affordable energy sources exist to supply all the energy we will need after current fossil fuel sources are used up.

3. We already know where and how we can grow all the food we will want for at least five times the current world population.

4. No particular raw material is essential, and each costs so little—except fuels—that we would not be badly hurt even if its cost (or the cost of doing without it) went up a hundred times.

5. Most raw materials have been getting less expensive. Even though we could afford to pay more for the minerals we take from the Earth, our experience is that minerals are getting less scarce—despite the great increase in consumption since industrialization and the population explosion began.

---

* The only significant change since 1980 is that the price of oil has gone down by about half.

Points 2 and 3 are explained in Chapters 7 and 8. Here we will look at points 1, 4, and 5.

What Raw Materials Do We Use? Food and Energy Dominate

Table 6 shows our 1980 raw material bill divided in the same way as this Part of the book:

TABLE 6
Use of Raw Materials in the U.S.

Item	Amount Used (per capita)	Cost per lb.	Tot. cost (per cap.)	Refer.
Food	2,000 pounds	25¢	$ 500	Ch. 7
Fuels	16,000 pounds	6¢	$ 950	Ch. 8
Drinking Water	2,000 pounds	.01¢	20¢	Ch. 9
Everything Else				Ch. 10
Metals	1,000 pounds	6¢	$ 60	
Wood	2,000 pounds	2¢	$ 40	
Miscel. Minerals	2,000 pounds	2¢	$ 40	
Stone, sand & gravel	20,000 pounds	.1¢	$ 30	
	45,000 pounds	**.4¢**	**$1,620**	

For explanatory comments see End-Table 6 on page 368.

This table comes from the ordinary statistics that everybody uses. These numbers are not controversial—although they are surprising. They show that buying all our raw materials requires only a small fraction of our average income.

When I first compiled this Table, I was amazed by the results. All the prices are so low. Most of the quantities seem low. But most of all, I was shocked that energy was such a big part of the total. I knew it was important, but I never would have guessed that fuels were over half of all the raw materials. And I was surprised that all metals together are such a small part of the total; and that they are not more than wood, which I thought of as old-fashioned and not important in a modern economy.

Let's consider for a minute whether the 1980 American raw material bill is a reasonable thing to look at in order to get a feel for how big a part of the world economy raw materials will be a hundred or a thousand or ten thousand years from now, and for the relative size of the main classes of raw materials.

Clearly, the details of our raw material menu are not relevant for the distant future. But our raw material bill is a better starting point than any other, because for the long-run future we need to think in terms of a rich world, probably two or more times as rich as America is today. Since the United States is the largest rich country, it is the closest model around for the long-run future.

But the important thing is that the only ideas we are taking from the current American raw material bill are the definition and relative size of the main categories of "everything else."

TABLE 7
"Everything Else"

Per Capita Use of Raw Materials in the U.S. (excluding food and fuel)

Metals	1,000 pounds	$ 60
Other Non-fuel Minerals	2,000 pounds	$ 40
Wood	2,000 pounds	$ 40
Stone, sand, & gravel	20,000 pounds	$ 30
TOTAL	**25,000 pounds**	**$170**

This permits us to focus on the following question: Could our need for these four categories of raw material grow much more than our need for food and energy? Could the effort needed to get "everything else" become as important as the effort needed to get food and energy? The answer is "no."

In 1980, $170 was a little more than 1% of the average income in the United States. Maybe these kinds of raw materials could become much more important in a rich world. (Fertilizers, which are an important component of non-fuel minerals, certainly might become much more important.) But it is very hard to see why our use of these kinds of materials should multiply *compared to food and energy, or compared to the non-raw material part of the economy.* The dominant trend, as we have become richer, is the inexorably increasing share of the economy that goes to services. If we satisfactorily take care of supplying food and energy, can anyone doubt that a bigger and bigger share of our work force (and therefore of our economy) will be devoted to services—to information handling and to other businesses based primarily on intangibles?

A rich world will not have an economy that is more of a metal-using economy than the United States is today in percent terms. Surely, when people have incomes of $30,000 they will buy more metal things, and spend more money on things made from metal, than people do today, when they make $15,000 a year. But they probably won't buy *twice* as much. It roughly follows from this that metals will be a smaller share of the world's economy when it is rich, than metals are of the US economy now. And it is very likely that the cost of making things out of metal will continue to go down compared to the cost of pure services.

In brief, although the American 1980 raw material bill is not terribly significant, the conclusion we are using it to demonstrate— that food and energy dominate the raw material problem—is valid.

Renewable Resources

This book follows the standard practice of virtually all statistical reports and other studies of raw materials, by including as raw materials (among other things): (1) field crops like grains, (2) animal food products, like beef carcasses, raw milk and eggs, and fish; and (3) lumber.

Some people would say: Grain, beef, and lumber are renewable resources; therefore they shouldn't be included in raw materials, because they aren't the kind of things that we should worry about running out of. By including renewable resources with finite resources, like coal and oil, in the category of raw materials you are distorting the picture.

In Appendix C, I consider the question of renewable

resources in a more careful discussion of the meaning of "extraction from nature." My conclusion is that most agriculture is not truly extractive because it doesn't reduce nature's ability to produce just as much next year. But since this view is out of line with standard thinking I do not follow it in this book.

Maybe, since wood is also a renewable resource, we should exclude it from the list of raw materials when we exclude agriculture. Many people would object because they are concerned about declining wood supply as a result of population increases and deforestation. They are afraid that in the future we will use so much wood that it will no longer be a renewable resource. However, there is also reason to think that we could produce plenty of wood on a renewable basis, even with a world population of ten billion people. In chapter ten, we will consider the question of forests in the future, which is particularly interesting and important because of its links to environmental quality and recreation. But, in any case, despite my arguments in Appendix C, I have included wood as a raw material, to be covered in chapter ten. If I had excluded wood it would have made the problem easier. So by following the conventional definition I am—as always—being conservative.

If we accepted the argument about renewable resources, and excluded wood and agricultural products from the list of raw materials, here's what the 1980 American raw material bill would look like:

TABLE 8
Use of Non-Renewable
Raw Materials in the U.S.

Fuels	16,000 pounds	$950
Everything Else		
Metals	1,000 pounds	$ 60
Other Non-fuel Minerals	2,000 pounds	$ 40
Stone, sand & gravel	20,000 pounds	$ 30
Total	**39,000 pounds**	**$1,080**

Raw materials altogether would be smaller, and fuels would be a bigger share of raw materials—compared with the conventional list. "Everything else" would be a bigger share of raw materials, but still small compared to the whole economy. Clearly, excluding wood and agricultural products from the list of raw materials wouldn't make the raw material problem harder.

Raw Material Prices and the Meaning of "Scarcity"

What does it mean to say that a material is "scarce"? It means that there isn't as much of it as people want to buy. But we know from experience that how much of a material people want to buy depends on how much it costs. So materials can't stay "scarce" for long—in this sense of the word—because the price will go up and people won't want to buy so much and soon there will be enough to supply everybody at the new price. (Also the higher price may make increased production possible.)

Experience confirms the simple conclusion that scarcity is very rare if it is defined as a lack of goods for a long time. What we see, for all materials, is that you can buy as much as you want—except in special circumstances such as war. This has been true almost all the time for almost all materials for generations. It is true for gold at $400 an ounce and for iron at $60 a ton. It is not just coincidence. It will always be true. There will be a price for any commercially significant material, and at that price you will be able, sooner or later, to buy as much as you want—and usually right away. In the United States and many other countries, there are millions of different products, and the everyday miracle is that there is almost exactly enough of every single one of them.

But even if the primitive idea of scarcity doesn't have much meaning, maybe the concept can be used to make comparisons. For example, can we say that gold is scarcer than iron? That depends on how you define scarce. If you define scarce as referring to a material which there isn't much of, than gold is scarcer than iron; but six-hole notebook paper is scarcer than gold. That's pretty silly. There must be a better definition of scarce.

There are several meaningful definitions of the scarcity of a material, and all of them are based on the price of the material or the difficulty of acquiring it.

Definitions based on quantities or desirability just don't work. They don't mean anything. Desirability is always comparative. Quantity always depends on how narrowly you define the material you are talking about. Polka dot toilet paper is scarce, but not toilet paper, and certainly not paper.

Therefore we must accept the economist's insight: a material is scarce if it costs a lot. If it is cheap it is not scarce.

So the question "Will raw materials eventually become scarce?" really means "Will raw materials become expensive?" (Will they become more expensive than they are today? Will they become more expensive than we can afford?) These questions too have their complexity, but we can work on them. It is clear that they force us to look at prices and costs.

One thing about prices and costs; they are the result of a great human tug-of-war. People care about prices. Buyers work to make them lower, sellers work to make them higher.

Nobody cares about total quantity; people only care about the quantity they buy or sell themselves. But everybody cares about price. Not only the buyers and sellers, but also the people who might buy if the price were low enough, or who might sell if the price became high enough. So quantity is a coincidence and price is the result of great human concern and attention.

What Can We Learn From Our Experience With Raw Material Prices?

Since increasing scarcity means increasing prices, we can find out whether there has been increasing scarcity in the past by looking at how prices have changed.

In 1955, the organization called Resources for the Future (RFF) was created, partly because of the great concern at that time about potential shortages of raw materials, which even led to the establishment of a Presidential commission. RFF did a tremendous amount of work to find out the prices for raw materials in the United States all the way back to 1870. RFF's technical studies of all these thousands and thousands of prices were published in a series of technical volumes which are generally accepted as the best work on the subject, and as a reasonably reliable summary of the history of raw material prices in the United States.*

The conclusions of these volumes were summed up in a small book written for RFF by Harold Barnett and Chandler Morse. It was called *Scarcity and Growth,* and published in 1963. This book was so important that RFF arranged a special symposium fifteen years later to reexamine its conclusion, and to see whether the facts had changed after it was written. That symposium, which was published in 1979 as *Scarcity and Growth Reconsidered,* made it clear that the additional fifteen years hadn't changed anything substantial. History still pointed in the direction that Barnett and Morse had described in 1963 on the basis of the mountains of RFF studies of commodity prices.

Barnett and Morse examined two kinds of prices to evaluate the popular idea that raw materials must be getting more scarce as a result of more and more of them being used.

One kind of price is the physical cost in labor and capital required to produce each raw material. Barnett and Morse used this kind of price to test what they called the "strong hypothesis" that, as we use more and more raw materials, more and more labor and capital would be required to extract them.**

It was natural to believe, as some economists had argued, that people would first use the materials that were easiest to extract, and when these were gone the materials used to replace them would be harder to extract. (A form of this theory has been used about farmland, arguing that the best land would be used first, and therefore new farmland would be very expensive or undesirable.)

Here is the evidence. From 1870 to 1880, the labor and capital

---

* Naturally specialists have many points of technical disagreement with the RFF studies of past commodity prices. But no one argues that there is a better overall judgment about what prices have been, nor would anyone argue that the RFF historical studies are far off the mark.

** This "strong hypothesis" is essentially the same as the popular view that, as we use up more and more of the Earth's supply of raw materials, naturally we will be forced to use more difficult and expensive sources.

required to extract things from nature (i.e. to produce the average unit of extractive product) increased slightly. From 1880 to 1890 the cost stayed roughly constant. Since 1890 the cost in work/hours and capital has fallen by more than half.

The decline in agricultural costs was about the same as for all extractive products—agriculture, minerals, and forest products— taken together. (Agriculture is the main part of the total.) But the cost of forestry products almost doubled from the late 1800s to 1919 and declined only 15% from 1919 to 1957.

The fall in the cost of minerals was much more dramatic than that of all extractive products together. The cost of extracting minerals went down to only a quarter of what it was in the late 1880s. This experience is especially significant because the quantities of minerals used multiplied much more than that of agriculture and forest products. Also, minerals are the most purely extractive products. Agriculture and forestry resources are mostly renewable. So, increasing scarcity should be a bigger problem for minerals, yet so far the opposite is true.

The original calculations for the United States that Barnett and Morse used have now been extended from 1957 through 1970. During these thirteen years the labor costs of extracting raw materials continued to decline at the same rate. But from 1960 to 1970 capital costs fell more slowly than they had for the previous twenty years (but about as fast as they had fallen from 1910 to 1920 and from 1930 to 1940).

In 1979, Barnett summarized the US price experience after 1957, and that from other parts of the world, concerning the strong hypothesis of increasing scarcity. He reported, "Productivity in mineral production not only does not decline, but increases rather strongly and somewhat persistently in all five of the regions for all four of the mineral classes."

The second kind of raw material price that Barnett and Morse summarized is the price relative to other kinds of goods and services. They used these comparative prices to examine what they called a "weak hypothesis" of scarcity. This hypothesis is that the labor and capital costs of raw materials have been declining not because raw materials are less scarce, but because the improvement in the efficiency of labor and capital has been so great that it overweighed and hid the effect of increased scarcity.

This weak hypothesis of scarcity is tested by comparing the prices of extractive products with the prices of other products. If increasing scarcity were acting like a brake, slowing the speed with which improvements in the efficiency of labor and capital could reduce the cost of extractive products, then the price of extractive products should not go down as fast as other products. In other words extractive product prices should rise in comparison to other products.

Here are the facts about the weak hypothesis of increasing scarcity. The relative price of all extractive goods in the United States increased 4% from the end of the nineteenth century to 1919. Then, from 1919 to 1957 the relative price of extractive products fell by 13% compared to other products.

The relative prices of minerals declined by 10% in the generation before 1919 and then fell by half from 1919 to 1957. These data have been extended to take into account prices up to 1973. They continue to give little support to the weak hypothesis of scarcity.

Will Future Price Trends Go the Other Way?

Some people have astutely pointed out that the fact that prices have gone down in the past does not prove that they will always go down in the future. Since history does not reliably answer for us the question about future prices, is there anything we can use to answer it?

As we will see in Chapters 7 and 8, there is a pretty good basis for saying that right now we can see, in general ways, how to keep the main raw material costs—food and energy—from rising to dangerous levels over the next centuries and probably for some thousands of years, even if our population multiplies by ten and our wealth by a hundred times.

Raw materials other than food and fuel now require only a small fraction of our time and money to produce, and many of them are among the most common materials there are. Also, modern technology has great abilities to avoid dependence on particular materials.

It is quite possible that raw material prices will stop going down, and then start to go up. But there is good reason for confidence that raw material prices do not have to rise to dangerous levels in the next several millennia, neither because of the greatly increased use that we can see coming, nor because of the finiteness of the Earth.[9]

In the mid 1970s grain prices, and many other commodity prices, rose sharply and a number of "experts" said that the basic limits of the Earth's capacity were beginning to be felt. Perhaps because of the false alarms only a few years earlier about worldwide food shortages, the main theme of the agricultural doom-sayers in the 70s was rising prices. ("How would poor countries ever be able to pay for food imports?") But most agricultural economists understood the situation and said at the time that the rise in the price of grain was temporary.*

Today, there are thousands of bankrupt or near-bankrupt farmers to testify who was right in that debate. The political problem of agriculture will be for many years, as it has been in the United States for at least fifty years, how to protect farmers from falling prices of what they produce.

Also, it turns out that for some time at least, the biggest buyer of food grains will not be a "poor" country, but the Soviet Union; which recently has needed to import twenty to sixty million tons a year (nearly a pound per person per day) on a continuing basis.

Some of the key poor countries have learned that if they don't enact laws to hold down the price of farm products, and if they stay out of war, their own farmers can usually grow most or all of the

---

* There was a clear disagreement among those who wrote about the significance of grain and commodity price rises in the 70s. One group said that it was the first stage of a permanent process of increasing prices. The other group said that it was an ordinary short-term fluctuation, and that prices would soon fall. The second group turned out to be right about those price rises.

This experience does not prove that all commodity price rises have to be temporary. But it suggests that if someone over forty tells you about impending shortages and price rises, you might want to ask what was his view in the '70s. If he was wrong then it might be helpful for him to explain how his analysis had been adjusted to avoid repeating the same mistake.

food they need, avoiding the need for non-luxury food imports. (Japan and Switzerland import a lot of food, but not because their people are hungry.)

Conclusions

The only practical meaning of scarcity is related to high prices. So far the prices of most raw materials (and especially minerals) have been declining. But it is possible that extractive products could begin to become more expensive, that is scarcer, in the future.

But, looking specifically at food and energy, the main raw materials, we will see that they do not need to cost dangerously more, even if the population gets much larger and richer. And the other materials, apart from common ones like stone and iron and aluminum sources, don't require much money now. So even if they did get much more expensive it would not be a dramatic burden on mankind.

How Pollution Fits In

Pollution is a turned-around question—that is, we worry about having too much instead of about having too little. The conventional form of the pollution question is whether we can get and use the resources we need without causing too much pollution. All the calculations in this book are done on the basis of avoiding any net increase in pollution. In fact all the discussion in this book is consistent with a decline in pollution. As we shall see, it is not very meaningful to talk about a single "pollution level," but it can be used as a rough synonym for "quality of the physical environment."

The overall pollution question is considered at length in chapter eleven. As a temporary expedient, I can respond to the pollution question by turning it around. Then it will fit into the general analysis of resource scarcity. You can say that pollutants create the need for resources that can trap, absorb, destroy or dilute pollutants; enough so that the environment isn't harmed. The pollution absorbers, destroyers, converters, or diluters, can be thought of as raw materials. Many of the reasons why we don't have to worry about running out of other raw materials also apply to pollution absorbers, converters, etc.

SEVEN

Feeding the Exploded Population is a Task Not a Problem

In the long run—pretty soon—the food problem everywhere will be what it is here: fat people and broke farmers.

I N THIS CHAPTER I WILL SHOW YOU WHY we can be confident that we can produce all the food we will ever want, even if we had to use only the science and resources we already know about. I will explain why nothing about the finite nature of the Earth has to stop us, and why no physical limit that nature now imposes upon us will determine how much food we can produce. (As I said before, I am talking here only about ten to thirty billion people. Also there are some real dangers that should be recognized, which we'll discuss in Part III.)

Of course, I am not saying it will be easy. Much brilliant work will be required to make possible what I will describe. Millions of farmers and others will have to work hard and intelligently to achieve the necessary production. Immense amounts of capital will have to be invested in machinery and factories, in land improvement and agricultural facilities of all kinds. This will not be possible unless there is a reasonable degree of peace in large areas most of the time. Nor will it be possible unless appropriate economic systems continue to exist in much of the world.

But what is required is not more than what we have done in the past. No new international order is necessary. Mankind does not have to become more honest, intelligent, cooperative, creative, generous or wise than Americans, Europeans, Japanese, Koreans, and others are today. Nor is there any reason to think that other peoples lack the human qualities that are needed. (As we have discussed in Part I, individuals and societies in much of the world have to learn how to be more productive and have to accumulate capital, but there is no reason to think that they are incapable of doing so.)

Nor am I saying that if you gave an order tomorrow to produce ten billion tons of grain in 1997 it could be done. But we won't want ten billion tons for at least a century, and we won't want it all of a sudden.

If it is as easy as I say to provide all the food we will need in the future, why is there so much hunger today? Why are we seeing television spectaculars to relieve the suffering of people stricken by desperate famines?

Hunger in the World Today

Many millions of people in the world today do not have enough to eat. Some will die of starvation. Many more will be so weakened by hunger that they will die of diseases that would otherwise not have been dangerous. An even larger number of people are stunted in their growth or damaged in their physical or mental development by lack of food. Large numbers of other people are forced by lack of food to stay almost completely passive and still for much of the year to conserve their strength for the seasons in which they eat extra to be able to work in the fields.

Lack of food produces a vast amount of human loss and suffering in the world. Many people do not have enough food. (In this sense there is undoubtedly immense scarcity.*)

* Despite the vast numbers of hungry people, the UN Food and Agriculture

While the number of people in the world has been growing rapidly, the number of people severely harmed by hunger, and the number of people dying in famines, has been going down each generation. But our concern here is the reason for hunger, not the amount of it. There is too much. (Although there is less than there used to be and there will be much less in the future.)

Here we must ask why widespread hunger exists. Is it evidence that the world cannot produce enough food? (Or at least an indication that the limit of food production cannot be too far away—even though new techniques and better management can somewhat increase world food production?)

The answer is that widespread hunger is not at all related to the ability of the world to produce food. The reason is very straightforward. The great bulk of the people who are hungry today do not have enough food because they do not have enough money to buy it. If they had more money to buy food the food would be there for them to buy.

Today the real cause of most famines is not drought or other natural disasters—it is war and politics. (Botswana's recent drought was as bad as the drought blamed for the famines in Ethiopia and elsewhere in Africa, but there was no famine in Botswana. Since Botswana is a democracy its government had to buy the food needed to prevent famine—well under a $100 per person per year—or it would have lost the next election.) Famines come when a government wants or is willing to accept starvation in order to get people to do what the government wants them to do. Local food shortages usually come from government programs to establish communal farming systems or to hold farm prices down.

Organization (FAO), the media, most international public figures, and many experts, manage to greatly overestimate or exaggerate the amount of hunger or starvation in the world.

The word "malnourished" can be used in so many ways that any debate about the extent of hunger in the world quickly degenerates into argument about definitions. For reasons explained above, we do not need to know the extent of hunger today to consider the issues of this book. But it is worth noting that the common idea that one-quarter of the people of the world go to bed hungry every night are extreme exaggerations. The quantity of human suffering from hunger is large enough without being exaggerated. If the word "hunger" is used the way most people picture it in their minds, it applies to under 10% of the people of the world.

Obviously, if all the hungry people were suddenly given more money, enough additional food to satisfy them would not appear overnight. But with any imaginable rate of increase in money for the poorest people, the farmers would have no trouble keeping up with growth in demand for food. (Nor is there any reason to believe that a rapid increase in the demand for food would greatly increase food prices for long.)

Do you doubt that there are many people who want a Cadillac and who do not have one? In that sense there is a shortage of Cadillacs. But if the number of people who can afford to buy Cadillacs increases, General Motors would be delighted to increase the number produced and could be counted upon to make one for everybody who is ready to buy one. There is no shortage of Cadillacs in the sense that everyone who goes to a dealer with enough money has no trouble buying one.

For a long time most of the foreign aid/economic development community didn't understand this fundamental point. They thought that the problem was how to grow enough food. Much of their effort was addressed to this "problem" of growing more food, even though that is no more the real problem than the difficulty of producing enough Cadillacs. The real problem is for people to have enough money to pay for food. When they do, the farmers will be just as accommodating in supplying all customers as General Motors is. (Of course farmers can always use help in the task of growing more food, which is not so easy. Since governments often stand in the way, the biggest help government can give in a number of countries is just to get out of the way, for example, by allowing the price to rise to the point where it makes sense for farmers to do what is necessary to grow more—but more positive help can also be useful.)

Famines today—like that in Ethiopia—have primarily *political* causes. They are not the result of physical difficulties in producing food. Starvation results from massive disruptions and population movements related to war and revolution, or from governments either deciding to starve part of their population or being too embarrassed to let others know that their people need food.

The largest famines in recent years occurred in China in the

1960s, when some thirty million people died from lack of food following Mao's reorganization of Chinese agriculture. Part of the reason for this starvation was that the Chinese government limited the facilities and arrangement for the movement of goods between provinces. The result was that when a province had a bad harvest, perhaps because of normal weather fluctuations, the people of that province starved even though there was more than enough food in the neighboring provinces.

Of course, there was ample food available in the *world* to prevent that starvation, but the Chinese government did not want to admit that its people were dying of starvation. Moreover, they might have had a problem arranging enough transportation to deliver and distribute the food to where it was needed.

Now that China is changing its farm policy, it is able to take advantage of new agricultural technology and to grow more than enough food for its people.

In many of the countries that are not growing as much food as they need, the primary reason is the political decisions taken by the government. The primary mistakes are keeping resources away from the agricultural sector (to favor the people living in the main city, who are politically more significant); favoring industry and the military; and imposing agricultural collectives or other inefficient farming practices for military, political or ideological reasons.

Also, there is less famine in the world than is often supposed. For example, there was much talk of the famine in the Sahel in the 70s—everybody has seen the picture of the emaciated dead cow. But despite the fact that UN Secretary General Waldheim talked about over one hundred thousand deaths in the "Sahel famine," the United Nations experts who examined the situation and the statistics in detail reported that there had been only an insignificant increase, or none at all, in the normal death rate during the "famine;" although the margin of uncertainty in the statistics was large enough so that there might have been a slight increase in infant mortality.[10]

In brief, if you want to judge the prospects for agriculture from today's newspapers, the significant items are stories about falling agricultural prices and growing surpluses, not the pictures of famines in Africa. The American farmers facing bankruptcy are in trouble not because they cannot not grow enough, but because they are facing increased low-cost competition around the world. This has lowered the value of farmland they bought at prices which were too high partly because of false expectations of food shortages.

Will We Have Enough Food in the Future?

Any agricultural expert can tell you about many problems and difficulties—some of which may now seem unsolvable—that we would have if we were to try to raise production of grain-equivalent* from two billion tons to ten billion tons now. I am not saying that anybody today knows how we will solve all of the immense problems that will arise as we multiply our food production by nearly five times over the next one hundred or two hundred years. It is an immense and complex enterprise, and the solutions to all the problems that will arise are not ready on the shelf.

It is a little like when a young friend moves to a city where you have never been. You can't tell him which neighborhoods would be good to live in, or what price to pay for a place to live, or which real estate agent is best, or how long a commute will be necessary. You know how frightening and difficult it is to be alone in a place you don't know, but you also know that everything that is needed will be there on a reasonably satisfactory basis. And even if he has never had to find a place to live he will be able to learn what he needs to learn (although undoubtedly with mistakes along the way). You don't know prices there, but you know that if he is single and has a reasonable job he will be able to afford what he needs. Similarly, I can't tell farmers, and those who produce the goods and

---

* I use the idea of "grain-equivalent" just to simplify discussion and calculations by having a single measure for all crops that we use directly or indirectly for food. We Americans now eat an average of 200 pounds per year of grain in the form of bread, cereal, etc. We eat another 1200 pounds in the form of meat and dairy products based on grains. All the other foods we eat have as many calories as do 700 pounds of grain. So I say that we each eat 200 + 1200 + 700 = 2100 pounds of grain-equivalent per year. (The calorie yield/acre of some crops is very different than that of grain. But since such crops don't provide a large share of our food, the error introduced by calculating as if all of our food came from grain is not large compared to the uncertainties of our estimates, and certainly is not large enough to affect our conclusions.)

services farmers need, how to solve all the difficulties they will face in multiplying food production, but I can be confident that, when they get there, they will be able to find the answers, even if there are no geniuses among them.

Multiplying food production by five times over the next one hundred or two hundred years will be easier than multiplying it by over seven times as we did in the last two hundred years. No miracles, no scientific breakthroughs, no unknown lands or unexpected new resources, and no reforms of human character or government are required. All that is required is a continuing use of current evolutionary processes in technology and in economic development; and as much peace as we have had in the last century.

How Much Food Will We Need?

How much food will we need and where will it come from? In brief, we will need to multiply the production of grain-equivalent by approximately 2.3 times because there will be more people; and we will have to multiply again by a little more than another two times so that everyone can eat as much as Americans do now (because now the average person in the world eats less than half as much as Americans do). Altogether, we need to multiply grain-equivalent production by five times, from two billion tons per year to ten billion (for a world population of about ten billion people).

One way to make it easier to show where we can get the food we need would be to say that we really won't need or want so much food. Americans eat much more than necessary, mostly because we use so much meat, requiring a large amount of grain-equivalent for every calorie that we eat. Also, we live in a colder climate than the average person, and we may continue to be larger than the average person in the world. (The average Japanese eats about 20% fewer calories than Americans or Russians; and it is not because Japanese are too poor to eat more.)

But I am not going to show that we have enough by arguing that since we eat so much and so wastefully, we can use conservation to close part of the gap. Of course, it wouldn't be at all surprising if the average person, when the whole world is rich, eats much less grain-equivalent than Americans eat today. But with our usual conservatism we will ignore that possibility. We will assume that everybody consumes as much grain-equivalent as Americans do today, and so we will need ten billion metric tons for ten billion people. If people eat less, the ten billion tons would be enough for more people.

There are three methods we might use—in some combination—to produce ten billion tons of grain-equivalent per year.

(1) Conventional crops grown in conventional ways—that is, normal evolutionary development and expansion of today's agriculture; or

(2) Conventional crops grown in new ways, e.g. hydroponics; or

(3) New kinds of foods produced entirely differently—perhaps more like manufacturing than like agriculture.

Today, grain or its equivalent is not manufactured, i.e., grown hydroponically or in factories, except in special situations, because it is cheaper to grow it in fields. But, using currently known techniques, grain equivalents could be mass produced artificially for approximately $100-$300 per ton. Undoubtedly there would be difficulties and unforeseen costs if we tried to produce billions of tons this way. But there probably would also be some technological developments that would permit costs to be reduced. Therefore, it is not unreasonable to think that the cost of manufactured grain-equivalents will be no more than three times larger or smaller than the current cost of grain-equivalents. That is, if we manufactured all of our basic food it might cost $450 per ton.

Another possibility is that we or our animals might get some or all of our nutrients from artificial ingredients not grown at all, and not forms of current foods.

Americans now spend about 1%-2% of our average incomes for the raw material for our food (that is, the grain-equivalent we use). In the long run, the world is likely to be richer than the United States is today, but people won't be eating more than Americans do today. And most of the evidence suggests that the very long downward trend of the cost of producing grain will continue. A century or two from now it seems likely that people will spend less than 1% of average income to pay for food raw materials. But even if food raw material costs changed direction, and more than doubled, to $450 per ton, only a small part of people's income would be needed for the food we grow.

We can produce so much more than ten billion tons just by using conventional agriculture that I only mention the other possibilities, although there is good reason to think that each of them could provide a major share of what we need.

Since most of what we grow we feed to animals, there is no particular reason to stick entirely to familiar foods, although we could. (I can already see the triply-misleading headlines if I talked about the prospects of new sources of nutrients: "Researcher says there is enough food because people will eat seaweed and algae."

But What About the Next Few Generations (the short-run)?

You will have noticed that I am only addressing the long-term food question—whether we should expect that there can be enough food for a large, rich world population beginning over a century from now, and lasting indefinitely.

Some people may be concerned about whether we will have enough food to get to the long-run. Although it is not the subject of this book, we can note that, since the amount of food produced in the world per person has been growing steadily, and population growth rates have been declining steadily, the short-term problem has been growing smaller.* (And, unfortunately for the American farmer, prices for food crops have been coming down as a result.) This is only one of the reasons why it is very unlikely that there will be a major food production problem before we get to the long-run. If we do, it will not be because of natural scarcity or pollution problems, but because of bad political decisions. In any event this book is about the long-term perspective—for which you don't have to spend a lot of time poring over complicated details, although you do need to learn a different way to look at questions.

* Even per capita food production in the developing countries has been increasing through the period when population was growing fastest; it increased by 14% from 1952 to 1980. Although total food production grew faster in the developing countries than in the industrialized countries (2.9% compared to 2.1%) the much greater birth rates in the developing countries made the average food production per person grow more slowly in those countries.

Aside on Some Mystical Ideas
about Food and Farming

1. Farmland produces crops.

The special feature of farming that distinguishes it from other kinds of production is its use of land. In fact, the implicit sense many people have is that it is the land that produces the crop. People see the land as fertile, giving birth to corn, and the farmer as a midwife.

The perception that grain is the product of land is profoundly misleading (although like many other misunderstandings it is based on a correct fact). It is much more realistic to think of grain as the product of man's work and of other components, most of which are also manmade. Man has shown that he can multiply the output of the land by ten times. Why should the land get the credit?

Only about one quarter of the value of the farm products sold is earned by the land (with the rest being credited to labor, equipment, and purchased goods and services). More than half of farm income in the United States comes from the sale of animal products which are no more tied to the land than are manufactured products. (While cattle are often pastured on large areas of land for convenience and economy, the use of pasture or range is not at all necessary; if the price of pasture land gets too high, cattle and sheep can be raised without it, and the cost of meat and milk will only increase moderately. Chickens and pigs don't graze at all.)

2. Farmland is natural.

The perception that farmland is natural, rather than manmade, is as erroneous as the perception that land produces crops. The acres from which we now harvest our crops required a tremendous amount of work to become as fertile as they are. They had to be cleared of trees, bushes, and rocks. Many of them had to be drained, irrigated, to have the soil treated, to be fenced, etc.

For most cropland, the value of the work invested in making it ready to farm is well over half of the value of the land.[11] While some land has been made worse over the years, the great majority of the land we harvest is much better (for farming) than it was when we came to it.* The cost of these improvements are a large share of the present value

* According to the Soil Conservation Service our farmland is still getting better. They

100

of the land.

So we can see that our supply of fertile, productive farmland today is more the result of people's work than it is a gift of nature. And, as we shall see, nature has waiting for us another land gift, bigger than that which we have already taken and used to build our current supply of arable land.

Summary Correction of the First Two Mystical Ideas

In brief, most agriculture is the product of man not of land, and most farmland is the product of man not of nature. Therefore, almost all food raw material is the product of man not of nature.

3. Farmland is being reduced and is in short supply.

But many people are worried about the long term sufficiency of food production partly because they are afraid that less land will be available for farming. They are concerned when the number of acres harvested in the United States declines, because they think the decline results from erosion and from paving over farmland for parking lots and housing tracts.

For a while the US Department of Agriculture was saying that in the 70s there had been a distressing acceleration of the rate of conversion of agricultural land to other uses. They based these cries of alarm on a survey of the Soil Conservation Service (SCS) that used some questionable estimating procedures (the results of which were contradicted by other evidence). Because of academic criticism of these reports, the SCS issued a new survey in 1982 that showed that their original concern was uncalled for.[12]

Other people say that declines in agricultural acreage are the result of using farmland more efficiently. How can anyone tell who is right? Are different points of view on this issue all more or less valid? No. One view is correct. You can tell which is correct by looking at the details of year-to-year changes in specific categories of land, such as sales for non-farm uses, changes in how much of the cropland on farms is actually used for crops from one year to the next, etc. More fundamentally you can see how misdirected is the concern about declines in farmland by thinking about the basic economics and facts of farming.

If you asked American farmers to increase production by 25% they

---

classify cropland in eight classes, and the fraction in the three best classes grew from 83% in 1958 and 1967 to 86% in 1975.

wouldn't say, "We can't do it because there isn't enough farmland left."*
Any careful analysis of what is happening on U.S. farms shows that there
is no shortage of land to grow crops, and that the land lost to roads and
housing tracts is very small compared to the farmland we use for crops,
or for the additional land we could use for crops if necessary.

A farmer can increase the amount of food he grows either (1) by
using more fertilizer and other inputs, or (2) by improving his own
farmland, or (3) by buying other farmland, or (4) by buying non-farmland
and converting it into farmland. Which he does depends on the relative
costs of all these different ways to increase the crop. Roughly speaking
public policy doesn't care what he does, anymore than it cares what kind
of tractor he uses. All these ways of increasing the crop are morally equal.

The amount of land being farmed declines when it is cheaper to
grow food on less land by using more labor or other inputs. If the amount
of farmed land increases it means it is cheaper to use less labor or other
inputs and to use more land. So we know that if the amount of land
used for farms is declining it isn't because more farmland isn't available.
It is just not true that the lack of good farmland is preventing us from
growing more food. The amount of food grown is determined by what
price the farmers expect to be able to sell their crop for and the cost
of growing food. The price is determined by how much of each food
people are willing to buy at various prices.

The supposed fallacy of being guided by short-term profits.

You could say, "That's the trouble with short-term thinking. Suppose each
year it is profitable for farmers to farm more intensively and to use a
little less land, and they sell that land to people who pave it over and
permanently destroy its agricultural potential, and this process goes on
and on until there is practically no farm land left. Couldn't we paint
ourselves into a fatal corner in this way?" The answer is "no" for several
reasons, such as: we aren't diverting agricultural land very fast; most
diversions can be reversed; prices do eventually reflect future problems
and so produce self-correcting forces (at least for slowly developing
problems). So we can't "fall over a cliff" on the supply of farmland. In

---

* If you asked American farmers to double production in ten years, they might say
that they couldn't do it, but if they did say so they would be wrong. I believe that
most agricultural economists would be happy to bet that if farm prices were
guaranteed at twice today's (depressed) levels for 20 years (inflation adjusted),
production would double within ten years. On reflection, I think most farmers would
agree.

fact during the last generation more farmland has been added than has been subtracted; the worldwide total has been increasing about 5% per decade.

As citizens we don't need to be at all concerned about whether the amount of land being farmed is increasing or decreasing. All we care about is that the price of farm crops doesn't go up, at least not so much that we can't comfortably afford to buy the products we are used to having. (Agricultural specialists may, as a technical matter, be concerned about wastage of farmland increasing costs unnecessarily. But that issue does not rise to the dignity of a citizens' issue.)

4. "Farm Labor" is unique and critical.

Just as some people talk mystically about how much farmland there is, other people talk mystically about farm labor. They say things like, "In underdeveloped countries there are so many people in rural areas that labor-intensive agriculture is possible, or is essential, or is desireable."

But as a practical matter farm labor is always available if you pay enough. (It may take a few years to expand the labor supply with particular skills in a particular place, but it can almost always be done.) So there can't really be a shortage of farm labor for labor-intensive farming. And, if there can't be a shortage, it doesn't say much to say that there is enough. On the other hand, the fact that there are many unemployed people in some rural areas doesn't mean that farm labor is free or even cheap there. There is always some cost to people's labor. At a minimum you have to pay people enough so that they are willing to give up leisure or whatever else they could use their time for. Also you have to pay workers at least the cost of the extra food a person needs to eat if he is working. If their labor doesn't produce very much, compared to what could be produced without it, then even a very low rate of pay for farm laborers will be expensive.

What it comes down to is that farm labor of a particular kind in a particular place may be cheap or expensive or in between. In this way farm labor is like land or water or fertilizer or transportation to market or fuel or machinery or anything else used in producing crops.

The usefulness of farm labor for producing crops can vary immensely depending on the quality of the labor and other factors. Therefore the value of farm labor of various qualities in a particular area at any time depends on the value of the different crops that could be planted, and on the cost of other things that can be used in different amounts to increase the crop. And all the costs and values are continually changing. So the efficient decision about how much farm labor to use in producing crops in a particular place depends on the cost and quality of the labor, and the costs of other things that can be combined with labor in different ways to produce crops.

5. The "Demand for Food" depends on how many people there are.

Sometimes people are mystical about the demand or need for food, as if it were different than other goods. Of course food is essential for life, but so is arsenic (.4 grams), and lots of other things. So the fact that food supply would be a matter of life and death if most food production disappeared, doesn't affect things very much on a day-to-day basis. A large part of the world's population could live very well on half as much food crops as they use now. Most practical decisions concern fairly small changes in food production, 1% or 10%. These are in the range where food consumption is a matter of preference or price, not life and death, or even health.* The farmer or agricultural planner doesn't care about how many people there are. He might care about the demand for food, except that people don't buy "food" in general, they buy particular commodities. The production plans of farmers and other growers are influenced by the demand for wheat or bananas or milk. And demand means the same thing to them as to the manufacturers of screw drivers or bow ties, "How much of my product are people ready to pay for?" So if you want to know how much food will need to be grown, don't ask how many people there will be, ask how much money they will have and what foods they like to eat. For each specific food—eggs, chicken wings, peas, etc.—there will always be what the economists call a demand curve, a line on a piece of graph paper which reports how much people will buy at any price. You can't answer the question "what is the demand for wheat?" by stating a single amount as the demand. ("People will buy three million bushels of wheat this week.") How much people will buy

* One of the confusing things about living in a rich society is that words change meaning. We talk about "necessities" and "luxuries" but the discussion is peculiar. Clearly food is a necessity. But for the average American only a small percent of the money he spends on "food" is a necessity. First he eats much more than he "needs" (meat is an especially unnecessary use of crops because it takes about 6 calories of grain to produce 1 calorie of meat). More important, most of the food bought is not so much food as it is convenience, fashion, entertainment, etc. And most of the value of the food part doesn't come from the cost of growing crops but from processing the crops after they have been harvested. The average American today can have a diet as tasty and varied as that of the great majority of happily well-fed people throughout history, and meet all the requirements of good health, at a cost of less than a quarter of what he now spends for food, if he is willing to use a reasonable amount of time preparing his food.

depends on the price. At a high price much less will be bought than at a low price. Therefore the only way to describe the demand is by a list of prices and a statement of how much would be bought at each price, or by a line on a piece of graph paper that gives the same information for all possible prices.

How Many More Acres Can We Harvest?

If we are going to use familiar ways of growing food, the only way we can increase production is by some combination of increasing the amount of land we use for growing food, or growing more food on each acre that we harvest.

The world now harvests its food from about 2,800 million acres of land. All of the most detailed, thorough, and unbiased studies indicate that there are at least another 5,000 million acres, comparable to those now being used, that could be used to grow food.

What about the fear that shortages of farmland will result from paving over "prime farmland" for suburbs or for roads?

Human settlements now occupy less than 1% of the land area of the world—and farmland less than 10%. About another 15% of the land area can be made into farmland at reasonable cost. (Half the land area is regarded as uninhabitable—deserts, high mountains, polar areas, etc.) Even if world population triples or quadruples and people want to spread out a great deal more than they do today, it is hard to be frightened at the possible competition for farmland. If population triples, human settlements would still occupy less than 6% of the habitable land area of the world.

What about roads? Using the great tools of multiplication and division we can get some perspective on whether a vastly expanding road system threatens to deprive us of the farmland we need. The United States, which is quite rich in roads, has a little over three million miles of paved roads in about three million square miles of area (not counting Alaska). By a great feat in division we see that in the United States, there is roughly one mile of road, on the average, through every square mile of land area. (But in Maine there is an area of about 3,000 square miles with no roads through it.)

Most of the roads are rural secondary roads. (The federal interstate highway system is less than one half of one percent of our road mileage.) So we can think of the average road running through the average square mile of land taking a swath about fifty feet wide out of the square mile, which is by definition 5,280 feet wide, so the road takes less than 1% of the square mile.

How Much Farmland Can be Made?

The most thorough study is one done a few years ago by a team of Dutch soil and agriculture experts who conducted a laborious analysis using the best recent soil maps of the world. The team, led by Dr. P. Buringh, looked at each of the 222 regions into which the soil maps divided the world. They considered the soil conditions, climate, topography, amount of sunlight, and vegetation of each region.

Since most of the regions were big and diverse, the study group, which was from the Agricultural University of Wageningen, had to evaluate each of the more than ten thousand smaller soil units into which the 222 regions are divided. (A typical soil unit would be less than 100 miles square.) One at a time they estimated how much potential arable land there was in each soil unit area; excluding areas where the soils are too poor, too stony, too steep, or too shallow; and excluding land already in use (10%-30%). They also excluded poor land used for extensive grazing, some forested areas, and swamps that can't be reclaimed. In their total they also excluded true deserts and also some large areas that could be farmed if there were water but for which no water seems to be available. And they excluded areas that are too cold or don't have enough sunlight to grow crops. They left plenty of room for other land uses—at least 30% and mostly over 50% of each region.

The result of all of these evaluations and estimates by Buringh and his Dutch colleagues was that there are 8,500 million acres of potentially arable land on the Earth, of which only 3,500 are now farmland. (80% of the current farmland is being used to grow food crops in the average year; the rest is fallow or idle or being used for non-food crops like cotton or tobacco.) Therefore they conclude that we could add another 5,000 million acres of farmland, almost tripling the area now being used to grow food.*

Most knowledgeable writers now accept Buringh's numbers as about as good as any estimates available today. There are some people who seem to have very different estimates, but when you read the fine print it turns out that usually there really isn't much disagreement about the basic facts. It is just that they are using some special assumptions or definitions—which may be perfectly appropriate for the question they are looking at, but which shouldn't be used except for those special purposes.

SOME TIME AGO it was generally believed that much of the humid tropics had "lateritic" soil which couldn't be used for farming because if you cut the forest down and exposed the soil it would turn to "laterite" which is like rock and can't be farmed. This would mean that almost none of the huge areas of humid tropical forests could be used for agriculture. But in the last twenty-five years soil scientists have learned that the "laterite" problem is much rarer than was first thought, and that much of the tropical forest areas have great agricultural potential.

As we shall shortly see, the question of exactly how many acres of potential farmland is available is less important than the question of how much can be grown on each acre. So if you allow for a margin or error of say 25% either way, it is reasonably safe to use 5,000 million acres as the best estimate of how much potential new food cropland there is on the Earth.

---

* Several prominent studies that were done before the Buringh work, including the first report to The Club of Rome, used an estimate of potential farmland that had been made eight years earlier by the US President's Science Advisory Committee. The American and Dutch estimates were almost exactly the same for Asia and Africa, but the Americans were 14% higher for South America, 12% lower for North America, and 34% lower for Europe than Buringh's group. But these differences almost balanced each other and the American total was only 6% lower than Buringh's.

The similarity of the overall conclusions reached by the Buringh group to the earlier results has two implications. It makes the people who did the American study look good; because they got almost the same answer as the Buringh group did, without the much more detailed work of the later study, and without the benefit of new research that had not been available when they did their study. Also the closeness of the Buringh result to the independent estimate that had been made in the United States earlier, lends some additional credibility to the Buringh conclusions.

Buringh, et al., estimated the average cost of making the potential arable land ready to grow crops. About one third of the land that is not already being used for farming would cost less than $500 per acre (in 1981 dollars) to make ready; about one third would cost around $1,000 per acre; and the worst third would cost close to $2,000 per acre. This money would pay for things like clearing forests, soil conservation, terracing, leveling and/or draining, etc. These costs are not decisively different than the current costs of agricultural land. Paying such costs would not multiply the cost of food, indeed might not increase it at all.

If we used *all* the agricultural land the Buringh group defined it would take about 22% of the land area of the world. But some farmland is much more productive than the average, and some much less. Therefore if there were some kind of shortage of land, we could take a large share of the less productive farmland away from food production without greatly reducing our ability to grow food. Certainly we do not need to use more that 10% of the Earth's land area for growing food for ten billion people.

Sequential Cropping

The growing season for any particular farmland is determined by the length of time that there is enough sun and no frost. The number of crops that can be grown, one after another in the same year, on one acre, depends on how long the crop takes to grow and how long the growing season is. Of course a second or third crop can't be grown unless there is enough water at the right time—either from rain or from irrigation—and also enough fertilizer and whatever else is required to maintain the soil. A substantial share of crop land, especially in the tropics, has a growing season long enough to grow two, three or even four crops.

Taking all these major factors into account, the Buringh study concluded that there are 4,000 million acres that could produce at least one additional crop per year by sequential cropping (double cropping). This includes third crops in some places now growing two crops, and second and sometimes third crops in places now growing only one; where sufficient water and other requirements are potentially available.

In effect, sequential cropping could add as much grain-equivalent as an additional 4,000 million acres with a single crop. (The usual practice is to consider sequential cropping with other ways of increasing yield per acre. But we are including it here with potential sources of increased acreage.)

Summary of Ways of
Increasing Number of Acres Harvested

We now grow our food on 2,800 million acres. We can add 5,000 million acres of land not now used as farmland, and we can add the equivalent of 4,000 million acres by the use of sequential cropping. This is a total potential increase of 9,000 million acres of food harvest. If we used all these additional acres, we would be harvesting more than four times as many acres to grow food as we do now.

Allowing for a margin of error in these estimates, and also for some increase in the amount of land used for non-food crops, a conservative conclusion is that the area of food crop harvests can be multiplied by at least three if necessary.

How Much More Food Can We Grow
on an Acre of Farmland?

Farming is such a complex and varied enterprise that one is rarely interested in overall averages. Some acres grow one hundred times as much as others. People cannot have direct knowledge about overall averages, only about particular kinds of crops, grown in particular kinds of soils and other conditions, with particular farming practices. But when the farmers are all finished at the end of the year, you can look around and see that they grew a certain amount of food, and you can see how much land they used to do it. If you divide the first number by the second you will have the average yield per acre for the year. Similarly if we want to estimate how much food can be grown by conventional agriculture, we have to see how much land is available for growing food and multiply it by some number to get total possible conventional food production.

Before considering past and current average yields, and

potential future increases, we should review briefly the major things that affect how much each acre yields.

Inputs

You'll have to excuse the use of this bland and offensive word, which happens to express perfectly the broad idea that needs to be discussed here. That idea is that if the farmer puts more into the effort to grow food on his land he will get more food out. The general category of inputs includes: fertilizers, pesticides, herbicides (weed-killers), machinery, and labor. (Some inputs, like improved seeds, we will consider separately.)

Farmers are very interested in the question of how much more they can get out of their land by spending more for fertilizer and other inputs. They have tried hundreds or thousands of combinations, on many kinds of fields with many different crops. Many American farmers, and others too, use as large an amount of each input as makes sense for their situation. They will spend an extra $1,000 buying inputs only if it will increase their harvest by a $1,000 worth of grain.* But most of the land being farmed in the world is using much smaller amounts of inputs than efficient American farmers. So we can know with reasonable confidence approximately how much average yield per acre would be increased if economic conditions were suitable and all farmers applied the knowledge gained by modern farmers about the benefits of using more inputs.** The studies of this question have indicated that the

---

* It should be noticed that this is a very dynamic question. If the price of the crop goes up, or the cost of the input goes down, it makes sense to use more inputs (and vice versa). But usually with the amount of inputs that a modern farmer uses fairly small changes in prices won't change the yield per acre much.

** There is a certain amount of controversy about various farming practices. Some people argue that it is better to use various methods to reduce the quantities applied, particularly of some kinds of pesticides and fertilizers. And there are arguments about the wisdom of tillage and plowing techniques that prevent erosion. But the conclusion that the world could grow a lot more food on the same land just by using more inputs, according to the practices of the most efficient farmers today, does not depend on who is right in those arguments about appropriate farming technology. Mostly it is a question of what kind of which input to use. It would take a rather extreme outcome from those technical arguments to make a significant change in the rough judgement about how much more food could be grown if farmers used more inputs.

amount of food grown on the average acre used all over the world could be increased by 80% just by using more inputs according to the best practices of today's farmers. In other words, just by using more stuff on the same land we could multiply food production by almost two times.

During the last generation we have not only increased the amount of inputs used by farmers, we have also found better ones. There is no reason to think that we won't continue to find better inputs for farmers to use. But our estimate here doesn't use any future discoveries. Undoubtedly there will turn out to be more problems with the inputs we are using now, especially as their use is greatly expanded. So we will only assume that any future discoveries are good enough to keep us even—that is, to make up for defects and problems with the current stuff.

How can we know that there will be any future discoveries, or that they will be good enough to make up for all the problems about current agricultural inputs? We can't. We could bring together the one hundred greatest experts and let them study the question for a year. They could say a lot more than I can; but they wouldn't be able to give a very different answer, certainly not with much confidence.

Better Seeds

During the last twenty years or so we have learned how to systematically develop improved forms of natural crops like rice and corn. (I am not talking now about the more recent scientific work with recombinant DNA.) Already a number of new "high-yielding varieties" (HYV) of rice have been developed and used by ordinary Asian farmers on millions of acres. HYVs of wheat, corn, sorghum, cassava, peanuts and many other crops have also been developed. The techniques of developing new HYVs have become reasonably standardized, and their use has just begun. There are already a number of institutes and other organizations applying these techniques to get all kinds of improvements in many different crops. The people who are doing this work have no doubt that by applying the techniques already developed they will be able to produce dozens and dozens of improved varieties of food crops.

111

The new techniques for designing improved varieties of seed can be used not only to increase yield. Sometimes they can be used to make the crop hardier, or easier to grow. For example, one of the new varieties of rice has shorter stalks so that it is less vulnerable to winds.

Of course these techniques are not magic and cannot produce miracles. There are significant biological or physical limits to how much improvement can be made in each kind of plant. Usually it is only possible to develop qualities that can be found in nature. The desirable qualities can often be combined in new species but they can't be completely invented. Within these limits, there is room for tremendous improvement when compared to most of the seeds that are used now. All that is required is a continuation and extension of the work now going on.

One of the most exciting, fastest moving areas of science today is the work growing out of recombinant DNA research. This involves a deep understanding of genes, the mechanisms of heredity, and much of the "code" with which nature combines a relatively small number of basic building blocks to produce the immense variety of life forms. The new knowledge is also beginning to make it possible for people to carry out some deliberate manipulation of genes and thus purposely to change varieties of plants and animals. When these kinds of techniques can be used they are much more efficient and powerful than the well-developed methods of producing HYVs discussed above.

So far the new recombinant DNA knowledge has not had a big impact on agriculture. But few experts in this work doubt that it will have immensely beneficial effects, and that the benefits will begin to be seen within our next generation. It is, of course, much easier to use these techniques on plants than on people, but no estimate of increased yields in this book is based on the use of this new area of science. The same estimates could be made, with a sound foundation, if the structure of the DNA molecule had never been untangled by Crick and Watson and others. However, it is safe to say that the new capabilities that will be developed because of the DNA research are likely to be valuable insurance in case unexpected problems develop with more conventional seed improvement techniques.

I am not excluding the effects of recombinant DNA research on agriculture because I have any doubts about it. It is just an extreme conservatism of calculation, plus a desire to keep this book simpler and less truly controversial. I don't want it said that the rejection of the scarcity perspective documented in this book depends on faith in future science. I have that faith, but I will leave it to those who are more informed than I am to try to convince people that it is justified. In this book, we are seeing how the scarcity perspective can be rejected simply on the basis of continued application of well-developed techniques and existing practices by ordinary farmers, businessmen, and technicians.

Some people have been concerned about the risk of using new varieties of seeds. They have visions of the whole world's wheat crop being planted with an exotic new seed which could be wiped out by some insect or disease. But these fears are out of perspective. Undoubtedly there will be mistakes and some new forms that look wonderful at first will turn out to have weaknesses that are only recognized after millions of acres have been planted. But there is no reason why all farmers should use the same variety of seed (in fact, given the differences in soil, climate, etc. they can't use the same varieties everywhere). The process that develops one new variety of rice for a particular setting can develop two or three different new varieties. It will take longer and cost more, the second and third new varieties may not be quite as good as the first, but we don't have to put all our eggs in one basket. Genetic vulnerability is not a price that must be paid to get the benefit of new HYV of seed.

Altogether it is a reasonable, conservative estimate to say that improved seeds can double average worldwide yields per acre. Some of the improvement will come from more wide-spread use of better seeds that are already available, and some from new seeds developed by the process that has already developed many successful new varieties of crops.

More Irrigation

In chapter nine I discuss the inefficiency of much use of irrigation in the United States. But those facts do not lead to the conclusion that irrigation never or rarely makes sense. The point is only that if irrigation decisions are based on mystical ideas about water, and made without any consideration of price and economics, they can be wasteful and produce a misleading impression of shortages. In many areas of the world reasonable irrigation projects can greatly increase yields per acre.

Now, about 450 million acres are irrigated. According to the Buringh study, as well as others, there are more than another 500 million acres that could be irrigated. This doubling of the irrigated acreage is without use of groundwater, desalination, or diversion of major rivers from their basins.

For the purpose of rough estimates of how much economically justifiable irrigation could increase world average yield per acre, we use a multiplying factor of 1.15. In other words, we estimate that increased use of practical irrigation could add about 15% to the average yield per acre.

Improved Inputs and Techniques

We have already noted that yields can be increased by using more fertilizer and other inputs. Yields can be further increased by using better inputs. As with seeds, this is partly a matter of a wider use of the better kinds of inputs now being used, and partly a matter of continuing the current pattern of gradual improvement in the best agricultural equipment, supplies, and techniques. (One of the most important inputs is agricultural labor and management, and there is much that most farmers can do to make their fields more productive.)

An example of new techniques are those that have been developed to farm black, sticky, vertisol soils, of which there are more than 700 million acres, principally in India, Australia, and the Sudan. Much of this land was thought to be too difficult to plant; now some of it is yielding three crops a year.

A substantial portion of the world's food harvest never gets to people's plates. It is spoiled along the way because of lack of storage facilities and for other reasons, or it is eaten by rats or insects. Effective yield can probably be increased by 10%-15% by wider use of measures to avoid these losses.

The question of improving yields is somewhat different for the animal products that we eat, which account for two-thirds of our estimate of how much grain-equivalent the world will need. To the extent that we can increase the yield of animal products per ton of grain we can reduce the amount of grain we will need. This increases the effective yield per acre. At present, America's grain-fed meat animals consume between four and eight calories of grain for each calorie of saleable retail meat.

The process of converting grain to meat (or dairy products) may be made more efficient at a number of points between the field and the fork. For example, one possibility might be the more widespread use of the beefalo, a hybrid between a cow and a buffalo that eats cheaper feed than the typical cow, gains weight twice as fast, is healthier and produces leaner meat. If we decide that we like beefalo meat we may be able to get 400 pounds of retail meat for perhaps 2,500 pounds of grain or less. This would mean a 25% increase in effective yield per acre measured by meat per acre, or calories per acre, or percent of food needs per acre, even without any increase in the number of bushels of grain grown per acre.

Usually the possibility of increasing the number of crops grown each year on the same land is discussed as a method of increasing yields. However we have already covered this in our discussion of the possibility of increasing the number of acres harvested for food. If sequential cropping were considered as a way of increasing yields it would offer the possibility of multiplying average yields by more than 1.5 (instead of increasing the area harvested by 4,000 million acres).

Summary of Yield Gains

Kahn, Harmon, et al., in their book *World Food Prospects and Agricultural Potential* (Praeger, 1977), summarized their review of the evidence about potential gains in yields by estimating that HYVs could multiply yields by two, irrigation by one and a half, and fertilizers and other inputs by 1.8 times. This would mean a total multiplication of today's average yields by 5.4 times.

While the specific multipliers that Kahn & Harmon use may not be right—for example I would not use such a high number for irrigation, and they don't take credit for what I call "peripheral and indirect increases"—their overall estimate of a potential multiplication by 5.4 times seems roughly correct. A potential gain in average yields of close to five times today's average is entirely consistent with past experience, recent trends, and the current momentum of agricultural technology. (Of course we are not likely to need such a large increase in average yields per acre, because acreage is likely to expand and non-conventional sources of nutrients may provide some of the supply.)

Over the last fifty years grain yields in the United States nearly quadrupled, while yields in Australia and India tripled and doubled respectively. Already average US yields are twice the world average. Record yields for a number of major crops are six or seven times the world average. (Although these records are achieved in special conditions which could not be generally reproduced.) In the most recent decade grain yields for the world as a whole continued to grow at over 1.9% per year. Improvement is continuing.

We can have very high confidence that a tripling of world-wide average grain yield per acre over the next century or so is entirely feasible. We can also have substantial, but slightly less, confidence that current agricultural science could also increase average yields by at least half again, if that were needed. In addition, there might be gains in ways we have not thought of. In the even longer term (say two to three hundred years) there is good reason to believe that a further doubling of agricultural yields per acre—to ten times the current world average—would be possible if there were a demand for it. But that is a more speculative conclusion.*

* We can't assume that in 150 years the currently used food cropland could yield ten times as much as it does now. But if at that time the world chose to use only the best 1,400 million acres on Earth to grow food (half as much land as is used today), average yields could almost certainly be ten times as high as they are today, i.e., eight tons of grain-equivalent per acre per year, enough to feed ten billion people at current US levels.

Whether 150 years from now the world will get its food from 1,400 million

In summary, if currently known techniques and more inputs are used wherever they are applicable, worldwide yield of grain-equivalent could be increased from the four-fifths of one ton per acre we are getting now to almost four tons per acre. This would be five times current levels, and would mean there would be no need to harvest any additional acres to reach the food supply goal we have been discussing. If this growth in average yields were accomplished in the hundred years between now and when we might need so much food, it would mean average yield per acre gains of 1.6% per year, which is about as much as average yield has been increasing in recent years.

Of course things are not as simple as I seem to be suggesting with these crude numbers. These simple calculations are not predictions. Much work will need to be done to respond to the requirements of such a large increase of the world's agricultural enterprise. Changing technology, taste, and price structure may change yields per acre or the practicality of adding agricultural land. Or we may grow less grain and manufacture more. There will be many problems that we will have to overcome. We cannot see now what all the problems will be or how to overcome them.

Some kinds of more intensive farming will increase the amount of pollutants that will need to be disposed of. New seeds and new techniques will have new vulnerabilities as well as new advantages. Many mistakes will be made before all the problems are dealt with, and the human and social cost of these mistakes will be high. But there is no reason to think that it will be harder to multiply food production by five times in the next two hundred years than it was to multiply by seven times in the last two hundred years. On the contrary, now population growth is slowing and we have many advantages that we didn't have before to help us to deal with the difficulties.

---

acres with yields of eight tons/acre, or from 5,000 million acres with yields of two tons/acre, depends on the economics and trade policies of the future, which are unpredictable. Both combinations, and all combinations in between, are possible without any scientific breakthroughs.

Conclusion: Plenty of Food for Everybody

With conventional agriculture we can at least triple the number of acres harvested for food, and we can at least triple the effective yield of the average acre. New science may add to our ability to grow food—as well as providing protection against unforeseen problems—and our ability to manufacture new kinds of nutrients for animals provides further insurance.

Therefore there is good reason to be confident that we can grow nine or ten times as much food as we do now, using only conventional agriculture—without damaging our environment and without spending more than a percent or two of our income.

Over the very long-term it is quite reasonable to believe that we could grow or produce enough food for high quality diets for 100 billion people—not just the ten to twenty billion we are considering in this chapter. The requirement of producing food doesn't seem to limit the population of the world below fifty or one hundred billion people.

E I G H T

Energy in Transition

When you think in terms of centuries, fossil fuels are clearly on their way out. (Although it is also true that when you think in terms of centuries fossil fuels are just on their way in.)

I T IS CLEAR THAT WE ARE APPROACHING a major transition in our energy supply. But nobody can know how this transition will develop. There is a big uncertainty about how much energy we will want. There is a big uncertainty about just how much of each of the fossil fuels are really available and at what costs. There is a big uncertainty about whether people will decide to use a lot of nuclear energy. There is a big uncertainty about how fast good solar technologies will develop and how cheap they will be. (Similarly for nuclear fusion, geothermal energy, and other potential sources.) And there are several new huge potential sources of methane that may turn out to be practical.

Does all this uncertainty mean that we're in trouble? No. There is little doubt that it will always be physically and economically possible to produce all the energy we need. And for the next one hundred or two hundred years we can get most of it from known sources with currently known technology. But neither is there any doubt that the energy transition is one of the things to which attention must be paid. It is one of the physical tasks from which it is most easy to imagine trouble coming.

The uncertainty means that we might get into trouble if our mistakes are bad enough. But that is no news. You can say that about anything. If you are perverse enough you can starve to death in a supermarket, but that doesn't make starvation in supermarkets a danger.

Long-Term Energy Supply

This chapter on energy will be divided into two sections. This section asks: Can we solve the long term problem of finding enough energy essentially forever? The second section asks: Will we have enough energy to last until long-term solutions are achieved?

The question we have to ask for the long term is: Can we find some source of energy which we know will be large enough, and won't cost too much?

If we can find some source of energy that would be good enough, we don't have to know whether we will actually use it or whether in fact we will use something else. We would only use something else if it were better for us. But here we don't care about better. We are just trying to see whether we are doomed to an energy disaster.

We don't have to try to say what energy will cost in the future or how much of it we will need. Nor do we have to decide whether any form of nuclear energy will be safe enough and politically acceptable enough to use in very large quantities. Those questions, like most questions about the future, are difficult or impossible to answer with any confidence. Fortunately, however, some questions about the future, including many of the crucial ones, can be dealt with on a reasonably solid basis.

The conclusion of this chapter will be: Yes. There is an energy source available that assures that we needn't ever have a disastrous shortage of energy. That source is solar energy, which everybody agrees will be available for millions of years in very large quantities.

This does not mean that I predict or recommend that we rely on solar energy. I do not. There may well be better sources of energy. But here we need only to find out whether there is one source that is *good enough*. The consideration of possible better sources is left to books on energy; this is a book on the Earth's sufficiency.

We only want to be confident that there isn't any danger of not having enough energy available at acceptable costs. If solar energy is good enough to ensure that that danger doesn't exist, we don't have to look further.

Many people who talk about fairly long-term issues make the mistake of being overly influenced by current economic conditions. They "think poor." For the long term, which is where the real danger of running out would be (if it were anywhere), it is better to "think rich."

We'll use a worldwide average income of $25,000 per person (in 1980 dollars). This would be a world roughly twice as rich as the United States is today. The world might not be as rich as that, but if so it wouldn't need as much energy. As we have seen in Chapter 3, there is every reason to assume that in 200 years the world will be much richer than it is today, and that by then the great majority of people will live in countries that have enough money so that almost all of their people can afford modern human lives.

Of course the world might become even richer. To discuss very long-term energy needs, you could use almost any average income hypothesis from $10,000-$100,000; that is, a world from four to forty times as rich as it is today. Although it would probably take more than 200 years to reach the higher numbers. (The reason it is not blind optimism to speak of the possibility of such high average incomes is that even low growth rates eventually produce high incomes.) No one can have any real understanding of such worlds, but the best guess is that they are possible if people—on the average—continue to choose to make the sacrifices of leisure and other values necessary to further increase their wealth.)

Today the world uses about 10%-15% of its income to buy raw energy. Clearly when we are much richer we could afford to use a bigger share of our income for energy. We wouldn't be hurt badly if, when we are ten times richer than we are now, we had to use 30%—or even 40%—of our income to buy our raw energy. (This assumes that if the raw energy cost so much, it wouldn't come to us in a more inconvenient way than the raw energy we use now comes to us.)

The world now uses about one-third Q of energy each year.*

---

* A "Q" is a very large number. It is equivalent to the energy in 180 billion barrels of oil, or 10 to the 18th power BTU.

If we are going to be using twenty-five times as much goods and services we might need twenty-five times as much energy—say eight Q a year. But most people who think about energy policy believe that in the future the world will use less energy for each dollar of GWP,* just as in the United States for the last fifty years we have used less and less energy for each dollar of GNP, even during the long period when falling energy costs were enticing us to use more and more energy. This view makes sense because as the world gets richer more of its money will be spent on intangibles (e.g., art, entertainment, fashion) which don't consume as much energy as cars, houses, etc. Also, new technology is often more energy efficient. So it is reasonable to think of our very long-term energy needs, beginning say 200 years from now, as something like four Q per year.**

Consider the alternative possible energy budgets shown in Table 9. It is apparent that our energy costs can go quite high by today's standards without crossing the danger line. These energy budgets are for a world that produces fifty times as much as we do today, and with energy costs per unit as much as four times as high as we pay today. Still the energy bill does not go above what we could afford to pay.

In Table 9 higher prices tend to go with lower quantities because as energy prices rise there is more incentive to find and to buy more efficient ways of using energy, and to economize on the use of energy. The conclusion is that it would not be disastrous if 200 years from now we had to pay even six times as much to produce a unit of raw energy as we do today. Of course we are not talking about quick changes. We are concerned with what can be done gradually, over 200 or more years. In the past, new energy forms have taken about a century to go from 1% to 50% of the total energy market. (*Energy in a Finite World*, I.I.A.S.A., 1981, p. 276.) So

---

* See Endnote 4 for a discussion of those unfortunate terms "GNP" and "GWP."

** Some scientists prefer to talk about long-term energy needs in terms of power capacity instead of energy units. (Power is the ability to produce energy.) Four Q of energy is the amount of energy that would be produced by about 130,000 big electric power plants (written 130 TW or 130 x 10 to the 12th power watts) of power capacity if they were used full time all year long.

TABLE 9
World Energy Budgets

	GWP	Energy Effic.**	Energy Amount	Price of Energy	Total Cost of Energy	Energy's Share of Total GWP
Current Actual Budget						
1980	$ 10 (trillion)*	$30 tr per Q	.3 Q	$ 4 tr. per Q	$ 1.2 (trillion)	12%
Alternative Hypothetical Budgets for 2200						
"W" (Base Case)	$500	60	8 Q	$ 8	$ 64	13%
"X"	$500	30	16 Q	$ 8	$128	26%
"Y"	$500	120	4 Q	$16	$ 64	13%
"Z"	$500	60	8 Q	$16	$128	26%

*A "trillion" is one million times one million
(it is also one thousand times one billion).
**Energy efficiency is the number of units of GWP produced by a single
unit of energy. The higher the efficiency of energy, the more GWP it
produces (and the less energy is necessary to produce a given GWP.)

it doesn't seem incredible that solar energy could go from 1% to
100% in two centuries. Multiplying by two is much easier than
multiplying by fifty.

An "All-Solar Energy World"

Now we will consider whether it would be alright if after 200 years
from now the world had to get along with only solar energy.* We
have to ask:

1. Is there enough solar energy?
2. Can it make the kind of energy we need?
3. Will it cost too much?
4. Is there any environmental or other obstacle that would stop
us from using so much solar energy?

* Again it must be emphasized that I am not predicting or recommending that we
rely on solar energy. This discussion is only to show that we *could* rely on it if we
had to. By seeing that we *could* rely on solar energy, we avoid the need for
considering the advantages and disadvantages of the other possible sources—which
I believe will provide most of our energy supply for at least many hundreds of years.

1. Enough energy?

No one will say the problem is that there isn't enough solar energy here. About 3,000 Q hit the Earth in the form of sunlight every year. We only need about one tenth of 1% of that.

Some people talk only about the fraction of the energy that strikes the land, but there is no reason to assume that if we needed it we couldn't usefully capture some of the solar energy that hits the oceans.

Furthermore, if it were necessary or efficient, we could also capture sunlight that doesn't hit the Earth or its atmosphere but passes nearby. We could do it either by using space stations to collect the energy then transport it in a concentrated form to Earth, or by putting up huge mirrors (essentially huge sheets of tin foil) to reflect additional sunlight onto solar collector areas—or in other ways. Such ideas seem difficult or expensive now. But even with presently known technology they appear to be clearly feasible, although perhaps ten times too expensive. It is not likely that any scientific breakthrough is required to make such projects practical in two hundred years. (Although it is quite possible that scientific breakthroughs leading to undreamed of technology will make such current ideas unnecessary and inferior.)

2. Right kinds of energy?

For example, will we be able to have electricity when and where we need it (not just during the day in the tropics)? Will we have forms of energy that can be used for cars and planes? Here are some of the ways that solar energy can be used:

- **Directly—to heat homes, hot water, etc.**
  This category includes various methods for storing and distributing the heat more conveniently—such as water circulation, rock walls, etc.
- **To make electricity**
  The main ways solar energy is used to make electricity is by photo-voltaic cells, like those now used in space vehicles and wristwatches, and by generators that use focused heat like a boiler.

Electricity is the most convenient form of energy. It can be used for almost any energy need. Even though it is expensive to make we have been using an increasing share of our energy in the form of electricity.* Today there are optimists who think that, after the current technology is worked out and produced on a large scale, electricity can be produced from solar energy in one of these ways at costs less than twice current electric plants. Despite such optimists we need to assume that it might take eight times current costs—which we could still afford—although it seems unlikely to be that expensive after 200 years.

● **To make a fuel like hydrogen**

Hydrogen is a fairly convenient fuel for storing and shipping energy. It could be used if, for example, it is convenient to capture the solar energy from deserts or other out-of-the-way places. And, of course, hydrogen is a good clean fuel for vehicles. It can also be made into liquid fuels or other forms of hydrocarbons.

Some people have calculated that hydrogen could be made from solar energy on a large scale with essentially current technology for only about twice the price of oil, but such estimates may well be too optimistic.

There are other possibilities as well, such as using the sunlight to grow special crops that can be burned, or to drive other biological processes that produce hydrogen, or taking energy from wind or waves.

Altogether, it is quite safe to say that if there are no special problems, the solar energy that strikes or comes near the Earth can be turned into all the forms of energy we need in ample quantity.

3. Cheap enough?

The problem is that this plenitude of solar energy is so spread out when it strikes the Earth that it must be concentrated to be convenient for most purposes, and the work of concentration costs a lot of money.

It is impossible to say how cheap (or expensive) solar energy will be. But we aren't asking, "How much will it cost? Can we afford it?" We are going the other way and asking, "How much can we afford? Will it cost more than that?" At the beginning of the chapter, in the discussion of world energy budgets, we concluded that, if two

---

* Technically electricity is very "high quality" energy. That is why we make increasing amounts of it even though we now have to use nearly three BTU of fuel to get one BTU of electric energy.

hundred years from now the average cost of our energy were no more than four or six times as high as the average cost of the raw energy we produce now, it would not be more than we could afford. So the question is, "If we needed to get all or most of our energy from the sun, would the average cost of solar energy be more than four or six times as high as average energy costs are today?" (Today's cost is about $4/million BTU.)

It is not possible to make such an estimate specifically. One of the main reasons is that forms of energy in an all-solar world and in today's world are too different to think about together. On the production side, for example, the whole pattern of costs for hydropower (which can only supply a small fraction of the total) is very different than that for coal. Similarly, on the user's side, different forms of energy have very different values. People can and do pay many times as much for a BTU of energy in the form of electricity than for a BTU in the form of heat for a house or for a steel mill.

And if, in over 200 years, we gradually moved to an all solar energy economy, we would increasingly shift to ways of operating that make sense for solar energy, so the pattern of energy use would become very different than it is today. Therefore it is much more meaningful to compare the average cost of a BTU in 1985 with the average cost in 1975 than it is to compare the average cost in 1985 with the average cost in an all-solar energy world 200 years from now.

But, when we were talking about the average grain yield per acre for all kinds of crops on all kinds of farms all over the world, we said that at the end of the year you could add up all the production and add up all the land used, then divide one number by the other to get average yield per acre. We can do more or less the same thing with the different forms of energy. We can add up all the raw energy produced and all the money spent for it and when we divide one of these numbers by the other we will get an average cost per BTU of energy produced. Our question is whether that number would be more than four or six times as high in an all-solar energy world than it is today.

The answer is that there is good reason to believe that the

number will be less than four times as high as today. Even if you are pretty pessimistic about the prospects for reducing the costs of solar energy you can still be confident that they will not be six times as high. Of course there is no guarantee. There are good people who will argue that solar energy will be much more expensive, even after 200 years of work to reduce costs. Unfortunately this is such an unusual question that there hasn't been much serious work done to answer it. But I believe that we don't have much cause for alarm about it, even though we don't yet have any reliable answer.

4. Environmental or Other Insuperable Obstacle?

IS THERE ENOUGH LAND? Yes, although we probably don't need to get all our solar energy from land. If we need it, there is enough land that is not usable for other purposes to produce, from sunlight, all the energy the world will need in the form of electricity. (For example, we might use 100,000 big solar electric power plants in or near the tropics—which might occupy some 2,000 million acres.)

Will taking the solar energy change the climate, or harm the environment? It is hard to see how. We would need to take only a fraction of one percent of the energy that comes in. This is less than naturally-occurring changes in the past. While there might be some ways of taking solar energy that would have a bad effect, at least locally, we need not use such a harmful approach, we could use a different method.

If a threat to the climate arose, from either the use of solar energy or from some other natural or manmade source, there are a number of measures that we might be able to use to counter it; by collecting additional heat now passing by or by artificially radiating more energy away from the Earth or in more subtle ways.

There is no reason in principle why anything we do that accidentally threatens to harm the environment cannot be balanced by things we do on purpose. Presumably things done on purpose are more efficient. Also there are so many different ways of producing whatever we need that nothing is apparent that locks us into a harmful method. (If we had to take 10% or 20% of the solar energy striking the Earth there would be reason to look at this question more closely.)

Perhaps the greater chance of harm to the climate or environment is the possibility that we will hurt it by trying to improve things or to counter some theoretical danger. We are more likely, I believe, to have the ability to deliberately produce effects to balance the accidental effects of our economy than we are to understand what is happening and what is needed.

WILL WE HAVE ENOUGH MONEY? The task of building all the equipment required to get so much solar energy is immense. Since with solar energy, like hydro-power, the "fuel" comes for free, most of the costs are capital costs that have to be paid in advance. This will require many trillions of dollars, even if during the next 200 years we figure out more clever ways than we know now.

But there is no reason to be frightened of this huge expenditure. The solar energy costs we have discussed take into account the capital costs. Therefore, since we can afford the cost of the energy we can afford the cost of the capital to produce it.

It shouldn't be surprising or distressing that providing energy requires huge amounts of capital. We are making the conservative assumption that energy might be one-third of all we produce, and probably the most capital-intensive part. Why not? It isn't as if someone can say "Look how much capital we will need just for energy; and we still will need everything else." Energy is the key to everything else. There is no close second that might make almost as big a demand on our budget as this size energy demand, just as there is no close second to the impact of oil on our economy. We will be able to afford it, even though we might not be able to afford three like it.

Two hundred years is a long enough time to allow slow growth, with several generations of mistakes and corrections and improvements.

WILL WE HAVE THE MATERIALS WE NEED? If we were to build all this solar energy equipment today we might want to use some rare materials. A calculation might show, for example, that many times more gallium (or some other exotic material) than exists in the world would be needed. But such a calculation no more indicates that we will be unable to get the solar energy we need than does the "disastrous shortage of Singerium" imagined in chapter ten.

The cost estimates include the cost of materials. These estimates do not depend on any particular rare materials being available at current prices. There is no material that we will not be able to do without if necessary. In any event, raw materials are likely to be only a fraction of the costs of solar energy. Most of the capital cost is likely to be some form of labor. Also, if the cost trends of the last century discussed in chapter six continue, metal and mineral costs will fall compared to other costs. (Although gallium, or something else might be an exception.)

Energy Before the Long-Run

Generally people use "long-run" to mean anything after twenty to fifty years, or sometimes to mean anything after the next election. Here we are using it to mean the thousands of years after world population and economic growth more or less level off, beginning perhaps 200 years from now. This raises the possibility that we won't have enough energy to get to the long run—which would make it pretty uninteresting.

It may sound paradoxical that we could have enough energy for thousands and thousands of years, but not have enough for the next 200 years, but that is not inconceivable. For example, if we really were going to rely on solar energy in the long-run, we would need to ask whether we have enough energy to last until we can economically produce the very large quantities of solar energy that will be needed.

The basic reason that we need to consider an energy transition is that the world now gets 90% of the energy it uses from fossil fuels like coal, oil, and natural gas. And it is possible that there are not enough of these fuels to meet our needs for another 200 years.* One task we may have to succeed at is finding other primary

---

* There is a possibility that there are sources of methane (natural gas) that are large enough to supply our energy needs for thousands of years. But while there is a chance that such large methane sources exist, it is much too unlikely to count on. (If these very large new sources of methane really do exist, and are economically

energy sources—and we may have to find them within a century or so. Because, even if we don't run out of fossil fuels so quickly, there is a reasonable chance that within the next century we will want to begin to get a much larger share of our energy from other sources for political, economic or pollution-avoidance reasons.

Nuclear Energy: A Life-Saver, But Not Essential

If we were to consider only economic and resource factors—including public health—nuclear energy could fill most or all of the need for a replacement for fossil fuels. Furthermore, using nuclear energy as the primary replacement for fossil fuels would almost certainly reduce the number of people killed or injured as a by-product of producing and distributing energy. Moving to greater reliance on nuclear energy would probably also result in an even bigger reduction in environmental pollution.

On the other hand, if we replaced most fossil fuels with nuclear energy, the cost in death and disease from producing energy would be paid in forms that many people find much more distressing. The human cost of producing nuclear energy is much less acceptable to many people than the almost certainly larger human costs of energy from coal because the deaths from nuclear energy are more concentrated—that is, they may come in larger numbers per incident—although occurring much more rarely.** (There are also differences in the form of the slow harms from nuclear energy compared to the slow harms from producing and burning coal.)

---

recoverable—perhaps from hydrates—they do not come from the decay of living matter as coal and oil do. So they would not be "fossil fuels"—although like fossil fuels, and other minerals, they would be extractive rather than renewable resources.

** The following hypothetical numbers illustrate this idea. Although these numbers are not correct, the basic relationships among them are probably reasonably realistic:

	Big nuclear energy industry	Equal size fossil fuel industry
Number killed each 80 years:	80,000	160,000
Fraction of world population:	(1 in 120,000)	(1 in a 60,000)
Largest number killed in a single incident:	25,000	500

This book assumes that neither nuclear fission nor nuclear fusion will become a major source of our energy supply. That assumption is made because people might decide to refrain from using nuclear energy—because of the undesirability of energy casualties coming in large groups, or in unfamiliar ways, or because of the possibility that a large increase in the nuclear power industry would increase the spread of nuclear weapons, or to avoid political controversy and fears, or for some other reason.

The fact that this book assumes that the world will decide to do without nuclear energy does not mean that I advocate or predict that it will do so. I don't. I use this assumption just to make the argument more conservative. I don't want to have the conclusions of the book depend on the nuclear energy controversy. This is part of the strategy of sticking as much as possible to technical points that are not truly controversial.*

The net result of this is that we may have to find a new, major source of energy as soon as a century or so from now. And that would be a big job, indeed.

The Problem *Might* Take Care of Itself

On the other hand, energy may turn out to be not even a problem, much less a danger. The reason is that various forms of solar energy, or other long term energy sources, may begin to be used very extensively before the cost of producing and using fossil fuels begins to be too high.**

---

* What I mean when saying that I try to stick to points that are not truly controversial is that, although people may argue—perhaps correctly—that some statements in Part II are not exactly correct, I don't think that it is possible to make a reasonable argument that any of them are far enough from the truth to affect the conclusions they are used to support. (At least not many of them.)

** For example, a number of materials have recently been invented that are super-conducting at 200 degrees below zero, which is the temperature of liquid nitrogen, which is reasonably cheap. If one of these materials—or a newer one—can be produced on industrial scale with reasonable mechanical properties, it might be possible to make devices that would make it economical to store and transport large amounts of energy economically. This would completely transform the economics of producing and distributing energy, and might make both solar and hydropower more competitive than they are today—as well as permit the use of immense gas resources that are now being wasted.

There are lots of reasons why people may spend enough to make other forms of energy competitive even if they are not needed. Most things are developed without the pressure that comes when some necessity becomes much too expensive. In other words, products are often developed when they are not needed.

Therefore even if we don't make any public policy decision, long-term forms of energy might become relatively attractive before they are "needed." As a result, there might be no sharp energy transition. Instead there would be a gradual change in the mix of energy sources as a result of normal market and political factors, and without any great concern about the long-term future. (Just as there has been during the growth of the use of oil and electricity.) During this transition fossil fuel's share of our energy supply would gradually be reduced, and permanent or very long term sources would gradually increase, and price fluctuations would be no larger than normal.

Whether the transition to a new pattern of energy sources comes as a natural result of changing technology and normal business and technical decisions—or whether it comes because governments decide that there is an urgent need to find new sources—the job of meeting our energy needs in the future is immense. In fact supplying energy will be an immense job even if it turns out that there are enough extractive fuels for a thousand years and so we don't have to make an energy transition at all. Even if there is much more oil and gas than people believe, we are likely to have to go quite deep to get it, and probably move it long distances; and all in a world with more stringent and expensive environmental protection requirements than we have been used to.

So, a noticeable share of our capital and our brain-power will have to be devoted to producing the energy we will need—while limiting damage to the environment and to human health. This effort will be a major challenge to our scientists, technologists, and businessmen. It will also be a major challenge to our political systems (that is to ourselves) because we will have to make the key decisions about health and environmental concerns and have to continue to provide a framework for large scale international transactions and operations.

Fortunately there is no reason to doubt that plenty will be available. Although we might need as much as 500 Q during the next two hundred years (1,500 times as much as we are producing this year), we have a pretty big selection of ways to get it. If the build-up of the solar or other longterm energy source is steady, starting one hundred years from now and growing to four Q per year, that would mean that it would provide some 200 Q. Table 10 shows the sources from which we could take the other 300 Q. It is also possible that much less energy will be used because of better energy conservation. There are a number of ways in which we now

TABLE 10
Possible Sources of Energy for the Next 200 Years

Conventional Oil	10 — 20 Q
Conventional Natural Gas	10 — 20 Q
Coal (including lignite)	100 — 200 Q
Very Heavy Oil (including tar sands)	10 — 40 Q
Oil shales	30 — 2,000 Q
Hydroelectric	10 Q
Nuclear Fission	500 Q
Unconventional and uncertain potential sources of methane	0 — 10,000 Q
Nuclear Fusion, Geothermal, and other potential long-term sources	50 — 500 Q

720 Q — 13,000 Q

Note: The ranges reflect uncertainty about how much is available. For those sources that aren't already providing a lot of energy, the limit may be the rate at which new technology can be installed. Where the expansion rate is limited, the amount that can be produced in 200 years depends on how soon it begins to be used on a large scale.

This Table is taken from H. Kahn & W. Brown, *The Next 200 Years*, N.Y., Wm. Morrow, 1976.

unwisely encourage energy consumption, and if we more fully included all the costs in the prices that energy buyers pay, less energy would be consumed. The only reason this discussion hasn't paid more attention to energy conservation is to make sure that no one gets the idea that conservation is a necessity or a moral obligation. Wasting energy is no more or less sinful than wasting any other resource—including time. (And if energy production is not subsidized, the price is the measure that lets us compare resources.)

It is apparent that if the lowest estimates for the fossil fuels turn out to be correct, then we will have to use some nuclear energy. Of course this is only true because I set the total energy demand during this period so high. If my estimates are too conservative we would not need nuclear energy, even if the low estimates for fossil fuels turn out to be correct. (But the examples of France and Japan suggest that there will be a lot of nuclear energy produced in the world, even if the United States continues to be reluctant to use it.)

N I N E

Water "Shortages" and the Power of Innumeracy*

Often "cheaper than dirt."

P EOPLE IN THE SOUTHWESTERN UNITED STATES may be wondering why this book has so far ignored the key restriction on major growth. Where are we going to get the water for so many more people and so much more food?

The public discussion of water powerfully illustrates the insidious appeal of various forms of the scarcity error. (A high portion of the professional discussion is based on the same misunderstandings, although this is partly justified by the fact that. for most practical purposes the public misunderstandings must be treated as if they were truths, because they have been embodied in laws and political constraints.)

In much of the American West it is assumed that water is very valuable, in short supply, and a major factor limiting development of energy resources and further population growth. The facts are that in the West, most of the water is used by people for whom water has so little value that they would not pay a penny to save a whole ton of it. The evidence that the users of water do not value it highly is found in their actions. They do not use well-known ways of saving water which cost less than a penny per ton

---

* "Innumeracy" is to numbers as illiteracy is to words. Unfortunately some dictionaries do not contain this handy word.

of water saved.* Also, in the American West there is plenty of additional good water that could be made available at a cost of a dime a ton or much less.

Water is indeed essential for life, and in that sense it is valuable. But arsenic, iron, and Vitamin C are also essential for life. Thousands and thousands of sailors have died from scurvy because they didn't have lemons, but we do not regard lemons as if they were particularly valuable, even though they cost much more than water. We do not worry about a shortage of Vitamin C, because we can manufacture Vitamin C. We could also manufacture water. That is, we could make drinking water out of seawater at a cost of something like seventy-five cents for a year's supply of drinking water for one person. But, of course, it doesn't make any sense to manufacture water—except in very unusual circumstances.

The water we drink is only a tiny fraction of 1% of the water that the country uses. And in fact all domestic and commercial uses of water, in houses, stores, offices, etc., comprise only about 10% of our total water consumption.

Water in Agriculture

Most water is used for industry and for irrigation on farms. (Not counting rainwater that provides natural watering of crops.) But farming is an essential activity. We need the food the farms grow, and they need water to grow the food. Here is the error. Much of the irrigation water is not needed. If less water-wasteful irrigation practices were used, much of the water would not be needed. In many cases more advanced irrigation techniques, now used in places like Israel, would save more than half of the water now used.

But the more water-saving irrigation techniques would cost the farmer, or the agency that stores and transports the water, more

---

* The more usual units for talking about water are larger than a ton. They are the acre/foot (enough water to cover one acre to a depth of a foot), which is about 1,300 tons of water; and 1,000 gallons, which is about four tons. (So a "penny per ton" is the same as $13/acre foot.)

A typical home uses about 400 tons of water per year and pays 25¢ per ton, even if the water agency gets the water from the river without paying for it. (Less than 1% of the water in the typical home is used for drinking and cooking.)

money. True enough. And now we see what the true shortage is. It is not water for drinking. It is not water for farming. It is water to allow farmers and others to save money for themselves by using water-wasteful irrigation methods. They can do this because taxpayers pay most of the real cost of the water which is wasted.

The apparent water shortages come from the way we have decided to allocate water. Because of these laws, many users have come to rely on getting water for free, or at a very low price, which is often far below the cost of providing the water (i.e., less than one-half cent per ton). The result is a large constituency for rejecting the information that plenty of water can be bought at a price that most users can easily afford to pay. Public understanding of the price of water would threaten farmers and others who now depend on getting water at a small fraction of its cost, and more important, it would threaten the communities that depend on those farmers.

There would be no technical difficulties for the United States to produce the same quantity of all agricultural products that we now grow, while using less than half as much irrigation water as we now use; and with a total cost increase of at most a few percent. (According to the Iowa State University model, if we had used less irrigation our crops would have cost *less*, not more; the irrigation produces no net gain, but a net loss.)* Of course, such a reduction of the use of irrigation water would help some people and some agricultural areas while hurting other people and other agricultural areas; and cause a great deal of conflict and shifting around unless it were done over a very long time.

Whole communities have come to depend on the agricultural patterns that depend, in turn, on the use of large quantities of water in ways that are not valuable enough to justify paying the true cost of the water, even if it is as low as a penny a ton. I am certainly not suggesting that these communities should be destroyed just because it did not originally make economic sense—from the point of view of the country—for those communities to grow in those locations. Just because their development in that location was only

---

* This implies that many irrigation projects have the effect of transferring money from taxpayers to a set of farmers and others.

possible because of water prices that were originally irrational, does not mean that these prices should be changed now.

But the fact that there are many communities that need and should continue to get super-cheap water shouldn't be allowed to confuse us about the real value and availability of water.

If decisions about future development use a realistic value for water there will be plenty of water available, and most users will be able to afford the true cost. This is true even if current use patterns continue to be subsidized, so long as the amount of subsidized super-cheap water is not greatly increased.

The study of agricultural land potential by Buringh, et al., (referred to in chapter seven), estimated that, without any irrigated lands, conventional world agriculture could produce twenty times as much grain-equivalent as it does now.

Water in Industry

Industry, which is the other big water consumer, is also a big water waster. Fortunately much of industry's water consumption can be changed with very little effect on where industry is located.

Nationwide, industry takes about 40% of our water (but it returns most of what it takes). However, in any place where the price of water to industry gets much above a dime per ton, factories change the way they use the water so that they need much less of it. Commonly they go from systems that use the water once and then dump it, to systems that recycle the water over and over, drastically reducing requirements (but not significantly increasing the cost of production). Even if industry had to pay full cost for the water it used, water would rarely be an important share of industry's costs. So a major share of our water goes to allow industry to save a little money by using water-wasteful methods.

ALL OF THIS IS A STRIKING ILLUSTRATION of the power of innumeracy, which is a lack of facility for understanding numbers and for doing simple numerical operations—such as multiplication and division. Because most people don't multiply and divide they don't know how little water costs. As a result, special interests frighten people about water shortages that don't exist unless we are talked into peculiar ways of counting.

IN BRIEF, in the "water-short" western United States, water is cheap, not valuable (it usually costs less than dirt). We now have more water than we really need; and we can get as much more water as we might want, at a cost we can easily afford.*

* To be fair I should note that we use so much water, that we spend 4% of our GNP producing, protecting, and delivering water. Only a small fraction of this cost is the raw material or "extractive" cost of the water; the rest is the equivalent of processing cost.

TEN

The Misplaced Concern About Other Raw Materials

There are only sixteen metals on which we have to spend as much as a dollar per person, to buy all we need in this country for a year.

IN THIS CHAPTER WE WILL CONSIDER the possibility of dangerous shortages of any other kind of raw materials than food, water and energy.

It is apparent that the category "Everything else" takes only a small fraction of what we pay for raw materials, which is only a small fraction of our average income. Most of Everything else is very common material like sand and stone and iron. Materials that might conceivably become truly scarce are only a small fraction of Everything else. Therefore, the amount of money we spend to buy those raw materials that might conceivably become truly scarce is a small fraction of a small fraction of a small fraction of our income—perhaps one half of 1%, probably less, for all such materials together.

If, when one material runs out there are other materials that we can use directly or indirectly, just about as well, then nothing really happened when we ran out of the first material. Since we are only interested in materials because of what they do for us, we don't care about running out of any one particular material if good substitutes are available. Our question must be whether there can be a severe shortage of the materials needed to serve some human purpose—such as traveling, communicating, building, keeping warm, etc.

But, people have the idea that there are a number of materials that are critical to modern technology, as vitamins are critical to human life. This perception seems to lead to the conclusion that if we run out of any of these special substances we would be in deep trouble.

Here again is the table showing American use of raw material:

TABLE 6
Use of Raw Materials in the U.S.

Item	Amount Used (per capita)	Cost per lb.	Tot. cost (per cap.)	Refer.
Food	2,000 pounds	25¢	$ 500	Ch. 7
Fuels	16,000 pounds	6¢	$ 950	Ch. 8
Drinking Water	2,000 pounds	.01¢	20¢	Ch. 9
Everything Else				Ch. 10
Metals	1,000 pounds	6¢	$ 60	
Wood	2,000 pounds	2¢	$ 40	
Miscel. Minerals	2,000 pounds	2¢	$ 40	
Stone, sand & gravel	20,000 pounds	.1¢	$ 30	
	45,000 pounds	**.4¢**	**$1,620**	

Technically informed people speak portentously about how every ton of steel for jet engines depends on small amounts of cobalt or molybdenum, and how some of our most advanced industries would grind to a halt if suddenly the source of a relatively few tons of special metals disappeared. But this is the mistake of "small step thinking." Certainly we couldn't operate the way we do today if some materials that we have learned to make good use of suddenly disappeared. But to think that means that we couldn't operate at all if those materials grew very, very expensive (which is what "running out" means as a practical matter) is like saying that there would be no United States if George Washington's father had not met his mother. George Washington may have been essential, but if he hadn't been born someone else would have been essential instead.

Tungsten is a pretty good example of the kind of thing that people have in mind when they think of critical metals. A number of uses of tungsten are indeed important. But in the three years after 1950 when the price of tungsten quadrupled (because supplies from China were cut off as a result of the Korean War) US consumption fell from 7,000 tons to 2,000 tons without affecting the economy or the war effort. And the demand for tungsten recovered very slowly when the price eventually fell back to a more normal level.

Take cobalt for example. How bad could it be if we ran out of cobalt? Do you think we would still be living in the middle ages if only a thimble-full of cobalt had ever been created? Do you really think life would be noticeably different if there were no cobalt? So what difference does it make if we run out of cobalt? (Incidentally, it is generally believed that the nodules found on the ocean floor contain thousands of years' supply of cobalt.)

An English Professor named Wilfred Beckerman made the same point in the following way. Suppose I discover a new material, Singerium, which is wonderfully useful, and millions and millions of pounds of it are used every year in all kinds of products. Whole industries are built around Singerium. What an honor! But then it begins to be harder to find Singerium. It begins to get more expensive. People begin to worry, what would happen if we ran out of Singerium? Not to worry. Except for the honor, nothing would be lost compared to where we are today. But how is cobalt, or any other minor product, different than Singerium? It is not. (And most materials are much more minor than cobalt.) If they disappear it would be the same as if they had never been discovered or created—after the adjustment period while they are running out. (Such an adjustment might be a great challenge and create severe difficulties for the industries directly involved, but most people wouldn't even notice.)

Why Money Tells Us What's Important

Here is an illustration of the reason we don't need to worry about running out of materials on which we are only spending one or two dollars per person, however essential they seem to be to our industrial process.

If something like cobalt increases from $10/lb. to $50/lb. the country as a whole experiences two kinds of increased cost. One, obviously, is the extra money spent on buying cobalt at the new higher price. The other is the extra money people spend to reduce or eliminate their use of cobalt, because the price has gone up so far. This money goes to pay for the extra cost of having to use substitutes for cobalt (or substitutes for whatever cobalt was being used for), or to pay for whatever steps have to be taken to be able to do without cobalt.

For anybody who stops using cobalt the extra cost of doing without is less than the rise in price. Otherwise he would continue to buy cobalt, even at the new high price.

Together these two kinds of cost are the outer limit of the damage to us from running out of cobalt or some other material. There is no indirect damage from the loss of an essential material that is not reflected in these two costs because they cover the effect on all those who are buying the material—and through them, of all who are using it.

Therefore the cost to the country of an extreme case of running out of a material would be about the same as the cost of having to buy the same amount of the material and having to pay ten or one hundred times as much. (In the hypothetical example presented in Table 11, running out of X cost the country as much as increasing the price of X by thirty times.)

For this extreme scenario the total cost to the country of running out of Material X is a little over $3 billion per year. Even though the price of Material X went up one hundred times, the total of both kinds of cost to the country from the price rise was only about thirty times what we had been spending on X before it began to run out.

(The calculation goes this way: When the price increases to $20/lb., users of one million pounds stop buying. Since they had

THE EARTH HAS PLENTY

been paying $10/lb. we assume that their extra costs are $20 minus the $10 they had been paying before. One million pounds times $10/lb. extra is $10 million. The next two million pounds spends $30/lb. extra ($40 minus $10), a total cost of $60 million. The next two million pounds spends $70/lb., etc. (In summary: $10 times 1 million, plus $30 times 2 million, plus $70 times 2 million . . . etc.) The total is about $3,000 million or $3 billion.

TABLE 11
Hypothetical Material X

Amount now used in U.S.:	**10 million pounds**
Price:	**$10/lb.**
Total cost:	**$100 million**

Here is an example of what might happen if the price of Material X rises:

to **$20/lb.**	1 million lb. reduction in use
to **$40/lb**	2 million lb. additional reduction
to **$80/lb**	2 million lb. additional reduction
to **$200/lb**	1 million lb. additional reduction
to **$400/lb**	1 million lb. additional reduction
to **$600/lb**	1 million lb. additional reduction
to **$800/lb**	1 million lb. additional reduction
to **$1,000/lb**	1 million lb. additional reduction

After the price goes to $1,000 there are no users left. All the former purchasers of Material X are "doing without."

Even though we can say that we have "run out" of Material X, because there are no longer any purchasers and therefore no more production, we can still look at the cost of "doing without X." We do this by looking at what the people who had been buying X are doing to make up for the fact that "X" has "run out" — i.e., that no one can afford to buy it. (Although it is somewhat strange to talk about the cost of something that nobody uses. It is a little like the cost of my not having discovered "Singerium.")

Usually the situation is much better. Usually most of the people who are forced to shift from some increasingly expensive material to an awkward and expensive way of doing without it, gradually re-adjust either their production process or their consumption so that they are no longer doing without X. At that

145

point they are just living in a world in which X is expensive, like gold or platinum. They no longer think of themselves as doing without X, just as they don't think of themselves as doing without platinum and caviar, which they don't buy because they are too expensive.

Therefore if we are now spending $2 per person per year for something, the worst that could happen from running out is that we would have to spend $200 per person per year as the cost of doing without. Such a high cost is very unlikely, but it would not be a tragedy, since $200 is only a small percent of our average income.

There has never been an important commodity whose real price increased as much as ten times for a long time. (The real price of oil rose about eight times between 1973 and 1980, but it came down to about half that within a few years.) But, even though it is very difficult to think of a material which we couldn't do without for one hundred times the cost, we can't be sure that it can't happen. We should allow for that possibility.

The conclusion is that, fortunately, there is no raw material which we could run out of (apart from food and energy) which is important enough to make a real difference to us—even if running out meant that we had to pay one hundred times as much as we do today.

The magic number* is that there are zero minerals (except fuels) for which we spend as much as $20 per person per year. There are less than twenty minerals on which we spend as much as $1 per person per year. (The only metals on which we spend as much as $10 a year are iron and copper). Iron is so abundant that we will never run out of it, and there are good substitutes available for most uses of copper.

YOU WILL RECALL that on the average Americans now use 25,000 pounds of raw materials per person each year, apart from food and fuel. Together all of the many raw materials included in the 25,000

---

* "Magic number" is the idea that Ben Wattenburg used so effectively in his wonderful book, *The Good News Is That The Bad News Is Wrong.*

pounds now cost a total of $170 per year. Perhaps a more detailed menu—shown in the Table 12—would be helpful.

TABLE 12
Everything Else in More Detail

Per Capita Use of Raw Materials in the U.S.
(excluding food and fuel)

(typical year in early 80's)*

	Quantity	Price	Cost
Wood	2,000 lbs	2¢/lb	$ 40
Iron	600 lbs	2¢/lb	$ 12
Copper	20 lbs	75¢/lb	$ 15
Other high volume metals	80 lbs	15¢/lb	$ 12
Expensive metals	3 lbs	$ 3.00/lb	$ 9
Precious metals	.6 oz.	$20.00/oz	$ 12
Misc. non-metallic minerals *(primarily: lime, cement, sulfur, potash, gypsum, and phosphate)*	2,000 lbs	2¢/lb	$ 40
Stone, sand, and gravel	20,000 lbs	.1¢/lb	$ 30
Total (avg. price)	**25,000 lbs.**	**.7¢/lb.**	**$170**

Columns do not add because of rounding; the total cost column is the most accurate — the others are more approximate.

*Many of these prices and quantities fluctuate substantially from year to year. This table smoothes the fluctuations and calls itself a "typical year"

More important, the table can not be completely consistent about what stage of processing it is talking about for each metal. Therefore the prices and quantities of the different metals are not strictly comparable.

However, the only purpose of the table is to give a general feel about the scale of our use of raw materials, and about the relative importance of different items; and these numbers give a reasonably fair picture.

Producing Wood

Human use of wood is a story that has just begun. We are now at a point comparable to where our ancestors were when they began to cultivate grain. Today most of the wood that is used is cut from forests where it grew more or less naturally. Only recently have we begun to harvest a substantial amount of wood from planted trees. Now a small but increasing share of the wood we use is a cultivated resource. But all wood is still obtained from natural species of trees, although tree planters have done a little work to select better specimens of trees to plant.

No one who has looked at forestry and the current state of genetic science and plant biology believes that we will not be able to multiply the productivity of forest and woodland. One of the truly exciting and challenging prospects facing man is the gradual change of a major share of the world's woods and forests from their current largely natural state to the vastly improved condition that is likely to be possible in the next few centuries. With reasonable good sense we can get even more improvement in the recreational, aesthetic, and environmental values of the forests as we increase their material productivity.

Wood has been one of the few major raw materials whose real cost has risen over the last century. This probably is a result of the difficulty of reducing the amount of labor required to harvest and transport trees, and of the reduction in the amount of convenient free forests. It would not be surprising if this increasing cost trend continued for some time, although the likely changes in the nature of forestry are so great that it is impossible to be confident of any such prediction.

In the United States today, about half of the raw material cost of wood is the cost of transporting logs from where they fall to the nearby mill. This cost might just as properly be considered a processing cost rather than a raw material cost. We could say that $40 per person that we spend for lumber at the mills is really two different costs:

(1) wood as a raw material: $20.
(2) transportation to mills: $20.

Perhaps we can expect (1) to rise as people more fully occupy the Earth and there are increasing alternative claims on forests, although the tremendous potential for technical change makes this very uncertain. But the future cost of (2) is more likely to be influenced by technology rather than by raw material factors. It may well tend to decline like most crude material processing costs. (Increasingly trees and forests, and equipment to harvest and protect them, are likely to be designed together.)

Most uses of wood are invisible and serve purposes that could be served by metals or plastics without any aesthetic loss. So the possibility of the increasing cost for wood does not present a great danger to the aesthetic values that wood provides.

In summary, it is clear that there is no necessary danger in connection with wood's share of our raw material supply. (Although there is danger that we will miss opportunities to improve our world.)

Forests

Since forests are so much more than the source of wood we should give at least equal attention to their other values as we do to forests as a source of one of the major raw materials.

Forests now cover 30% of the Earth's land surface.* Since a few thousand years ago about 36% of the land area of our globe was covered by forests, man has already reduced the area of forests by about one sixth since he became civilized enough to destroy forests.

For comparison we can look at the American experience. Forests covered one half of the acres of what is now the lower 48 states when the white man first arrived on our shores. By 1920, the forest had been reduced to one-third of the total land area. But then the trend reversed. Now the fractions of our land covered by forests is back up to about 40%. So the United States now has one-fifth less forest area than it did two hundred years ago when the population was quite a bit smaller than it is today (that is, 40% coverage instead of 50%).

Since American forests are much younger (less mature) than they were two hundred years ago, they now contain much less wood than they did then. But much more wood is being added to our forests each year than was being added when Columbus arrived.**

* In some geological eras forests covered more of the Earth than they do today, and in other eras they covered less than now.

** More wood is being harvested from U.S. forests than ever before. But the amount

(By definition, a mature forest, like those that greeted the Pilgrims, adds very little if any wood each year—because it is mature, growth is matched by death.)

The broad interaction between the forests and the global environment is very poorly understood, but felt by some scientists to be potentially important. However it doesn't seem likely that any great global danger would result if we reduce the amount of land now covered by forests by less than one-third. And, if it is found that something bad would result if the area covered by forests was reduced from 30% to, say, 23% of the total land area, there is every reason to believe that acceptable ways will be found to avoid or counteract such bad results.

It is also possible that it would be wiser not to reduce forest area so much—although there is no reasonable evidence or theory now to support that conclusion. And it is quite possible that the area of forest coverage is not as important to the protection of the global environment as the amount of wood, or some other factor. If so the problem could be either easier or harder than preventing the area of forests from being reduced too much. (See the discussion of "sneaky pollution" in chapter eleven.)

There are also regional interactions between forests and the environment. These might be caused by rivers being overloaded by silt from erosion caused by forests being cut down, or perhaps by local weather effects. Presumably the world has already seen examples of the worst kinds of regional effects, because there are regions that suffered a total loss of forests many years ago.

While major losses have been suffered as the result of unwise destruction of forests, these losses have not endangered the global environment. Nor have such extreme deforestations always prevented rapid economic development in the region involved. Few

---

of wood growing in the forests is increasing faster than the amount of wood harvested. So the amount of wood in our forests is increasing steadily, although the forest area isn't changing much.

The steady increase in wood growth in our forests has already given the lie to five consecutive U.S. Forest Service predictions, the most recent of which was in 1970. (1979 was an especially interesting year because in that year U.S. forests passed, without slowing down, what the Forest Service in 1933 called the "ultimate biological limit," which they predicted would be reached in the year 2025.)

areas have been as thoroughly denuded of forests as the area of Israel, which since it was created has been one of the fastest growing countries of the world. South Korea, which is many times larger than Israel, also suffered an unusually severe deforestation; but in the last generation it produced more economic growth than any other country of its size (and has begun restoring its forests).

Therefore, it doesn't seem at all likely that protecting the planet from dangerous effects of cutting down forests is likely to be one of our great tasks for the future.[14] But, as we shall see, that does not mean that the future of the world's forests is not an important concern.

The Real Forest Task

Forests are a major recreational and aesthetic resource. The need for understanding this aspect of forests, and for wisdom in preserving and enhancing these benefits of forests, is one of the great challenges we face.

The total area of forest land is not what is most important for achieving the greatest possible human values from forests (recreational and aesthetic). The key factors determining how valuable the world's forests will be to people (apart from their use for supplying wood and environmental protection) are probably the following:

(1) Where forests are located,
(2) Their physical nature,
(3) Facilities—within forests and connecting forests to people,
(4) Arrangements for use of forests,
(5) The behavior of people in them, and
(6) How wealthy people are.

For example, a fifty-acre forest in the middle of an urban area, or a 500-square-mile forest near to a large population center (e.g., New York's Adirondack Park), provide much more recreational and aesthetic value than thousands of square miles of Northern pine forest or tropical rain forest in the middle of the Amazon Basin.*

---

* Of course people's values differ; I believe that the statements here are consistent

151

While the wilderness values of forests require substantial land area, they are more sensitive to purity of control than to total world forest acreage. There could easily be more wilderness in the world with 6,000 million acres of forest than with 8,000 million acres. (There are now about 9,000 million acres of forests.)

HINDSIGHT SHOWS THAT PEOPLE and governments are often selfish or imprudent in their decisions about forests. One tactic that some people use to try to protect against bad decisions about forests is to try preserve all forest anywhere; that is, not to trust human decisions on the subject. This book does not deal with difficult questions such as choosing tactics for avoiding waste or destruction of the human values of forests. That is a human problem, not a physical problem.

If we are not too foolish we can get all the physical resources we need from forests while multiplying their aesthetic and recreational values. On the other hand, if we handle ourselves badly we can get much less human value and fewer physical resources. The main challenge presented by forests is the opportunity to increase the pleasure that man gets from the Earth.

Metals

We can divide metals into three categories: cheap, expensive, and precious (see Table 13). Cheap metals cost less than ten cents a pound. Precious metals cost more than a $1 an ounce. And everything in between is an expensive metal.

Unfortunately, one of the most important metals—copper—is sort of in the middle. It costs more than ten times as much as most of the cheap metals, but much less than a number of expensive metals. It is important because we use a lot of it.*

---

with the values of at least 90% of Americans—when their values are applied with informed calculations. I say this not because I believe that most Americans are in precise agreement about environmental values or policy, but because my calculations are so understated that they are compatible with a very wide range of values— although not with all.

* Because of copper (and also titanium, zinc, and lead) the category "high volume metals" in Table 12 includes both the important cheap metals, and the few

TABLE 13
Metal Use in the United States
(typical recent year)

	approx. price ($ per pound)	total use (1,000 tons)	total cost (mil. $)	% of total U.S. metal cost
Cheap Metals				
Iron	.02	70,000	2,800	20%
Bauxite	.01	5,500	100	1
Manganese	.06	800	100	1
Expensive Metals				
Copper	.75	2,300	3,400	24%
Titanium	.60	1,000	1,200	9
Nickel	3.00	150	900	6
Zinc	.40	1,000	800	6
Tin	6.00	50	600	4
Lead	.20	1,200	500	4
Magnesium	1.25	100	250	2
Molybdenum	6.00	20	250	2
Tungsten	5.00	10	100	1
Cobalt	10.00	5	100	1
Precious Metals				
Gold	$300/oz	4 mil. oz.	1,200	9%
Silver	$ 6/oz	140 mil. oz.	800	6
Platinum Group	$400/oz	2 mil. oz.	800	6
All Metals (total or average)	$ .07/lb.	80 mil. tons	$14 bil.	100%

Most of these prices and some of the quantities fluctuate greatly from year to year. More important, it is not possible to be entirely consistent in choosing what stage in the extraction process to talk about. Therefore the table gives prices and quantities for metals with different amounts of processing included. Although the numbers here are somewhat arbitrary, they are a fair illustration of the pattern of our use of metals.

Also, because of rounding the numbers don't seem consistent.

"expensive" metals that we use a lot of, and which are "almost cheap," i.e., between a dime and a dollar a pound.

We can summarize the table by saying that: (1) in most years iron and copper together take about half of our total expenditures on raw metals; (2) almost all of the rest of our metal expenditure goes for fourteen metals each of which takes between 1% and 10% of the total (including three precious metals); and (3) this leaves only about a few percent of the expenditure for all other metals together. So altogether there are only about sixteen different metals on which we spend as much as sixty cents per person per year.

It is interesting to note that in some years we spend as much for the thousand tons or so of precious metals we use—which are usually measured in ounces—as we do for the seventy million tons of iron we consume.

The primary fact about the very long-term availability of metals is that iron and the sources of aluminum are so extraordinarily plentiful, in so many places and forms, that it's impossible to imagine running out of them.

Already these two metals are a major share of the weight and value of all metals used. Furthermore, aluminum and iron have between them most of the properties that are needed for most of the functions that metals now perform. Therefore, either aluminum or iron or both can be used in place of many other metals. One important example is that aluminum can replace copper as an conductor of electricity.

We don't need to go through all the other metals (but see the Annex to this chapter printed as Endnote 15). Many of the metals seem very plentiful, even in relation to thousands of years of use, but one can't be sure. Others seem to have a real possibility of being used up in a few generations or centuries—although that is also uncertain.

If we are interested in thousands of years there is no point in trying to make a judgement metal by metal. No one could put any weight on such judgments, no matter how thoughtfully or carefully they were made. We need to have a reasonable way to think about them as a group, to get an overall perspective on the possibility of a dangerous running out of some set of metals.

The following are the critical points:

(1) All metals taken together aren't a major share of the world economy.

(2) When you subtract iron and aluminum (plus those metals that could fairly easily be replaced by iron or aluminum) the metals that are left are only a tiny share of the world economy.

(3) Iron and aluminum ore are so plentiful that they can never become expensive.

(4) So far, our experience has been that metals as a group have been getting cheaper and cheaper to find and produce.

The long experience of falling costs for getting metals may change. It may have been the result of coincidence or luck or the fact that we still use such small quantities. But there are plausible theories which suggest that the pattern of falling costs for metals is the result of underlying factors that will continue. Of course one can also make theories the other way. Neither kind of theory can be proven. But we don't have to know which theory is right. We won't be in trouble even if metal prices in the future go in the opposite direction than they have in the past.

Miscellaneous Minerals

The "big six" miscellaneous minerals (minerals that are neither fuels nor metals) are:

lime	phosphate	potash
cement*	gypsum	sulfur

On average, Americans now spend between $4 and $8 on each of these minerals each year. That is, from 100 to 700 pounds per person at raw material prices of $20-$100 per ton (one to five cents per pound). (Don't multiply the high price by the high quantity,

---

* Technically cement is not a mineral. But it is treated as one in standard reports on minerals because it is made of combinations of several kinds of minerals.

because we use more of the cheap stuff because it is cheap.)

Most of this is such ordinary stuff that we could never run out of it. The only materials that conceivably could be of concern are potash and phosphates, both of which are fertilizers. (In 1970 the known reserves of potash were over five hundred times as much as all the potash that had been used in the previous twenty years. From 1950-1970, 4% of the known reserves were used and twenty times the reserves known at the beginning of the period were found. The experience with phosphates, which are more important, was twice as good.)

The other minerals that we use in large quantities are silicon, clays, salt, barite, and sodium carbonate. But these are all very common materials and none costs us more than $1 or so per capita.

Conclusion

We don't have to deal with the possibility that some day the world might be gravely harmed by running out of raw materials as a theoretical question. Despite all the uncertainties of the long-term future, the facts we can know today show that we will always have the materials we need, without having to spend a large share of our effort to get them. This remarkable conclusion is the result of the fact that raw materials (apart from food and fuel) are such a small part of our economy, and that so much of the raw materials we use are so common that they can never run out. (e.g., salt, sand, stone, iron, aluminum, etc.)

Concluding Note to Part II:
Can Anyone Believe All This "Optimism"?

My view is that my readers are people of good common sense. After going through the six chapters of Part II, the natural reaction of such a reader is: "Singer has an argument for everything—one ingenious theory after another. But how can any reasonable person rely on all of his theories being right? How can anyone make a judgement about the future of mankind for millennia on the basis of a pile of clever arguments? It can't be so easy." Fair enough. Here are some answers.

First, you don't have to accept all of these "clever arguments" to believe the overall conclusion of Part II. These arguments don't pretend to be an attempt to say everything there is to say on these subjects—that would make the book too long and dull. Instead, Part II is a report on an effort to look into all the critical issues, and to consider all the major challenges and concerns that have been raised by those whose work underlies the gloomy views that are so widely distributed.

I believe it is fair to say that the conclusions presented here are the result of cautious and conservative analysis, in some depth, using the work of the most serious scholars and informed professionals—and taking into consideration the arguments of those who have different points of view. But I don't claim that this analysis is all presented here. I haven't tried to take the reader back and forth on scores of related disputes. Instead I have tried to find common sense ways to present the overall conclusions and to give reasons why they should seem plausible (not conclusively proven). More important, I have tried to focus on the fundamental issues for thinking seriously about whether Earth has the resources man will need—so one can put into perspective the particular scare stories that keep coming out, many of which are true but not really significant.

Some of the fundamental issues can not be definitively resolved—like whether we can produce enough energy at a low enough cost. And for most issues I have only been able to close the loop by using a broad view, and avoiding details. But if my attempt to give a complete answer, solving all basic problems, isn't entirely convincing (how could it be?), where are you left? If I haven't proved everything, does that mean that the opposite is true?

Of course not. Maybe you should decide that the conclusions here are reasonable but not proven. Maybe the answer is unknowable. Maybe the view presented here could be reasonably proven, but only with more detail and complexity than presented in this book. Any of those reasonable judgments are a long way from the standard discussion in our media and in our schools.

Certainly it doesn't make sense to jump from a judgement that the arguments in Part II don't prove that everything is going to be all right, to the commonly heard conclusion that we are heading sooner or later for dangerous shortages, and that if we are to act responsibly toward future generations we must mend our ways.

The basic message of this part is that, as best we can tell, the great dangers facing mankind are not any limits imposed by our physical environment but the things that we may deliberately do to each other. The opposite view is widely accepted. Most of our young people are taught that we have been damaging our environment, that the world is getting less capable of supplying our needs and more dangerous, and that we must drastically change our ways in order to survive. To counter that common view, which I believe is profoundly wrong, I have tried to show a solution to virtually every potential physical problem that mankind can have for thousands of years. And I have tried to do it using mostly facts that are widely known or uncontroversial—without using technical arguments or anything else that an ordinary person couldn't think about on the basis of his own experience and common sense. It's not surprising that such an ambitious goal should require at least some stretching, some unfamiliar ways of thinking.

If you are not satisfied with the arguments presented here, don't jump to the opposite conclusion. Instead look into the matter more deeply. Appendix F discusses sources of further information and analysis.

PART III

Problems and Dangers—Real and Imaginary

THE MESSAGE OF THIS BOOK is not that everything is fine and there is nothing to worry about. The message is that many people are being led to worry about the wrong things. The result is inadequate attention to realistic dangers and a wrong approach to real problems—as well as a misleading view of the world.

This part will discuss some major realistic dangers and tasks with which we ought to be concerned, and which provide an important part of a sensible overall perspective. Its title points to the critical distinction between problems and dangers. "Problems" are challenges that many people must work hard at, but which the rest of us shouldn't worry about; if they are ignored or bungled the worst result is that we won't be quite as well off as we might be. "Dangers" are what all of us should worry about, because these are what might produce drastic or even absolute harm. Look at it this way:

Distinguishing Between Problems and Dangers
*(Whether they are caused by human activity
or unrelated to human activity.)*

Problems	Dangers
Results are a matter of *degree* —better or worse, not life or death.	May result in *decisive* harm.*
Solvable.	May be beyond our powers to deal with.

Of course problems and dangers affect each other. While problems are defined as challenges that can be solved—with human performance no better than normal standards of the past—the fact that they can be solved doesn't necessarily mean that they will be solved. Some may represent a potential danger that we will fail to do something essential for survival—even though nothing is

---

* Of course this distinction only makes sense because we are talking of the world as a whole. From some points of view there is decisive or irreparable harm when a single person dies because of a mistake.

stopping us from doing what we need to. I think that it is quite unlikely that there will be dangerous failures to solve any of the problems discussed here, although costly mistakes are likely. But it would be wrong to forget that our continuing success depends on our own efforts, and grievous failure is possible.

E L E V E N

Pollution: Not Dirtier Than We Decide

Tokyo had become a great industrial center—but its skies had grown grey and brown and its citizens were choking on the air. One day Emperor Hirohito sadly commented to his Prime Minister that he missed the beautiful butterflies that no longer flitted about in his imperial garden.

Since this was Japan, the Prime Minister took the Emperor's hint as a command and launched a vast program to improve Tokyo's environment. Not many years later the Emperor was heard happily describing the beauty of the butterflies that had returned to his imperial garden.

In this little story we see illustrated the following pattern or trend: First poverty and butterflies, then industrialization and no butterflies, then wealth and butterflies.

FEAR THAT THE WORLD WILL BECOME INCREASINGLY POLLUTED is a major theme in public discussion of prospects for the future. One sophisticated form of this fear is that we will have to sacrifice the quality of our environment to grow enough food, or to cope with the increased difficulty of getting the minerals we need. This chapter will show why these fears are fundamentally unnecessary and unrealistic (which is not to deny that controlling pollution is an important and growing task).

Thousands of scientists are studying questions related to pollution problems. Protecting our environment involves technical issues of terrifying complexity. And the problem is getting bigger and more complicated every year as the number of people and the amount of production increases, and the number of new chemicals multiplies. No one can hope to understand all of these complexities, much less the way in which they will change in the future. But let's see whether we can get a reasonable handle on the human implications of pollution without going very far into these technical issues. After all, most of us drive cars without knowing much about internal combustion engines.

Before we get started on a realistic description of the pollution problem let's do a little exercise for gaining perspective: How clean is your house? Could it be neater, better kept, cleaner? Why isn't it? Maybe you have children. Even so, if you spent more time and money on keeping your house clean, wouldn't it be cleaner?

How dangerous is your house? How many smoke detectors and burglar alarms do you have? Have you worked out escape plans and instructed everybody about what to do if you have a fire? Have you installed fire escape ladders? Have you checked to see whether there are internal air contaminants? Is all your electric wiring properly grounded or do you have a tangle of extension cords? Do you have "grab bars" to protect yourself from falling in the bath tub?

Even though the world's problems are not so simple as keeping a house clean and safe, we can learn something about the general nature of the world's problems by thinking about our houses. Basically, our homes are as clean and neat as we choose to make them. The choice is not expressed in what we say or think or how we vote. It is expressed by actions. The house would be cleaner if everybody who lived in it took an extra hour every week to keep things clean or took a few weekends to paint or repair. Our houses are not cleaner because those of us who live in them chose not to make them cleaner—we preferred to use those hours for something else.

We make the same kind of choices about how safe our houses are. We could make them safer by spending either time or money (or effort to learn how). We don't because it isn't worth it to us. We choose our level of safety by deciding when to stop spending time and money on making our houses safer.

Although the world environment is infinitely more complicated than our homes, one of the basic points of this chapter is that our environment, like our home, will be as clean and safe as we choose to make it. Almost certainly the thing that will keep it from being cleaner and safer will not be some inherent limit of nature— it will be human decisions not to exert additional effort to make it cleaner and safer.

In this chapter we will consider the three "catches" that ought to concern us about the analogy to our home environment.

Catch number one. Sometimes we can't avoid a danger because we don't know about it. For example, who knew that installing asbestos insulation might be dangerous? I call this problem— something that is more dangerous than you think it is—"sneaky pollution," and there is a section on it below.

There is no guarantee against sneaky pollution, and no clearly safer strategy for minimizing the risk. (That is, going slower with new technology may be more dangerous than going faster.)

Catch number two. We know that the cost of keeping our house clean is reasonable, but how can we know that the cost of keeping the environment clean is reasonable, especially in the distant future?

Good question. See below for a pretty good answer.

Catch number three. I can decide to spend the necessary effort and money to keep my own house clean (at least if I live alone), but our individual decisions aren't enough to keep the environment clean. Protecting the environment requires cooperation among many people, sometimes people in a number of different countries.

This is the "common property" problem, and it makes things much harder. But, as we shall see, it is not by any means the only or worst "common property" problem. We are dependent on decisions of others for many other things that are as important to us as the quality of the physical environment.

What Does Our Experience Suggest about Pollution in the Future?

Different people looking at the experience with pollution in the last generation come to opposite conclusions about the future. There are no obviously decisive statistics. Inevitably it is a mixed picture. Some places are getting better at the same time other places are getting worse. And since pollution includes many different things, any one place may be getting better in some ways and worse in others at the same time. How can we make sense out of such a complicated and contradictory experience?

Since particular facts point so many different directions, the only way to think about trends is to try to understand the overall pattern. (And there are good grounds to be skeptical of anyone who only deals with those facts that show things getting worse—or better.)

One common pattern is that old forms of pollution disappear while new forms arise. Horse manure in city streets was a big problem at one time; now it is not. Soot from residential use of soft coal and similar fuels was once the dominant feature of the air in many cities such as New York or London; but it is no longer a problem because different fuels are used now, only partly to avoid pollution. Dysentery germs in urban water supplies, once an even bigger problem, have essentially disappeared from advanced countries. But now sulfur dioxide and carbon monoxide from cars and modern industrial plants are problems.

Perspective on pollution is often affected by short memories. People notice today's problem and are led to think that most pollution is caused by industry and manmade chemicals. They forget horse manure, and that the hazard from the contamination of drinking water with human wastes and other natural pollutants, was many times as great as the harm from sulphur compounds, PCBs and other modern pollutants that cause so much concern today. (Which does not mean that we shouldn't be concerned about modern pollutants, just that we should have some perspective.)

Another common pattern is based on the effects of economic development. When a country moves from primitive, very poor conditions to the very first stage of economic development, pollution usually is reduced as plumbing and sewer systems and other basic measures for cleanliness become understood and affordable. The next stage of development often brings industrialization and increases in pollution. Later the industrialization often produces enough wealth so that the country wants to, and can afford to, take control measures that reduce pollution. The United States and England are both good examples of countries that during the last generation have, overall, become less polluted than they were. Of course the picture in those countries is complicated and mixed. But the careful and well-informed environmentalists who have tried to make overall assessments have agreed that the overall picture in both countries has been getting better.

Can other countries learn from the mistakes of the first countries to tread the path of modernization and avoid the phase of increasing pollution? Only partly. To the extent that our pollution resulted from ignorance, others can learn from our mistakes and avoid some pollution. However, much pollution comes from choice not from ignorance. When you are poor you often choose not to spend the resources required to prevent some kinds of pollution, even though you know very well how to do it. Just as the individual may not paint his house if he doesn't have enough money for meat for his table.

How Should We Understand the Basic Idea of Pollution?

The idea of pollution includes two different kinds of things: *dirtiness* and *danger*. We spend money to reduce pollution because we want to be cleaner and safer. We can think of wilderness preservation, the protection of scenery, and other concerns for the amenity values of the environment as forms of cleanliness.

There are two kinds of reasons why we choose to be cleaner and safer: preference and efficiency. That is, because we like it better or because it saves money or lives. For example, we may want to get some chemicals out of the air, even if we can't see them and they don't hurt us, because when they are in the air they increase agricultural or building maintenance costs by a larger amount of money than the cost of keeping those chemicals out of the air. This is an efficiency reason.

Or as a matter of taste or preference we may want to keep

167

the air quality in some areas so good that one can see for fifty miles, even though there are no health or economic benefits from doing so. While safety is often talked about as an absolute requirement, we shall see in chapter thirteen that, because of the extreme ability of modern science to detect infinitesimally small dangers, the decision about how much health-threatening pollution to allow also becomes a matter of preference or efficiency, not an absolute. (Just as we choose how safe to make our homes.)

Taking all these considerations into account it turns out that there are two quite different kinds of pollution problems that have to be dealt with. I call these "mass pollution" and "sneaky pollution."

With mass pollution you know what the pollutant is and that you don't like it. The problem is spending the resources to get rid of it. With sneaky pollution you don't realize how bad it is until it is already in the environment. The problem is knowing in time.

As a practical matter, of course, it is not so simple. Usually some people know the facts while others are ignorant or disagree, and sometimes only part of the harm from a pollutant is understood. Sometimes there is genuine technical uncertainty; sometimes there is controversy because people have different interests and values. And people can even disagree about whether something is harmful, harmless, or useful—like fluoride in the drinking water. But even though in some cases a mass pollutant will also be somewhat sneaky, it is useful to think separately about: (1) the problem of how to get something that is recognized to be a "pollutant" out of our environment; and (2) the problem of how to recognize what really is a "pollutant"—because if we let too much of it get into our environment it will cause harm, or maybe is already causing harm (here "harm" means either dirtiness, ugliness, unhealthiness, or danger).

Mass Pollution

Most pollution now is mass pollution; that is, we know what is causing our problem—either dirtiness or danger or both. But it is expensive to get rid of the pollutant or to prevent the pollution.

The basic fact about mass pollution is that in the long run we will have only as much as we decide to have. It is our choice. Cleanliness is like other products: you can buy as much as you want and have money to pay for.

Of course the avoidance of pollution, which is community cleanliness, is a common property, like defense or a stable currency. Individuals can't buy such common properties, only groups can. Some pollution avoidance can be bought by the group that lives in an "air basin," in other cases by those living in a river basin, and in other cases only by the people controlling a whole region or even, in a few cases, the whole world.

There are several problems that come from the fact that community cleanliness is a common property. The community may buy more or less than any individual would prefer. You can't please everyone.* Also buying cleanliness is more complicated than buying potatoes. It is often hard to know what is the efficient way to buy it, and the best way may be one hundred times cheaper than the obvious way.

Some ways of buying community cleanliness tend to put the cost on a particular part of the community while an alternative way, for example, of reducing the amount of sulfur in the air, would put the cost on a different group. Naturally everybody agrees about who should pay: "the other guy." The political resolution of such disputes, as well as the more ideological ones, often lead us to buy our cleanliness at unnecessarily high cost.

Reducing mass pollution—pollution that is recognized—is essentially a group buying process. Each country or region (and for

* To some extent people can vote with their feet. They can avoid local pollution by moving to a community that shares their standard of cleanliness. But that is a drastic solution, particularly if the "local" pollution extends over a large area. On the other hand the possibility of competitive pressure on communities to maintain higher standards is a potential counterweight to the natural reluctance to spend money.

a few pollutants, the world) has to decide how much cleanliness and safety it wants, and what actions are the best way to buy it. In practice, obviously, it is much more complicated to make this set of decisions than I make it sound; and often they are not made nearly as well as they might be.

Decisions about how to produce a common property like environmental cleanliness (whether, for example, we should reduce sulfur coming from electric power plants by installing scrubbers or by using clean coal) are made by a political process. Political processes are designed to preserve domestic peace and achieve democratic or other political values; so they are not usually good at finding the efficient answer to technical problems. (For example, the law in the United States now says that even if you are burning clean coal you must use very expensive scrubbers, paid for by the people who use electricity—not because that is a good idea but because the political strength of the people who sell dirty coal, and of others who had parallel interests, was greater than the political strength of the people who pay for electricity.)

If our political processes aren't working well enough, we may have a lot more pollution than many people want, and/or waste a lot of money on foolish anti-pollution measures. But presumably, if things get too bad, eventually people will decide to do whatever it takes to fix the problem. There is no reason to believe that political incompetence will produce disaster in pollution control before it produces disaster in war avoidance or tyranny avoidance or depression avoidance.

Since this isn't a book about pollution policy we will not deal with the hard questions of how to find efficient and popular methods of limiting pollution. These are difficult and genuinely controversial questions, because they involve the kind of complex interaction that I discuss in connection with risks in Appendix E (which describes the relation between the country's game-against-nature and the political competition among groups for economic benefits).

The Cost of Mass Pollution

Now let's look at the problem of dealing with mass pollution. Our objective is to get a sense of how the costs compare to other things we need to buy; and a sense of how the problem is changing as we get richer, more technically and industrially advanced, and more numerous.

In 1975, the research organization mentioned earlier, Resources for the Future (RFF), arranged for a four-year study led by Ronald Ridker and William Watson, of the resource and environmental consequences of different growth paths that the United States might follow during the next fifty years. The results of this study were published in 1980 with the title *To Choose a Future*.

The Ridker & Watson team (R & W) estimated the amounts of materials and energy that would be needed for many possible combinations of population and economic growth in the United States during the fifty years from 1975 to 2025. They then estimated the amount of pollution that might be produced by all of the necessary mining, manufacturing, power generation, etc. They also considered the effect of many different pollution control laws, including the 1975 laws, already scheduled changes in the laws and regulations, and other possible future pollution control policies.

Of course, the mass pollution problem imposes two kinds of costs on us. First, there are the "pollution control costs" spent to prevent the pollutants we produce from getting into, or staying in, the environment. Basically pollution control is like a production task, such as providing food and furniture and transportation. It involves designing and procuring pollution absorbers, pollution sinks, pollution-avoiding production technology, etc. (Sometimes it is better to use a different production process in order to avoid producing the pollutants in the first place, in which case the extra cost, if any, of using a "cleaner" production process is a pollution control cost.)

The second kind of cost of the pollution problem is "pollution effects costs;" including things like cleaning costs, damage to property as a result of pollution, health care costs, and the value of reductions in health caused by pollution.

Most of both kinds of pollution costs are very difficult to estimate, even when you know all the facts. When you are talking about complicated pollution patterns fifty years in the future, in a radically different technical and economic environment, the task of estimating is much more difficult. But even though no confidence can be placed on any one estimate (for example the cost of removing sulfur dioxide produced by 300 big coal-burning electric generators in 2025), the sum total of the many thousand of estimates is reasonably useful, even if each separate estimate is almost worthless.

There are a number of reasons why this kind of estimating process is useful if done by a careful, balanced, and sophisticated group. One reason is that many possible mistakes and things that can't be predicted produce underestimates, while others produce overestimates. If the estimators are not trying to push the results one way, the errors in each direction tend to balance each other. This balancing of errors can apply both to detailed errors in each of the thousands of specific quantitative estimates and to systematic errors. (There are many possible systematic errors. One example would be to ignore potential cost-saving from new technical ways to avoid pollution rather than cleaning it up.)

What Ridker and Watson did to pull everything together was to develop about seven different scenarios for the next fifty years within which pollution costs could be figured. These scenarios combined different possibilities for economic and population growth, high or low use of nuclear energy, high or low oil prices, etc. They then tested the effects of four different kinds of pollution laws—relaxed, strict, minimum, and efficient—on each of the scenarios.

For each possible combination of production scenario and pollution control law, Ridker and Watson estimated two kinds of results: (1) the total cost of the pollution control programs, and (2) the expenses caused by the pollution that was allowed to remain in the environment. The sum of these two costs—pollution damage cost and pollution control cost—is the total cost of pollution, as best it can be calculated.

For the United States in 1975, where R & W had real costs to observe, pollution control costs were about $18 billion and pollution damage costs were about $48 billion. Putting it in other words, R & W estimated that in 1975 pollution cost the country a total of $66 billion, which was about 7% as much as people spent for everything they bought. (It was about 4.5% of GNP.) So in 1975, the costs of pollution were like a tax of 7% on everything we bought.

Now let's look at what we can expect the "pollution tax" to be fifty years later, in 2025. R & W calculate that it will be between 4.4% and 6.4%. In other words, their detailed analyses show total pollution costs going down regardless of which growth path our economy follows, and whether our pollution control laws are at the relaxed or strict end of the range of possibilities that seemed reasonable to them.

For a "strict" set of control laws, R & W estimate that in 2025 control costs would be between $162 billion and $290 billion (in 1975 dollars) and that pollution costs would be between $12 billion and $32 billion. This calculation says that if we stick to strict pollution control laws, the amount of money spend on controls will go way up but the costs of pollution will go down; and the total of the two costs will go down compared to other things we buy.

The R & W conclusions were: ". . . environmental damages from the mass pollutants covered in this chapter are likely to remain the same or fall over time despite the growth in the economy and greater number of people at risk . . . . In all cases, after 1985 they fall over time on a per capita basis and as a percentage of consumption.

"Pollution control costs, though never a large percentage of GNP, will increase over time . . . in all scenarios. *The net effect is that total costs (damage plus control costs) as a percentage of GNP or consumption remain roughly the same or fall slowly over time* . . . . Clearly, control policy is central to achieving acceptable levels of environmental quality; indirect approaches that would alter population and economic growth can have little impact . . . ." In other words R & W concluded: *no matter how much we grow we can have less pollution damage than now by paying the costs requred to keep clean—and the costs won't be very high.* [My emph.—M.S.]

Ridker and Watson would be the last to argue that their calculations are correct predictions of anything specific. The future is too complex and unknowable for any specific calculations to turn out to be correct. On the other hand, it is a little bit difficult to see why we should believe that the future will be completely different than all of the many possibilities that they looked at, so it is reasonably likely that the general shape of their conclusions will be roughly correct. No one else has attempted such a careful and thorough study of future pollution costs. Nor has anyone looked at their work and argued that it was systematically biassed or given any reason for believing that it is substantially incorrect. It stands today as, by far, the single most thorough and substantial effort to evaluate long term pollution costs.

So the R & W study is the best evidence we have, and it says quite clearly that for the next fifty years in the United States, regardless of how fast we grow, mass pollution will cost less than it does today. If R & W are correct, that pollution costs are going down over the next fifty years in the richest large area of Earth, it is a powerful piece of evidence that further economic growth in the world in the long term does not have to increase the pollution tax that people need to pay to maintain the quality of the environment.

People who focus on improving the environment will always have something to complain about, no matter how much improvement we make in the quality of the environment. (Just as your house could always be cleaner or more elegant.) And there will always be environmental protection proposals that seem much too expensive. Anyone whose view is dominated by the current pollution control proposals that are being rejected because they cost "too much" will see pollution as getting worse in the future. And of course anyone whose standard of evaluation is the quality of the environment before there were people, and who doesn't rate human values highly, cannot have high hopes for environmental quality in the future.

Conclusion about Mass Pollution

It is necessary to choose a standard to make a judgment about the future. As one possible standard of judging, let's start with the quality of the environment as it is today. This standard may not be the greatest, but at least we all know what we're talking about. We've seen it and tasted it. We know we can live with it. My claim is that in the long-run we can, at a reasonable cost, keep the quality of the worldwide environment at least as good as it is today.

We are now spending less than 5% of our economy on pollution, and R & W estimate that in the United States these costs will decline over the next fifty years. Therefore it is not implausible to think that the world can keep itself cleaner than it is today without spending much more than 10% of its economy on pollution. If this is true the pollution problem need not be a disaster, which is really the appropriate question for this book—which is concerned with very long-term issues.

Of course we can do better. There are many ways in which I think we should do better. We should improve the quality of our environment, and we certainly should be more efficient than we have in our expenditures on environmental protection. I am not saying either that the environment today is good enough or that we will need to spend as much as 10% of the world economy on pollution when the world's population is very large and very rich. All I am saying is that it is a conservative judgment to conclude that we can keep the environment at least as good as it is today without having to pay excessive costs.

The fact that it is difficult to make good decisions about buying cleanliness doesn't change the basic situation; we the people, not nature, determine how much mass pollution there is. Nature will allow us to have all the raw materials we want at reasonable costs with about as little pollution as we choose and without spending a noticeable share of the economy for pollution control. While many people *seem* to contradict this basic point, in fact they have not examined this question and do not challenge this conclusion.

In other words, mankind—by its policies—will determine the level of pollution in the world. How clean and safe the environment is depends on how much cleanliness and safety we want, and on how smart or dumb we are about how we go about keeping the environment clean. There is no evidence or sensible theory which shows that we will have to pay very much to have an environment that is in better condition than the one we have today. This conclusion holds for tens of billions of people and very high living standards, with very large consumption of energy and everything else that goes with it.

Sneaky Pollution

With mass pollution the problem is deciding how much cleanliness to buy, and buying it efficiently; with sneaky pollution the problem is knowing what's happening.

Here is where all those who insist that there must be something to worry about can have their day. "Sneaky pollution" is defined as a category to give room for most of the "what if . . .?" questions that can't be answered.

We can't know for sure all the effects of what we do. I use the idea of sneaky pollution to bring together all the harmful effects that we are unable to predict (except some disasters which are discussed in chapter twelve.) So the discussion of sneaky pollution is a discussion of the unpredictable dangers and problems.

I define "sneaky pollutants" as any phenomena that turn out to cause more trouble than was originally thought. The concept is broad enough to cover not just chemicals and bugs. Television, for example, might be a sneaky pollutant if it turns out to make intelligent life on the planet impossible after several generations. Many germs or bacteria are good examples of sneaky pollutants; until we find out about them they cause many deaths.

One dramatic example of a sneaky pollutant is methyl mercury. At one time people believed that it wasn't absorbed by the human body and therefore that industrial wastes containing methyl mercury were not dangerous. The error was discovered only after hundreds of Japanese and others received deadly or disastrously harmful doses. Once the cause of "Minamata disease" was discovered the discharge of methyl mercury was virtually stopped almost overnight.

Various forms of natural pollution that produce malaria or dysentery or other diseases have been quickly limited once the danger from them was recognized; that is, as soon as they were recognized as pollution. Such natural sneaky pollutants have caused millions and millions of deaths.

We are especially interested in manmade sneaky pollutants. We want to know whether we will make things or do things that are surprisingly dangerous, perhaps cumulatively over a long time or to later generations. Will we do things that, if we had known what the results would turn out to be, we wouldn't have done them? To be blunt, will we make mistakes that kill many people? The answer is: Yes.

How can we be sure before we unleash some new chemical or medicine or research program or social reform, that it will not cause untold death and destruction? We can't always be sure. Our mistakes have caused millions of deaths in the past, and probably will in the future.[16]

By definition we cannot stop sneaky pollution—because we don't know what it is. As soon as we recognize it, it becomes mass pollution. So how can we estimate how big the problem of sneaky pollution will be and what can be done about it, since by definition we don't know what the problem is? More important for our concerns, does the problem of sneaky pollution get worse if the world population gets very large and very rich?

The short answer is that we can't know for sure how bad sneaky pollution might be. It is entirely possible that some form of sneaky pollutant will kill everybody and end the human species. And it is quite likely that sneaky pollutants will in the future, as they have in the past, kill millions of people.

Therefore I want to be very clear. I do not mean to say we don't have to worry about sneaky pollutants. There is no assurance that they will not cause immense harm. But, on the other hand, there is no reason for thinking that sneaky pollution is anything like the most dangerous problem we face.* And there is no way of knowing whether more population and economic growth will increase or decrease the total harm from sneaky pollution.

Dealing with Sneaky Pollution

Three things determine how much harm we will suffer from sneaky pollution. First is the number and nastiness of sneaky pollutants. Second is the speed with which technical people expose the sneaky pollution, that is how quickly they learn that a mistake was made.

---

* The phrase "no reason for thinking that" means exactly what it says; it does not mean "it is definitely wrong to think that."

Third is how quickly the society acts to correct the mistake once it is discovered.

It is reasonable to think that the more the world economy grows and advances technically, the more sneaky pollutants of every degree of nastiness will be produced. But that doesn't mean that sneaky pollution will cause increasing harm. The decisive question is whether our ability to respond to the sneaky pollutants grows faster than the sneaky pollutants do.

Presumably, our ability to find the sneaky pollutants will increase as the level and quantity of our science and technology rises; but after scientists found that feeding citrus fruits to sailors would prevent scurvy, it was thirty years before the British navy began providing limes to their sailors. And it was another forty years before the new technology of limes was transferred to the British merchant marine, although frequently 25% of a ship's crew might die of scurvy if the ship did not provide limes or some other source of Vitamin C.

It is harder to guess whether, when the world economy gets bigger and richer, we will become quicker or slower to act against pollution dangers after they are uncovered by scientists. It depends on what might be called "social wisdom." And anyone who thinks he can predict whether social wisdom will increase or decrease in the future is welcome to the job.

But there are some more predictable factors. Other things being equal people are more able to recognize dangers if they can see what needs to be done to deal with them and if they can afford to do it. So increasing wealth means that a little less social wisdom is necessary to respond to newly-recognized pollution mistakes. Also, as people get wealthier they usually decide to spend increasing shares of the income on safety and aesthetics. This is another way in which wealth may speed the response to sneaky pollution.

Conclusion about Sneaky Pollution

Sneaky pollution is a problem to which there are no guaranteed answers. It will be costly and it may be disastrous. But we have no good reason for thinking that it is a problem that will get worse as we complete the passage from natural to human worlds. Clearly we are likely to produce more sneaky pollutants, but equally clearly our ability to reduce the harm from any particular sneaky pollutant will also grow. It is the balance between these two effects that is unpredictable—although I would bet that our ability will increase more than the challenge.

When we turn from speculation about the future to decisions about policy, the danger of sneaky pollution does not provide much basis for action. It isn't clear whether this danger should make us lean more toward going faster or toward going slower. Obviously we should be watching out for sneaky pollutants, but we already are.

Sneaky pollution remains the category for the unsolvable problems. By creating this catchall category for those kinds of pollution we can't predict, we have made it possible to speak confidently about our ability to handle the other kinds of pollution that are the great majority of the pollution concerns.

Preserving Natural Amenities

"Natural amenities" includes beautiful scenery, wilderness, beaches, other parks and recreational areas, and places where the air is not only clean but so clear that one can see for fifty miles on a clear day. I use the term to cover many desireable things that can't be bought in the marketplace and which are difficult to quantify.

The problem is to make sure that as many natural amenities as possible are available to people in the future—despite the fact that there will be so many more of us to use them, and despite our rapidly increasing use of the globe to produce marketable commodities.

One of the things that makes this problem so hard is the difficulty of quantifying most natural amenities. It is hard to protect or to produce things that can't be measured. And because it is hard to arrange for people to own natural amenities, it is hard to use markets and prices to help us to ration and produce them.

The problem of providing the amenities of nature involves a number of subtle issues. For example, is an area wilderness if man has ever been there? Modern man or Indians? On foot, horse, canoe, helicopter, or jeep? How far away must civilization be for one to be in the wilderness? How many people can walk through an area and have it keep its character as wilderness? Does the world have more amenities or less if one thousand people walk through a big "untouched" forest in one year instead of only one person? Some would say more, because one thousand people have been able to enjoy what only one could before. Others would say less, because if one thousand people a year go through a forest it is not wilderness any more; they would say the amount of wilderness amenity had been reduced.

We all can observe from our personal experience at home and in our communities that how crowded and unpleasant a place feels doesn't depend only how many people are there. Whether crowds are unpleasant depends a lot on how efficient and understanding the arrangements are. And it depends on whether people behave with consideration.

For example, a few dozen people who ride snow mobiles and dirt bikes wherever they want can prevent thousands of people from enjoying a huge forest area. On the other hand, if sensible arrangements are made, and the rules observed, the same area can be used by thousands of dirt bikers and snow mobilers, and at the same time also by thousands of cross-country skiers, hikers, hunters, fishermen, and campers; with no one seriously interfering with anyone else's enjoyment.

The key to the protection and enhancement of many of the natural amenities of the world is not how many people there are—either in the world or the region. The key issues are how wise society is about devising suitable arrangements, and how courteously people behave. In other words the key is wisdom and social character, neither resources nor population growth.

Therefore the question of natural amenities—like so many other questions that seem to depend on the limited capacities that nature has given us—turns out to depend on how much we care, and on the wisdom and effort we devote to the task of getting what we think we want.

TWELVE

Natural and Other Disasters

**Nature can still make a much bigger bang than we can.
But she doesn't do it very often.**

W HY SHOULD WE HAVE A CHAPTER ON DISASTERS? Partly because I am so afraid of being falsely accused of being a "Pollyanna." When a book has a specific chapter on disasters no one can say that it doesn't take the possibility of disasters into account.

Even if there were no need to be concerned about avoiding the appearance of excessive optimism, it would be wrong to omit the question of possible disasters from any book designed to provide as broad a view of human prospects as this book attempts. Natural disasters that have happened in the past can happen again. More important, we can use the actual disasters that have happened in the past as examples to help us think about different kinds of potential disasters that might happen in the future—whether natural or manmade. And disasters give perspective to normal problems.

Our special interest is whether the possibility of disasters makes the general picture of the world described in this book misleading. Is the passage to a human world a "summer soldier," good only if the weather is fine?

The short answer has three parts:

1) Sure, a disaster could destroy the human race, preventing the passage to a human world, described here.

2) This possibility is so small that it should not influence our view of the world; it is much less likely than other dangers that we ignore.

3) Our best protection against disaster is probably the continued expansion of wealth and technology that is making passage to a human world possible.

The vision presented here is not a fair-weather picture, dependent on continued good luck; it can survive a lot of foul weather. But we have no guarantee that protects us against all dangers. We can be overwhelmed by forces beyond our power to resist or cope. Humans are not all-powerful, and our existence depends on a continuation of the basic physical conditions of the Earth as they have existed since the time of our first human ancestors.

Natural Disasters

We see small natural disasters, like earthquakes, floods, and the eruption of volcanoes, fairly frequently. But most of the effects of the natural disasters with which we are familiar are limited to the region where they occur. The worst disasters, which may occur half a dozen times in a century, kill as many as hundreds of thousands of people. Each of several Chinese floods are thought to have killed over one million people.

It seems likely that bigger earthquakes and volcanic eruptions than we have experienced are entirely possible. And certainly it is possible that we will be more unlucky about where these disasters strike—which would mean more casualties. So on the basis of experience we can easily imagine natural disasters that could kill a few million people. But even very large floods, earthquakes or eruptions are likely to have limited effect beyond the region where they occur. They are not likely to kill as much as one-tenth of 1% of the world's population—one person in a thousand—which is not enough to affect the general condition of the world, even temporarily.

But the worldwide effects of giant volcanic eruptions might be an exception. The dust clouds from some volcanic eruptions within our history were great enough so that it is conceivable that one or a few such eruptions would cause more harm to our atmosphere than human activities like supersonic planes, spray cans, or even the burning of fossil fuels.

There are pessimists who argue that modern economies are so technologically complex and interdependent—and modern cities so crowded—that we have become more vulnerable to natural disasters. Certainly there are new kinds of vulnerability. And it is hard not to believe that a sedentary office worker, with no experience at making or fixing anything other than a computer program, is less capable of taking care of himself, if caught in a natural disaster, than his father who worked on a farm, hunting and fishing, and building and repairing most of what he needed. No doubt the concentration of people in large cities makes it possible for many more people to be killed by a local event than was possible a few centuries ago when the largest cities had only a few hundred thousand people.

But the pessimists are probably wrong about the trend. Generally, modern wealth and technology puts us in a much better position to limit the number of people killed by natural disasters. Our system is not as vulnerable as it looks—as we found when all the electricity suddenly went off in New York City and most of the Northeast United States one night in 1965 and there were practically no casualties.

While individuals may not be very capable of responding to emergencies by themselves, modern societies are well-adapted to respond quickly and powerfully. We have an extraordinary kit of capabilities that swings into use whenever there is a disaster. Help can come quickly from great distances; applying immense resources, powerful technology, and brain power from all over the world. As a result, most wounded can be saved. And we are usually able to prevent the epidemics that historically were the major killer in many disasters.

While it is true that growing concentrations of people in cities makes it possible for nature to kill more people at one time, this is not saying much other than: When there are more people, more people can be killed. Even the worst urban disaster one can imagine, killing all the population of one of the giant metropolitan areas of the world, would not kill as large a percent of the world's population as the destruction of the large cities of the past.

In brief, it seems unlikely that familiar kinds of natural disasters can have a noticeable effect on human history—or that they are a significant risk to any individual.

We have to look at less familiar events to find a real threat to our society, or a reason to doubt that the rest of the passage to a human world will be traversed in the next few centuries.

Meteorites

There is very good evidence that the Earth has suffered a number of severe blows from meteorites. *The Scientific American* of September 1978, summarizes research on the Manicouagan crater in central Quebec. The scientists estimated that the crater was created about 214 million years ago when a stony meteorite about five miles in diameter hit the Earth travelling at about 38,000 miles per hour.

The study did not consider the effect of this impact outside of the local area. What can be observed today are three concentric rings. The outer ring, which is nearly one hundred miles across, is thought to be the limit of the disruption of the bedrock by the shock wave produced by the meteorite's impact. An intermediate ring, with a diameter of about forty miles, is thought to be the edge of the original outer lip of the crater formed by the material blown out of the center of the crater when it fell back down. And the inner circle, which is twenty-two miles across, is the edge of the cavity made by the meteorite when it hit what was to become Canada.

In other words, it is thought that a stone about five miles across hit the Earth at 38,000 mph and the impact released so much energy (probably equivalent to several million Hiroshima bombs) that it left a hole twenty-two miles across. What effect the meteorite's crash had on the environment beyond the crater is not known.

Dr. Dale Russell, in another *The Scientific American* article (January, 1982), presents evidence which suggests that about sixty-three million years ago a meteorite of asteroid size hit the Earth and somehow produced a biological crisis that caused at least 75% of the previously existing plant and animal species to disappear. While the evidence for the meteorite is fairly speculative, it does seem clear that all the dinosaurs and a number of other species became extinct at about this time.

According to Dr. Russell, if such a meteorite—estimated to be six miles across—had hit at sea it would have generated tidal waves five miles high. If it had hit on land it might have produced enough dust to make the atmosphere much less transparent for several years, and thus strike at the foundations of life by diminishing photosynthesis.

At about the same time Dr. R. Ganapathy, writing in *Science* (May 21st, 1982) argued that a meteor at least two miles in diameter, weighing at least fifty billion tons, hit the Earth only thirty-four million years ago and caused the extinction of a number of plant and animal species. Supposedly the impact of this meteorite spread one to ten billion tons of glass, commonly referred to as North American tektites, over a large fraction of the Earth's surface. (Other scientists give different explanations of how the North American tektites were formed.)

Less than eighty years ago a much smaller meteor was big enough to cause very widespread damage even though it fell in an isolated area. On the morning of June 30, 1908, an immense meteor exploded over the Stony Tunguska River basin of Central Siberia with the force of a ten megaton explosion. 700 square miles of ancient forest were blown flat. Men who were forty miles from the site were thrown down and seared by the heat. An article in the October 2, 1981, issue of *Science* suggests that in its passage through the Earth's atmosphere this meteor would have generated about thirty million tons of nitric oxide. This nitric oxide would probably have removed 30% to 45% of the ozone in the Northern hemisphere. There is evidence that the ozone was depleted about that much in 1909, and that it took several years before the ozone level of the atmosphere returned to normal.

WHILE WE HAVE TO GO BACK tens of millions of years to find examples of meteorite impacts big enough to be threatening to a large piece of the world, we only have to go back tens of thousands of years to find ice ages which produced a vast expansion of glaciers. Another such advance of the glaciers might pose a greater problem for people than a meteorite.

Changes in the level of the oceans, and continental

movements like those of the past could also present severe challenges to human society.

Mass Destruction of Species in the Past

While the causes are not known, scientists now are reasonably sure that during the 600 million years since life on Earth evolved into millions of different species, there have been at least five times when most species were eliminated in a short time. In one case as many as 95% of all species might have become extinct.

Thus the experience of life to date suggests that the elimination of species is as much a part of nature as the creation of species; because almost all species that have ever existed have already been eliminated. The recent concern about preserving all species of life—such as each regional form of the snail darter and every local variety of jungle insect—may come from misunderstanding of what a species really is, and of the history of species. (Of course this is not a reason for us not to work hard to prevent the extinction of a particular species that seems to have some actual or potential value.)

Obviously things that happen roughly every hundred million years or so are not very worrisome (although they are more threatening than the limits created by the fact that the Earth's resources are only finite.) They are mentioned here primarily to illustrate that bigger natural disasters than have been experienced in human history are possible.

The "Greenhouse Effect" Danger

Probably the main physical danger to the world now in sight is the possibility of what is called "the greenhouse effect." This is the possibility that so much carbon dioxide (plus a few other gases with similar effects) will be added to the atmosphere in the next one hundred years or so and that the atmosphere will act like a giant greenhouse trapping heat and making our climate substantially warmer and wetter, with disastrous effects on agriculture and on the level of the oceans. (Carbon dioxide seems to be added primarily by burning fossil fuels and possibly by cutting down forests.

However there are a great many processes, both natural and human, that add or subtract carbon dioxide and other gases, such as methane, to or from the atmosphere. The total amounts added and subtracted are large compared to the net changes in the total.)

There is still a great deal of scientific uncertainty about the greenhouse effect and the carbon dioxide question. The following are statements about which, I think, almost all those who have carefully studied the greenhouse question would agree:

(1) There is uncertainty about the extent to which the carbon dioxide released by the burning of fossil fuels is trapped by the atmosphere.

(2) The influence of the oceans on the amount of carbon dioxide in the atmosphere is not yet well understood and conceivably could be decisive.

(3) Nobody knows how much the world's forests are likely to be reduced during the next century or so. Nor does anybody know how much a reduction of forest area would add to atmospheric carbon dioxide, if at all. (There is more wood being added to the forests of North America each year than when the white man came to the continent—because the forests then were mostly mature, that is, with gains and loses approximately equal.)

(4) There is still uncertainty about how much heating effect results from any particular increase in atmospheric carbon dioxide—and how important trace gases, particularly methane, might be. So far research has increased confidence that there is some heating effect, but reduced the estimates of the size of the effect of current levels of coal burning.

(5) It is also even uncertain whether a heating effect would be harmful, neutral, or beneficial (for example, to counteract a natural cooling trend), but it is probably harmful.

(6) If there is a dangerous increase in atmospheric carbon dioxide, it is unclear whether the best response would be to reduce the use of fossil fuels, to stop the reduction of forests, or to take some countermeasure.

(7) Even at the worst, we have at least a decade to do further research before we have to decide whether we need to take any action and, if so, what action we should take to avoid this potential danger.

(8) It seems likely that, if it turns out to be true that the greenhouse effect will be seriously harmful, we will have time to take sufficient measures to prevent the harm. The appropriate action will probably not be disastrously onerous or expensive—that is, it is unlikely to cost as much as 5% of Gross *World* Product (GWP).

But, if action is necessary, it may well require a challenging degree of international cooperation.

Sneaky Pollution Disaster

The phrase "sneaky pollution"—which we discussed in chapter eleven—sounds as if it refers only to things that are manmade and slow-acting. But the definition is broad enough to include anything, either in nature or created by man, which is allowed to cause harm because the danger is not understood.

Sneaky pollution refers to that class of dangers which are the result of ignorance—rather than powerlessness, dangers that we might be capable of dealing with when their source is known — like anopheles mosquitoes, which carry malaria to people. Or like radon gases and other indoor pollutants that can become more harmful if we make our houses too tight in order to save energy.

In principle there is no limit to the potential harm from sneaky pollution. Just as we cannot be sure that mankind will not be wiped out by a natural disaster, so we cannot be sure that mankind will not be wiped out by some form of sneaky pollutant.

Both of the basic facts about a potential natural disaster apply to a sneaky pollution disaster as well: (1) it might destroy all of us regardless of what we do, or (2) its effect on human life might depend on how much resources and technology we have available to respond when it occurs—as discussed right below.

Especially in the case of a sneaky pollution disaster, the key to whether we are destroyed may not be either the size of the threat, nor the amount of resources we have available to cope with it, but our social wisdom—the ability of governments and other units of society to make the necessary decisions.

How Can We Be Cautious About Disasters?

I do not pretend that I have listed all, or even the most dangerous kinds of disaster. The main point of this review of disaster possibilities has been to emphasize that much bigger natural disasters than we are used to thinking about are possible, and to provide some illustrations of what is meant by natural disaster. There is no reason to think that the chance of any such super disaster occurring during the next few centuries is as large as one in a hundred. But that doesn't mean that we can be sure that one won't come tomorrow.

The phrase "being cautious about disasters," seems to imply trying to avoid or stay away from disasters—which is a good idea but not so easy to know how to do. Of course we could be very "cautious" about what we do, making every effort not to do anything that can turn into huge disaster—whether it is creating radioactivity or new genes or changes in the atmosphere. Other things being equal, the less we do, the less chance that we will do something disastrous. But other things are not equal.

Another way to look at being cautious about disasters is to think in terms of a struggle between man and disaster. If we can't prevent continuation of the climate cycle that caused the last ice age to send glaciers moving South or can't prevent a giant meteorite from racing on a collision course toward Earth, maybe we can do something to prevent them from hitting us with their full force. We might be able to break up the meteor or divert it. Possibly we could alter the path of some glaciers.

Even if we cannot halt or divert the forces threatening us, maybe we could prevent some or all of the harm to people from any such unstoppable force. We might be able to prevent a great natural disaster from being such a great human disaster. For example, we might be able to get precise warning of the point where a big meteorite would hit, and evacuate nearby people to safer areas.

More likely, we could take measures to cope with the effects of the disaster.

The idea of a struggle with disaster gives an entirely different perspective on how to be cautious. It tells us that we need to get ready, to increase our ability to respond to danger or disaster. But how can we get ready for unpredictable disaster? What do we need in order to be prepared? The short answer is: knowledge and money, that is, tools and resources.

Resources vs. Disasters

The wonderful thing about money is that it is flexible. It can be used to buy orchids or steam shovels, opera or dams. The first way to estimate how ready we are to deal with a disaster is to ask how much money we have, that is, how much money could the world spend next year to protect ourselves against a natural disaster?

In 1940 the United States produced a total of $100 billion worth of goods and services to take care of all the needs of the American people. During the next five years we produced a total of $360 billion worth of military goods and services—in addition to enough civilian products to take care of the needs of what we called "the home front." (These are 1940s dollars; multiply by six to get the equivalent in 1980s dollars.)

In 1944, the United States was able to divert almost half of all our production from civilian to military uses. During the peak year of the war we spent about $100 billion for the war in Europe and Asia—which of course used a very different mix of resources and talents than the economy had needed before. Presumably if there had been no war a similar quantity of resources could have been diverted to coping with or averting some great natural disaster.

Today the annual production of the United States is more than twice as great as it was in 1944, so we might be able to divert twice as much of our resources to respond to a natural disaster. Since we are richer now, we might be able to divert an even bigger share of our production. (It isn't clear whether the change in the content of our economy since 1945 increases or decreases our ability to convert from what we normally do to what would be needed to respond to an unprecedented natural disaster—perhaps it would depend on what kind of effort were needed.)

Of course the growth in annual production in the rest of the world since 1944 has been even greater than the growth in the United States. A reasonable estimate is that in the next five years, with a mobilization only one-fourth as effective as that of the United States in World War II, the world could spend at least as much as one year's GWP on special measures to respond to a worldwide disaster. That would be over $12,000 billion, enough to put twenty-five million people to work full time on the job for five years. That much work can produce large results. And more growth lies ahead. So the resources potentially available to respond to a natural disaster are very large, and growing.

What Needs Might a Disaster Create?

To see what could be done with so much money, let's speculate for a minute about what a really giant natural disaster would be like. (Of course there might be disasters so great or so sudden that everybody would be killed despite all our efforts; but let's consider lesser disasters.) Although we have no way of knowing whether there ever will be such a disaster, or what would cause it, we can think about how people would be affected by various types of disaster, and what they might do.

First are the relatively sudden disasters such as earthquakes or meteorite impacts. Second are the slower disasters such as new diseases, climate changes, or sea level changes. (These slow-acting disasters might be caused by a sudden action; for example if a meteorite impact or a volcanic explosion put enough dust or smoke in the atmosphere to create climate changes.)

Several kinds of disasters would have the result of requiring many people to move. For example people living near the ocean, if the oceans were to rise, or people living in the path of glaciers, if there is a new ice age. Or people who are part of farming economies in areas where a climate change makes farming impossible—or much less competitive. The costs of moving so many people, and building all that they would need in their new locations, would be tremendous.

Since so many people live near the oceans, rising ocean levels would produce an immense burden. Many billions of dollars worth of buildings and roads and other immovable facilities would become worthless. Whole new cities would need to be built. And if the rise were gradual, and people didn't know how far it would go, it would be difficult to locate harbor facilities and the cities that normally grow around them. But no reason is apparent why rising ocean levels would make it impossible for life to continue—assuming that much land would remain above water.

While sea level changes would hit cities hardest, climate changes might have a similar effect on many farming communities. Whole areas might become either uninhabitable or incapable of supporting more than a fraction of their population. Presumably new farming areas would have to be opened elsewhere to replace those areas hurt by the climate change, or some existing farm areas would have to be farmed much more intensively. The effect could be a big increase in the cost of food, at least until the adjustment was completed.

If the climate change resulted from a sudden event, like volcanic eruptions, there might be several years in which it was impossible to produce as much food as is usually used. If there were one or two growing seasons before the full effects were felt in all parts of the world, there would be a great need to grow as much as possible while there was time, and to put as much into storage as possible. Consequently, there would be a sudden jump in the need for food storage facilities. (Probably it would make sense in this situation to slaughter most cattle, so that grain for people could be grown instead of animal feed, and this would create a need for facilities that could store large amounts of meat.) (According to the Bible Pharaoh was able to use warning of impending crop failure, surplus resources of seven fat years, the technology of warehouses, Joseph's organizing skill, and his imperial authority, to protect the Egyptian people against the natural disaster of seven lean years.)

A disaster such as an epidemic that is even more severe than the AIDS epidemic raging today could make use of massive resources, even though the primary response might have to be the kind of scientific research that cannot be expanded rapidly, and so can only absorb limited amounts of money. It might require an unprecedented quarantine program, in which we had to find ways to take care of large parts of the population while they are kept separate from uninfected people and were unavailable to do their normal work. Or we might have to fix a large part of the world up with the kind of equipment and procedures we now use to keep advanced medical research labs sterile, at costs that now seem unbelievable.

Some disasters might make it necessary for everybody to live underground for a while—say two years. That would take a few bucks and some time, but it could be done—although it would not be as nice as Disney World, or home.

While we cannot predict what kind of disaster, if any, mankind may have to face, it is hard to imagine any disaster which doesn't kill everybody immediately for which no human efforts would be possible to significantly reduce the harm to people. A disaster against which our ability to struggle would make a difference seems more likely than one against which we would be absolutely powerless.

Are We In a Race Against a Disaster?

The effect on the human race of another big meteorite hitting the Earth may depend as much on the rate of technological and economic development between now and the date it hits, and on how far in the future it comes (ten years, 100 years, 200 years, 2,000 years), as it does on how large the meteorite is. In other words, if our wealth and technology continue to grow, perhaps we could cope with twice as big a meteor 200 years from now as we could today.

The AIDS epidemic is an example of how accelerated technical progress (apart from increased wealth) can increase safety. So far the fight against AIDS is primarily in the area of scientific and medical research. But the costs are already reaching the multi-billion-dollar level, and they surely will rise.

AIDS is the result, apparently, of a natural sneaky pollutant—a virus or family of viruses. But the extent of the AIDS disaster is partly the result of human actions. The spread of AIDS probably has been much faster than it would have been two hundred years ago because of modern wealth and life-styles; including extensive international travel and the fact that in the modern world many people have a much broader range of contacts than was common in the traditional natural world.*

If AIDS had come here twenty years ago we would not be nearly as far along the way to a prevention strategy or a cure as we are today. Most of the medical research being done to respond to AIDS is using scientific tools and knowledge that did not exist twenty years ago. If, in the interests of safety, we had held back research on recombinant DNA or other technologies, the response to AIDS would be far behind where it is today. Probably many more people would die before AIDS is brought under control if AIDS had come sooner, or if technical progress had been slower. This is one of the reasons why the danger of being "too safe" maybe at least as great as the danger of not being "safe enough."

We did not expect AIDS. We cannot know what else may lurk in our future, nor what we will need to cope with future menaces. One argument is that the only safe thing to do is to acquire as much wealth and technology as we can in order to increase the chance that we will be ready.

Conclusion

There is no way that we can be sure that we will not be hit by a meteorite—or some other kind of natural disaster—that will destroy all human life, regardless of how much resources we have to protect ourselves. Nobody can say for sure that our species will survive this year, much less the decade, century, millennium, or the much longer period for which our raw material supply is sufficient. Just as nobody can say that she will live long enough to die of old age. Any of us, however careful we are, can be hit by lightning, a bus, or cancer.

The two basic facts about a potential large meteorite impact, as well as other kinds of potential disaster, are: (1) it might destroy us all regardless of what we do, or (2) its effect on human life might

---

* Some people might argue that the promiscuous or "decadent" lifestyles which played a role in the transmission of AIDS (at least in the United States) are also an unfortunate by-product of wealth.

depend on how much resources and technology we have available to respond when it occurs.*

The Effect on History of Potential Disasters

At first thought it might seem that since either sneaky pollution or natural disaster could completely wipe us out, either of them could do enough harm to prevent economic growth, but this conclusion does not necessarily follow. It is true that we cannot specify any upper limit on how many people or how much wealth might be destroyed by sneaky pollution or natural disaster. But if there are a sizeable number of people left, it seems likely that economic growth would start again and world population and wealth would grow to more or less the same level as it would have grown without the pollutant or disaster.

We can imagine a scenario in which sneaky pollution or natural disaster didn't kill many people, but destroyed a large share of our capital stock. In effect this would be the result if we had to spend massive amounts of money to protect ourselves from the effects of some slow disaster such as rising ocean levels. Would this prevent us from completing the passage to a human world? Probably not, although no one can say for sure. More likely it would cause a delay, perhaps of generations. But the passage would be completed, although quite likely in a different way than we can expect without a great disaster.

The following numbers have only limited value—partly because they are worldwide totals or averages—but they are a reasonable illustration of such an extreme scenario.

In 1980 there were about 4.4 billion people in the world, and they used their work and about $30,000 billion of equipment and structures (capital) to produce about $11,000 billion of income. Suppose that there were a disaster that destroyed half of all the

---

* Professor Aaron Wildavsky and I have discussed this point for a number of years. He sums it up in a title he was considering for his new book, *No Risk Is the Biggest Risk of All.* (See Appendix F.)

capital in the world and required $2,500 billion each year thereafter for protective measures (almost twenty times the United States defense budget for 1980).

After such a disaster, world income would be down from $11,000 billion to something like $6,000 billion because there would be a smaller amount of capital working for us. Furthermore $2,500 billion of this reduced income would be needed each year for protective measures to deal with the results of the disaster. This would leave only $3,500 billion for other purposes. In other words the amount of goods and services available would be reduced by two-thirds (from $11,000 to $3,500 billion), and this would have to be spread among the same number of people.

If the disaster had come in 1980, and then, during the twenty-one years after the disaster, capital and income grew at the same rates as they did during the period 1960-1980,* by the year 2001 average income per person, after paying the continuing cost of the protective measures required by the disaster, would be about the same as it had been before the disaster struck.

One Percent Faster Growth Beats Almost Any Disaster

In other words, using these assumptions, if there were a disaster that wiped out a half of the world's capital, and made the environment so much more difficult to live in that an amount equal to the whole GNP of the United States is required each year for extra environmental protection, it would only have to delay the passage to a wealthy world about twenty-one years. But this calculation probably is too optimistic; a few years might well be required after such a disaster for reorganization, and growth might be slow for a few additional years. Perhaps it is fair to say that about one generation probably would be required to restore the economy of the world after such a disaster.

Of course there could be worse disasters or sneaky pollution catastrophes and we wouldn't necessarily respond with growth rates as great as those of the 60s and 70s.

---

* Although our experience with post-war Europe, for example, suggests that catch-up growth is usually easier than original growth.

196

Also the uneven distribution of wealth could make things worse. Right now, taken as a whole the world has almost enough income to meet our tests for a wealthy society. But the world isn't a single economic unit, and because of the division into separate countries, it is still a century or so away from completing the passage to general wealth. The date when the passage is completed is determined by when the slower countries pass the threshold of wealth, not by worldwide averages.

But, even allowing for distribution problems, we can probably say that the economic effect of even such a large disaster is probably less than the uncertainty about the future growth rates in the poor countries, without a disaster. Slowing poor country growth rates a percent or two would delay the advent of a wealthy world as much as such an immensely destructive disaster.

In brief, either a natural disaster or sneaky pollution could kill everybody and thus prevent economic growth. But even quite a large disaster, if it does not kill everybody, would not necessarily prevent the completion of the passage to a wealthy world in the next century or two. Of course we should take extraordinary measures to protect against potential dangers that threaten our whole species. Every possibility should be carefully evaluated. Even if there seems to be only one chance in a thousand that some suggested danger is really a danger, we should put large resources into checking to make as sure as we can whether it really is a potential danger.* We should not let the fact that the increased sophistication of our science lets us invent more potential "dangers" lead us to believe that human life has become more dangerous.

Discovering Dangers

Recent experience suggests that we can expect the following. A new danger will be discovered at least every few years. Each new danger will get a great deal of publicity and many people will be concerned about it. At first nobody will know the relevant facts or have

---

* Many years ago Herman Kahn suggested that the United States create a special organization whose formal assignment would be studying "unlikely but potentially catastrophic dangers."

considered the question sufficiently to know whether the danger is real. Then more scientific attention will be given to the question and some data necessary to evaluate it will be gathered. With this data and further analysis it will turn out that the danger is not real or is extremely improbable. This conclusion will be reached gradually by the scientific community and will be given relatively little publicity. Many members of the public will remember the stories about the danger and will not notice that informed people no longer consider it to be a real danger. Thus at any particular moment there will be a few dangers that nobody can properly evaluate, as well as a number of other dangers that have been scientifically debunked but which are still causing concern to the general public. At all times the unreal dangers will greatly outnumber the real ones that require serious research efforts, and even more greatly outnumber the dangers that will require further action.

So, as far as we can know today, it seems very likely that all of these potential natural disasters and sneaky pollution catastrophes together are much less likely to harm us or our children and grandchildren than war, tyranny, runaway inflation, or a drastic worsening of human society because of some disastrous set of mistakes about public policy.

THIRTEEN

Technology Is a Friend, Not an Enemy

**Life is getting less risky, but dealing
with subtle risks is a complex challenge.**

P RACTICALLY ALL LIVING SPECIES, plants and animals, have a
characteristic life span. If they live under perfect conditions
(whatever that means) all the members of a species will die
of old age at the end of their life span. Maple trees grow to eighty
feet and live one hundred years. Sequoia trees grow to three
hundred feet and live thousands of years. Persian cats live sixteen
years or so; elephants perhaps eighty years.

Recent studies have given very substantial evidence that the
natural life span of human beings is as fixed as that of other living
species. Death from old age comes at an average age of eighty-five.*
Of course, like height, the age of natural death varies a great deal
from person to person.

Life expectancy is something different; it is a practical statistic
that reports how long, on the average, people in a particular
community are living. Because of the results of bad living conditions,
only a small percent of the people of the world live their full life
span and die of old age. Life expectancy says more about the

---

* Much of this background material is derived from a wonderful little book called
Vitality and Aging, (W.H. Freeman, 1981), written by two doctors from the Stanford
medical school, James Fries and Lawrence Crapo. They do a beautiful job of
presenting to the lay reader the results and implications of a wide range of recent
scientific research bearing on longevity and the nature of the aging process.

conditions people live in than it does about natural human life span.

The idea of death from old age is a very common and correct idea. Now, in the United States and other wealthy countries, many people die of old age but very few death certificates list old age as a cause of death. Old age is not even included in the list of major causes of death, although it is responsible for about half of all deaths in the United States.* The reason is that old age is not a disease. Aging causes death by gradually reducing our organs' reserves of ability to cope with the kind of physical stresses that are part of normal life. The result of gradually reduced reserve capacity is that sooner or later we die of some disease—or accident—which gets the "credit" in the medical and statistical reports, although it would be more realistic to say that the death was caused by old age.

The life span of a species is the average age of death of the members of the species who die of old age. In *Vitality and Aging* Drs. Fries and Crapo present a lot of evidence indicating that the human life span is about eighty-five years, and that about 99% of all people who die of old age die between the ages of seventy and one hundred.

Since life span is a characteristic of our species, which was essentially fixed at least forty thousand years ago, the age at which people die of old age has been the same throughout human history. (But until recently almost everybody died of something else before becoming old enough to die of old age).

Our experience with the rapidly changing pattern of human life has produced two misleading impressions. First, the facts that our average age is much older than it used to be, that most of us are living longer, and that fewer people are dying at each age, seem to suggest that the human life span is increasing. This is not true. Our life span is not increasing. What has been happening is that fewer and fewer people are dying prematurely, from disease or accident, and therefore more and more people are living longer and dying of old age.

---

* The fact that the single largest cause of death is not included in the standard statistical reports illustrates the importance of thinking about questions independently of the form in which they are normally reported. Often the most important questions are ignored in standard analysis.

As a statistical matter people are living longer, because conditions are getting better, but the inherent, genetic characteristics of people that determine how fast their organs will be weakened in old age are not changing. Our species is no longer-lived than it ever was.*

Fries and Crapo report on a large amount of evidence that indicates that no one has ever lived to the age of one hundred twenty. They describe a number of investigations into stories about individuals and groups who were supposed to be unusually long-lived. All the stories that could be checked turned out to be incorrect. No reasonably reliable evidence of a person living to age one hundred fifteen has been found. Nor is there any evidence of a group with an apparent life span beyond eighty-five. Millions of people have died in countries where there have been good records for well over one hundred twenty years. Not one of these millions of people have lived to age one hundred fifteen.

So, despite increasing statistical longevity, the human life span is not increasing.

Let's look at exactly how much progress has been achieved so far towards one goal of medical science, preventing premature death. One simple measure is to ask how many years will an average person live. During any century before the eighteenth the answer would have been about twenty-eight. Most of the babies would have died young. Perhaps 5% would have reached sixty-five, and only a few would have died of old age.

When medical science achieves as much as it can, the average person will live about eighty-five years, and most people will die a natural death due to old age. Now the average person born in the United States can expect more than seventy-four years of life.

Since originally the average life lasted twenty-eight years and the best that can be done is probably eighty-five years, the most that could be added to life expectancy is about fifty-seven years. In the

---

* The exact age at which a particular individual who has taken good care of himself will die of old age depends primarily on two things: genetic factors that determine how fast that person's organs deteriorate, and chance which brings the small cause that finally tips the balance against a weakening body.

United States we have already gained at least forty-five of the fifty-seven years of possible additional life expectancy. So, here we have done about 80% of the total job so far.

Health is more difficult to measure than length of life. But one objective measure of the health of part of the population is the amount of time workers lose because of illness. In the United States now the average is six days per year, including time lost by older workers and by those with long-term injuries. Using this measure it is clear that we are not too far from the best that can be done.

Health, Wealth, and Life Expectancy

Practicing doctors and hospitals are not responsible for much of the increase in human life. Most of the gain comes from improved living conditions, from increased knowledge, and from public health measures such as protecting drinking water, vaccinating and inoculating people, and teaching people how to protect themselves. The major causes of premature death in the United States now are things that people choose to do—mostly smoking and excessive drinking and drug use (also murder, suicide, and dangerous driving). Therefore further big gains will have to come from increased knowledge and changes in behavior.

Roughly speaking, a poor country today can raise the life expectancy of its people to perhaps sixty-five without very many doctors or hospitals. The crucial requirement is sufficient wealth so that people can afford good nutrition and decent living conditions. There must also be enough money to provide public health programs and mass medical clinics. The society must be rich enough so that the people are literate and sufficiently educated to be able to take reasonable care of themselves, and the culture must sustain people's motivation to take care of themselves and their children.

Some wealth is needed for medical science, but that wealth does not need to be in every country, because most of the benefits of medical science spread from rich to poor countries. That is the reason that relatively poor countries today have much higher life expectancies than the United States or England had when we were as poor. They are able to benefit from our medical-science-producing wealth without having nearly so much wealth themselves.

In the United States we spend about 10% of our money for medical costs, an average of over $1,000 per person each year. We spend more on health care than most people spend on everything. Although we usually count medical care as a necessity, our experience shouldn't mislead us into thinking that everybody needs $1,000 per year worth of medical care. If $1,000 of medical expenses a year were necessary most of the people of the world would be dead.

From the country's point of view, the most accurate way to think of the purpose of almost all of the work and expenditure of hospitals and doctors who treat patients is to think of them as personal consumption services. They have very little effect on the health of the population. Most of the money used for medical treatment is related to the need for essential health care in the same way as the money spent for dinner in a fine restaurant is related to the need for essential nutrition. (From the individual's point of view there is one important difference. Expensive medical treatment has some small chance of making a substantial difference to the purchaser's health. People will consider time and money well-spent if they think it buys even a small chance that their own health will be improved. But when the country as a whole looks at the total health gain resulting from medical care it looks tiny compared to the cost.)

Aging Less

Another false impression we "learn" from our experience is that the amount of geriatric disability and chronic disease is increasing and will continue to increase. It is easy to believe that the increasing age of death dooms people to spend more and more years in feeble, diseased or disabled condition. It is common for studies of future medical costs or future welfare problems to assume that the burden of caring for disabled old people is going to keep on increasing without apparent limit.

Basically all these ideas are wrong. To understand why, let's look at the example of cancer. The number of Americans dying of cancer has multiplied in this century. The primary reason is not that there are more causes of cancer (apart from cigarettes) or that people are becoming more vulnerable to cancer. The primary reason for the increase in cancer deaths is that people who in previous generations would have died of flu or dysentery or tuberculosis or something else, are now living long enough to be killed by cancer, which is primarily a disease of the later years of life.

Real progress is being made in treating some kinds of cancer and so the mortality of cancer, to those who get it, is less than it used to be. But many people's impression about cancer is influenced more by the increase in the number of cases due to longer life (and to cigarettes) than it is by the progress in treating cancer.

The story is essentially the same with many of the infirmities and diseases of old age. Substantial progress is being made in learning how to cure, treat, or avoid many of the causes of debility and infirmity that often accompany old age. But this progress, like the improvements in cancer fighting, is hard to notice while we see so many more people suffering these conditions because they have been saved from dying prematurely.

Vitality and Aging gives us some good news in the form of a simple syllogism: "(1) Human life span is fixed. (2) The age at first infirmity is increasing. (3) Therefore the average number of years of infirmity must decrease." (In other words, since infirmity will start later, and cannot end later, it must become shorter.) There is no escaping this logic. It is extraordinarily good news.

This good news refutes the second common misimpression—that our population will spend more and more years diseased or disabled because of old age. At most this is a temporary trend. In the slightly longer run, the amount of time that the average person lives with severe infirmity due to old age will decline steadily.

A realistic projection of current scientific understanding and statistical experience is that it is likely that by the twenty-first century most Americans will die of old age in their eighties after an average of no more than a few years of severe infirmity or disablement.

The pattern of progress against the infirmities of old age is likely to be parallel to the pattern of progress against premature death. Most of the gain will not require the efforts of practicing doctors and hospitals. Medical and other science will make important contributions, but they will be implemented mostly by public health measures and by people learning or being taught what they need to do to avoid infirmity.

A large share of the improved vigor and health in old age that people can have depends on their own efforts.

Here is a dramatic table taken from *Vitality and Aging:*

TABLE 14
Reducing the Effects of Aging

Effects of Aging that We Can't Do Much About	Effects of Aging that We Can Influence	Actions Required
Arterial wall rigidity	Cardiac reserve	Exercise, nonsmoking
Cataract formation	Physical endurance	Exercise, wt. control
Graying of hair	Skin aging	Sun avoidance
Kidney reserve	Intelligence tests	Training, practice
Thinning of hair	Memory	Training, practice
Elasticity of skin	Physical strength	Exercise
	Pulmonary reserve	Exercise, nonsmoking
	Reaction time	Practice
	Social ability	Practice

We can also influence such physical characteristics as glucose tolerance, osteoporosis, serum cholesterol levels, and systolic blood pressure, with similar personal decisions.

To say that we can modify or influence an effect of aging certainly does not mean that we can control it completely.

The nature of the power that each person has over much of his own aging can be illustrated by a trivial personal example. I can now run three miles or so, certainly not ten miles. Thirty years ago I could have run ten miles. Today if I did a reasonable amount of practice I could still run ten miles. So the fact that I can't run ten miles now is not just the result of my aging. Mostly it is the result of the fact that I don't exercise and run much. If I cared about being able to run ten miles, I could do it. Therefore, how much I can run is determined by my effort, not by my age.

Aging reduces the outer limits of what the body can do. But practically nobody makes the effort necessary to go to the outer limits of what their body can do. It doesn't really matter to me that age has reduced the outer limit of my potential running ability, because, like most people, I don't make the effort to get near my outer limits. My outer limits don't affect my life.

As a practical matter, my capacity depends on my actions, not on the absolute limits set by my body or by aging. And this is true for almost everyone, and for most things that people want.

The message of modern science presented in *Vitality and Aging* is that with things like diet and exercise we can reduce or eliminate a surprising number of the feared effects of aging, just as by exercise I can eliminate my loss of ability to run long distances. (And for many things it is easier.)

Subtle Environmental Risks

This section focuses on subtle risks, like cancer-causing pollution, and mostly skips identifiable hazards, like auto accidents.

While no one knows in advance who will be killed by lightning or auto accident or drowning, as soon as someone dies from one of these identifiable risks there is no doubt what killed him. Therefore we can measure exactly how great identifiable risks are—that is, how many people are being killed by them. And if we do something to reduce such risks we can see whether our action is working. For this reason, the analysis of identifiable risks, while not quite as easy as shooting fish in a barrel, is not as much of a challenge as that of subtle risks.

The category "subtle environmental risks," does not cover the whole subject of risks. It doesn't include the risk that as soon as you buy fifty shares of IBM the price will go down, nor the risk, that you will lose your job, that your buying power will be decimated by inflation, that there will be a nuclear war, or that a meteor will hit the Earth with enough force to destroy human life, nor any of a number of other equally charming possibilities.

Subtle environmental risks produce "theoretical or statistical deaths." For example, although there is no doubt that cigarettes kill hundreds of thousands of Americans each year, there is not a single corpse about which the medical examiner can say for certain, "He was killed by smoking. If he had not smoked he would not be dead now." So, while we know precisely how many people were killed in auto accidents last year we do not know how many people were killed by cigarettes. We have studies which estimate how many people are killed by cigarettes. For a group of non-smokers we can see that seventy people died of lung cancer; when in another group, that is exactly the same by every measure we can think of, except that they are smokers, we see that 700 die of lung cancer, we can say that cigarettes killed at least 630 people in the second group. But we don't know which ones, and we don't know whether the correct number is really 630, or 430 or 690, because we don't know whether the groups were really exactly the same except for the second group's smoking.

With nuclear fallout from weapons tests (held before the agreement to stop weapons tests above ground) the situation is even more ephemeral. Even if you accept the high end of the range of scientific estimates of how many people are being killed by the fallout from the atmospheric weapons tests that were conducted before the test ban agreement—or how many deformed children would be born, or any other kind of observable damage—we can never know whether any deaths actually resulted. The calculations may show, for example, that the fallout should produce one thousand extra cancer deaths in the world per year, but no one knows exactly how many cancer deaths there were altogether last year. We believe that there were approximately four million, but that statistic is not accurate to the nearest one thousand. So we couldn't recognize an increase by one thousand in the number of cancer deaths in the world. Probably there were extra deaths. Perhaps there were nearly one thousand as the conservative scientists estimate. But it is also possible that there were none, as other scientists believe. No one will ever know, or even have any reasonable evidence.

One of the basic strange features of the subject of environmental risks is that it deals mostly with the special phenomenon of statistical deaths. But the emphasis on the distinction between statistical deaths and identifiable deaths does not imply that statistical deaths aren't real or aren't as important as other kinds. We have to act as if they are real.*

Smoking and More Subtle Risks

Here are some examples to show what is covered by the topic of this section—subtle risks to human health (particularly in the United States and similar countries).

The least subtle, and largest, risk in our environment is smoking, which probably is responsible for 300,000 deaths in the United States last year (plus or minus 30%). Although smoking is an example of a subtle environmental health risk, most of the policy issues raised by the harm from smoking are different from the usual risk issues. For the typical policy issue the number of people whose lives are in fact at stake is very uncertain. A wrong decision might mean zero extra early deaths or a million. We can't know when we make the decision, and we may not know the results of our decision even many years later if we try to look back.

So smoking probably sets the outer limits of our concern. It is a familiar hazard and very useful for perspective and contrast.

In most discussions of subtle risks the subject is divided by setting and regulatory authority. For example, food, drugs, and cosmetics are regulated by the Food & Drug Administration (FDA). Air and water pollution, the control of which is primarily the responsibility of Environmental Protection Agency (EPA) and its local counterparts. Occupational diseases come under Occupational Safety & Health Administration (OSHA) in the Labor Department. Nuclear safety belongs to the Nuclear Regulatory Commission. The Consumer Product Safety Commission protects against carcinogens in clothing or other products. At the national level these are the principle areas of controversy.

Some of the major political controversies of the kind we will address here are best evoked by familiar phrases: nuclear reactor

---

* This discussion has made the distinction between statistical and identifiable deaths sharper than it really is.

safety, saccharin and cyclamates, benzene and coke ovens, brown and black lung diseases, auto emissions, spray cans, acid rain, Love Canal. We will show how these controversies relate to other ways of saving lives and to the edifice of error.

Are Subtle Risks Important?

Apart from intellectual curiosity there are three kinds of reasons for being concerned about the policy issues raised by subtle risks.* First, it is clear that the kinds of subtle risks we will talk about are responsible for many thousands of deaths each year and that the number of deaths can be reduced if we have greater wisdom in dealing with these issues. Second, great areas of our business, government, and other activities are influenced—and often impeded—by efforts supposedly intended to reduce these risks. These costs could also be reduced, without increasing health risks, if we were wiser. Third, the policy controversy about how to respond to environmental health risks, and the social and psychological consequences of this controversy, has played a part in raising the edifice of error so high that it blocks out our vision of the world.

If we ask not just "How many deaths are caused by subtle risks?," but the more pointed question, "How many deaths could be postponed by better policy about subtle risks?" we have to face a large uncertainty. Subtle risks may cause about three-quarters of the 700,000 "early deaths" that occur in the United States each year. (Of that three quarters, smoking, drinking, and drug abuse probably account for somewhere between 40% and 90%.)

Although overall, the number of early deaths has been steadily decreasing, we must watch out for the danger that new risks could start to cause increasing numbers of early deaths. But the number of deaths from new causes that could be avoided by better public policy is even more uncertain than the number of deaths from familiar causes that could be postponed.

---

* The phrases "subtle risk" and "environmental hazard" are used interchangeably here, although strictly speaking they are not quite the same, because not quite all subtle risks are environmental. Also, some people make a distinction between "hazard" and "risk," but I don't.

For the short term I would suggest that anywhere from ten thousand to one hundred thousand early deaths per year could be prevented by better public policy, with the gains tending to accumulate over time. Unfortunately it is not easy to make better policy. And moving from understanding better policy to producing real changes in the world is another step, one which usually produces noticeable effects only slowly.

Early Deaths

Since death can not be prevented—it can only be postponed—environmental hazards don't cause deaths; they make them come sooner.

Our discussion of risks will focus on preventing "early death" which we define arbitrarily as any death before age sixty-five. While death can't be prevented, early death can. Focusing on deaths before sixty-five avoids the problem of having to tell apart natural deaths from the effects of hazards. (Of course many deaths after age sixty-five are also not natural death from old age but a result of avoidable hazards; but after age sixty-five there can be a question, whereas before sixty-five, all deaths are premature.)

The focus here on early deaths is not a judgement that only early deaths are important, or even that they are more important. Talking about early deaths is a convenient way of simplifying without distorting the discussion of policy about subtle risks.

The statement above that there are probably about a half million early deaths each year in the United States caused by subtle environmental hazards—including self-harming personal behavior—does not at all imply that most of these deaths could be prevented if the country pulled itself together and cleaned up its act. It is true that some of the deaths come from social mistakes which we could avoid; and other early deaths result from misdeeds by people who wilfully avoid responsibility not to endanger others. But most early deaths come from; (1) self-imposed risks like smoking, or drinking too much, (2) deliberate social decisions balancing values and accepting the statistical deaths, or (3) unknown causes.

THE SECOND MAJOR REASON for paying attention to policy about preventing environmental risks is that this policy affects a great many of our activities. In new and different ways, the EPA and the OSHA influence a very large share of our activities, not just a particular industry. There are very large, direct expenditures for equipment made to comply with environmental protection laws and with the standards set by the companies themselves. In addition there are major costs from uncertainty and delay. Many of these costs are probably transitional, that is extra costs of the period during which our practices are more fully adjusted to new standards, attitudes and knowledge about this class of risks. By definition, transitional costs will largely disappear as this area of policy stabilizes. But now and for some years we are in a period of paying high extra costs for doing a new activity on a large scale before we understand what we are doing.

By emphasizing the importance of the costs of trying to reduce environmental health risks, I do not want to suggest that these costs are too high in the sense that if we had a choice between giving up all the costs and all the benefits, or keeping them both, we should give up the program. That is not the argument being made here. The point is only that the costs are large enough so that this would be an important area of policy even if the opportunity for further life saving were quite limited. Furthermore there is plenty of evidence and agreement that the specifics of our policy to date have not been as wise as possible and that therefore, a significant fraction of the costs have been unnecessary. In other words, better policy could save both money and lives.

Effects of Risk Decision Making

The third area of concern is the impact on people and our society of the process by which we make decisions about environmental risk policy and of perceptions about that policy. These issues go both ways. We act to save lives not only because lives are important, indeed sacred. We also do so to express our feelings that we care about human life. Values are expressed through action. The values of our fellow citizens are an important part of our environment. So, some deaths are not only direct losses, but also may be seen as a failure of the community to care enough for its members, which weakens the community and reduces the value of our membership in it.

In a democratic political system, political support must be built in order to get action by the government. Getting action against risks requires making people aware of them, which is to say frightening people. The heat of the political battle sometimes leads people to argue and often to believe that those who disagree are selfishly motivated. Thus a large part of the policy process of deciding about environmental risks involves charges, in effect, that some Americans are deliberately endangering the lives of other Americans by inflicting poisons on them through the environment in order to make profits or for other selfish motives. While ours is a big country and I don't mind if there are a few Americans who are willing to endanger my life to make a fast buck, I would not feel good if I felt that an important number of my countrymen were so callous as to deliberately endanger me excessively in order to increase their profits. I don't think it is true. But one consequence of the increased debate about environmental risks is a large amount of public discussion pointing in that direction. The public discussion can also make the physical as well as the human environment seem less pleasant and more dangerous than it really is, which is both misleading and unpleasant.

These issues of public discussion and feelings are difficult to express, to measure, and to evaluate. Therefore they are usually excluded from scientific or analytic discussions of policy. I believe they are important. Therefore one of the things this book will be is a small experiment at taking such issues a little seriously.

IN SOME WAYS many of these risk disputes are like Rorschach tests; what you see in them has more to do with what is inside your head than with the "inkblot" that is in front of you. Typically, after the best scientific study of all the issues by the smartest and fairest people you can imagine, the genuine uncertainties overwhelm the analysis. An air pollution standard might result in anywhere between zero to 10,000 extra early deaths per year. The cost of complying with a proposed rule might be anywhere from negative (that is, compliance might *reduce* net costs) to hundreds of millions of dollars. An action proposed in order to save lives might instead, on balance, cause more early deaths than it prevents, and it might well be impossible to predict confidently which alternative is less dangerous.

Dominating uncertainty is not so unusual for policy issues. Certainly it characterizes many defense and foreign policy decisions, which have even more lives at stake. We should not be paralyzed by uncertainty. But if we want to make risk policy intelligently we have to take into account the kinds of uncertainty normally involved in environmental risks. It makes it impossible for politicians to do what is natural for them. That is, to say "don't take risks," "make it safe."

The nature of the practical political problem of developing policy to reduce these risks is briefly discussed in Appendix E.

Risks, Morale, and Related Perspectives

Much of our national policy about risks is determined by ideas that seem to be outside the area of risk policy. One reason is the "Rorschach nature" of subtle risk issues.

In relation to American public policy in general, the most important thing about subtle environmental risks is the way they interact with the question of American morale and perspective. The following are three major erroneous perspectives that are very influential in American policy making today.

The first misunderstanding affecting risk policy is the main structure of the edifice of error; that is, the scarcity error, the misunderstanding of the nature of modern productive wealth, and the failure to recognize where we are in history. If one sees the world today as making a great transition* from natural to human, one must also see that our country has challenging and important tasks that can engage our hopes and ambitions.

Risks may look different to someone who has this view of the world. The task of minimizing unnecessary death and suffering

---

* "The great transition" is the phrase that Herman Kahn uses to describe the passage from a natural to a human world. See especially his book *World Economic Development* (Praeger 1979).

will not be gone, but it will be one of several important tasks. Many will see our more important mission as advancing, protecting, and improving the passage that has been given to our generation, and a few before and after, to make. Reasonable risks can be justified because we have much work to do and important ends to pursue.

The second major error which now influences American reaction to risk policy questions concerns science and technology.

A baby born today may die as a result of any one of many newly-created, manmade hazards. Many people are dying today because of unknown effects of modern technology. People like Ivan Illich argue that even medicine is again doing more harm than good. Our public discussion is filled with debates about new or newly-discovered hazards to human health. In the last dozen or so years we have found it necessary to write much far-reaching new legislation to protect our health against manmade dangers. The new regulatory programs that have been required to protect our health are probably more extensive than all the regulatory programs enacted previously. Certainly our media is fuller of the many hazards produced by science than ever before.

Therefore many Americans are getting the idea that economic and technical progress is harmful to health. The impression has developed that science and business (and even government in the military-industrial complex) are out of control and endangering our lives. Some people feel that many Americans (not just the tobacco industry) are busy spreading cancer to make a buck, and that the country is going in the wrong direction—even leading the world astray. This is a destructive error. It is almost always harmful to confuse your friends with your enemies. In fact technological development is on our side—on the side of life. (Like most friends, and even loved ones, technology has its flaws and dangers and cannot be absolutely trusted.)

Is Technical Progress Dangerous?

Perhaps the easiest way to describe this second fundamental error that influences our risk policy is to give three summary sentences that partially encapsulate some of the ideas that are distressingly common.

214

(1) Complex modern technology, including new chemicals, is being introduced into the world at a rate so rapid that a full evaluation of the dangers is not possible, and as a result there have been, and will be, many people killed by things that man introduces into the environment. Often when we introduce a poison into the environment and only later find out how harmful it is, there is no way to get it out again.

(2) New technology is potentially so dangerous, and so difficult to control because of the vested interests that it creates to support itself, that on average it is likely to do more harm than good. (Partly this is because the harm from new technology is truly harm, but the good is only a new consumer convenience, like electric toothbrushes or video games.)

(3) We can't be too careful of new technology. Before it is introduced we must really establish its safety before it gets out of control.

These ideas are often simplified to: (a) modern technology does more harm than good, or at least (b) further new technology is likely to do more harm than good.

These ideas of course raise several subtle issues that need to be dealt with carefully. Many of the ideas are at least partially true. (Statement (1) above is true—although it does not imply what many people think it does, because it omits the benefits.) But other truths have too often been lost sight of in the discussion of these issues. For example, it *is* perfectly possible to be "too careful"; that is, it is possible by being too suspicious of new technology to lose more lives than are saved.

The relationship between suspicion of technology and risk policy is a two-way street. Either too much or too little suspicion of new technology can lead to bad risk policy decisions (even if we make the mistake of having no values other than life saving). The risk policy system as a whole—controversy, decisions, education, and policy—can cause excessive (or inadequate) suspicion about future technology.

Similarly, if individuals have either excessive or inadequate suspicion of technology they may well make personal decisions that unnecessarily endanger their lives.

PART OF THE PASSAGE to a more human world is the transformation of the health problem described earlier in this chapter. The clear-cut fact is that economic growth and new technology, as a package, are making our lives incomparably safer and healthier. The new dangers being created hurt many fewer people than the old dangers they protect against. This is part of the process of humanizing the world. We are reducing nature's influences on human life, including its dangers, and becoming increasingly influenced by mankind's creations, including the dangers we create. In the area of health and life expectancy we are gaining in this exchange, and we can confidently expect to get further ahead as a result of this process.

To some extent we have to take the good parts and the bad parts of this package together. But there is much that can be done to reduce the harm that is the price of the greater gains.

There are real dangers to health from technology. The number of people who will die as a result of these dangers (and the number who will die because of the absence of potential new technology) depends on the amount and quality of our efforts to protect ourselves.

In brief, an important requirement of our environmental risk program is that it not teach wrong lessons about our relationship to technology and how to respond to its dangers.

Issues That Go Beyond Environmental Risks

There is another set of perspectives that is crucial to the way we deal with subtle risks—and with other issues as well. Although these perspectives are rarely discussed explicitly, they underlie much of the debate as well as the reactions of many people to subtle risks and a wide range of issues. Therefore it is important that we formulate and consider this set of influential perspectives.

Safety vs. Profit

If the choice is between safety and profit, the public interest is clear. For many people this formulation leaps to mind because of the ideas they have about profit, business, and the American experience.

The following are some of the widely accepted partial truths that influence public and political attitudes about risk policy decisions: The purpose of production, construction, and other business activities is to make a profit. When these activities create risks, society must balance these risks against the corporate interest in its right to make profits. In a dispute that is too complicated and technical to understand, the only way one can decide which side to be on is to evaluate the people or organizations on the two sides. If the people on one side are paid by corporations and are motivated directly or indirectly by a concern for corporate profits, and the people on the other side represent the public interest in safety either through the government or a public interest group of some kind, then it is better to side with safety against profit.

One of the major reasons why many people in the United States and around the world find it difficult to feel good about the United States is that much of American life is supposed to be based upon the profit motive. Much American activity at home and abroad is carried on by large corporations, which are also supposed to be organized and operated according to the profit motive.* The profit motive is selfish. In view of our wealth and all the problems and suffering in the world, how can one think well of people who dedicate their lives to getting richer? How can one expect decent behavior from an organization devoted to accumulating more wealth? How can one feel committed to defending, supporting, and getting moral and emotional sustenance from allegiance to a country dominated by a selfish pursuit of profit?**

* We will not here get into the question of how much corporations are really dominated by the profit motive, nor will we address the deeper question of the extent to which, in fact, people who do actively seek profit act out of a selfish spirit. George Gilder, for example, argues that entrepreneurs are the true creators and that creation involves giving, or at least generosity of spirit. I do not wish to take a position here on any of these issues. Here we are talking about the feelings of those who find the profit motive distasteful, and it doesn't matter too much whether they are accurate in their understanding of those they dislike. In presenting the view of the distaste-for-profit people I do not endorse them.

** This is not the place to deal with this set of ideas. In brief they have two problems. First they are terribly crude about the relationship betwen selfishness, profit, and the system. Second, they ignore the immense gains for society and people from the use of profit.

"Good Guys" vs. "Bad Guys"

Many people in their personal life (including business) make it a practice to rely on people they can trust. They want to hire, work for, or do business with people they feel are on their side (or at least share their basic values): members of the family, friends, alumni of the same school, people from the same neighborhood, members of the same national or religious, age, or sex group; or whatever. It is an everyday experience, producing much folk wisdom, that one cannot understand all the issues and know all the necessary facts, so one decides by lining up with or following the advice of those whom one trusts. And trust of this kind is based primarily on judgement about motivation. For many people it is very hard to understand how people and organizations who admit they are motivated by profit can be doing things that benefit somebody else and are in the public interest. Abroad, and even among some Americans, that wisdom leads to great suspicion of the United States.

These attitudes are important for risk policy because a large share of the actions that raise risk issues are actions that are taken by big corporations or by government. American government, particularly the branches of it that do things and build things, doesn't get much more trust than big business in many circles in America. So, often, risk issues come up in the context of a government agency or corporation wanting to do something and being challenged by non-profit organizations resisting action on the grounds that it is too risky. In these situations many people decide their vote by choosing between the "good guys" and the "bad guys."

A few words are necessary about this good guys-bad guys perspective. It is possible to talk in a high-minded way about balancing conflicting interests and increasing risk efficiency, etc.; but if we are going to be realistic it is important to recognize that the public is right: there are bad guys. They can be defined as people who (1) selfishly pursue their own interest without due regard to the interests of anyone else, and/or (2) try to get what they want by using improper means, such as lying, bribing, forging documents, or otherwise deliberately using phony evidence and arguments they know to be specious .

There are two problems about voting for the good guys. First, the good guys can be on either side of the risk issue* even if it is between a corporation and a public interest group. Civil servants, politicians, and public interest group leaders also have personal interests that can be pursued as selfishly and cynically and with as much disregard for the interests of others as those of corporate profit-seekers. They are also equally capable of using illegitimate tactics.

More fundamentally, it is not necessarily true, even in a case where the good guys are on one side and the bad guys on the other, that it is in the public interest for the good guys to win. There can be a case, for example where a corporation wants to sell a product that is in fact safe, where they try to get the sale approved by using improper methods without due regard for assurance of its safety, and are opposed by genuinely public-spirited groups genuinely concerned about the safety issue. It is quite possible for there to be a genuine, even careful, concern about the danger from a product which is in fact safe. In such a case the public interest is for the product to be allowed even if the good guys are against and the bad guys are for it. (The opposite situation is of course also possible.)

Punishing the Guilty vs. Helping the Needy

Another common attitude that hurts policy making about risks is the preference for condemning and trying to punish the guilty rather than helping the needy. This attitude is more an undertone, less central to most of the risk policy debates than the ones discussed above. Essentially the same spirit (greater enthusiasm for punishing than helping) influences a variety of policy issues, such as tax policy, policy about human rights violations in other countries, concern about welfare cheats, anti-discrimination programs, and many other policy areas. (On the other hand, despite the fact that concern for punishing the wicked can be carried to such excess that it hurts those

---

* For a nice example of Ralph Nader's understanding of excessive or mistaken concern for safety, see his defense of sodium azide quoted in the Wall Street Journal, Sept. 20, 1977, p.20 (cited in Julian Simon's *The Ultimate Resource*, Princeton, 1982.)

it is designed to help, such punishment often serves important public functions, such as deterrence or expression of public values, even when the immediate victim is not helped.)

Fundamentally, risk policy decisions are a matter of balancing—conflicting evidence, advantages and disadvantages, and various costs and risks to different parties—so when the problem is approached as a search for villains its essential nature is distorted.

Of course there are villains, of various kinds and degrees; and a single-minded search for villains and for intentionally hidden dangers is a necessary part of the process of protecting the community. But carrying this spirit to excess produces three kinds of costs to the community. First, it can lead to wrong decisions, that is decisions that sacrifice too much benefit to the community because of excessive attention and concern about potential harms and suspicion that the advocates of action conceal or don't understand the harms. Second, it can interfere with relationships in the regulatory and decision making process. It gets harder for the producers to cooperate with the regulators if the producers feel that the regulators see them as villains and are pursuing them vengefully, and that therefore they need to protect themselves. The process becomes healthier and more effective the more each group sees the other as having an equally respectable role to play in a common community effort to reach the best balance of action and risk avoidance. This view is of course too idealistic to be fully achieved. But it is the right ideal to hold up, and tendencies that too strongly fly in the face of this ideal and weaken it more than necessary are harmful. Third, operating the policymaking process in a way that teaches the community that villainy is a large part of the risk problem, and that there are lots of villains, hurts community morale.

Wallowing in Villainy

The sense of villainy is a persistent undercurrent in modern social science and policy debate.* There is a strong tendency to write with

---

* I should use the modifier "American" because that is the only literature with which I am at all acquainted, but I don't want to assert that American writers and thinkers are worse than their foreign counterparts.

anger and accusation, and to assume that most troubles—like poverty or pollution or war—are the result of misdeeds by greedy businessmen or by governments that are not "progressive."

The health and safety branch of the environmental movement in the United States has demonstrated the result of the predisposition to focus on villainy. For many years they have missed one of the most dangerous environmental hazards—radon seepage into homes—because it is nobody's fault. Radon comes from nature not from industrialists.

Over the last twenty years both the government agencies, and the non-governmental "watchdogs," responsible for protecting people from environmental hazards have created scores of mini-crises about manmade "hazards" in our food supply, work place, and the air we breathe. Tens of billions of dollars have been spent evaluating and debating, and then removing "hazards" whose casualties have been either theoretical or probably less than a few thousand people a generation. (Of course the environmental-industrial complex has also done useful work against a few substantial killers.) Recently it has been noticed that radon seepage into basements may be causing as many as ten thousand cancer cases a year. But our environmental protectors have been so busy chasing or looking for villains, especially in industry, that they failed to notice one of the biggest dangers—a danger against which there are useful steps to take.

The tone of the discussion of dangers to human life—as well as most of its content—gives the impression that modern science and industry, abetted by business villainy and government failure or corruption, is making our lives more dangerous. But if we ask what are the substantial killers in our lives today, the answers are: smoking, drinking, driving, drug use, unhealthy lifestyles, and radon. Compared to these hazards, nuclear reactors, hazardous waste dumps, all artificial food contaminants, and all work place hazards, together produce tiny amounts of human harm.* But these political targets produce immense amounts of accusations, bad feeling, legislation, interference with productive activity, and expenditures.

* While lead and asbestos are also substantial killers, the number of lives to be saved by further actions against these two hazards is now small.

The conclusion seems to be that those who claim to be trying to protect us from environmental hazards are too bound up in the search for villains to do a good job.*

THE FIELD OF ECONOMIC DEVELOPMENT is as misdirected as the field of protection against environmental hazards. The recurring themes are: lack of progress and hopelessness, insufficient foreign aid appropriations, disastrous population growth, exploitation by the advanced countries and by multinational companies, remnants of colonialism, unfair terms of trade, and crushing foreign debt.

What are the basic truths? The background is tremendous progress and almost certain success—although perhaps fairly slowly. The real obstacles are the normal resistance of human beings and human societies to change, the difficulty of maintaining reasonably stable political environments, and—most significant—the strong tendency of governments to pursue harmful policies. (Not only policies that deliberately sacrifice the nation's welfare to the interests of those in power, but perhaps even more often, policies chosen as a result of misunderstanding.) Again the community of experts and idealists are led astray by their basic view of the world.

The problem is that the real solutions are dull. Poverty is abolished by people learning how to work better, producing per capita growth rates of 2% per year for a century. The first steps to industrialization are rural development, which results from farmers being allowed to sell their crops for their market value. The most important jobs of the government in speeding this process are: keeping peace, providing a legal system that permits contracts to be made and enforced, maintaining a stable currency and building transportation and communication infrastructure. Its toughest task is to limit the number of government employees, redtape, and corruption. But there does not seem to be any romance in these useful efforts. Idealists, especially young ones, are too often

---

* Ironically, in the one major area of policy where something very like villainy is at the heart of much of the problem—the role of Soviet Union in international politics—the same intellectual mainstream rejects villainy as a subject of serious attention. There is contempt for a President who talks about the "evil empire." And anti-communism is called "conservatism," or "hard-line, right-wing ideology," and regarded as outside the bounds of sophisticated discussion.

captivated by pursuit of dramatic successes and of villains who are thought to be blocking progress—even if progress is not blocked at all, but coming at quite a reasonable pace.

The biggest enemy of poor people may be the reluctance of idealists and intellectuals to work for dull ideas.

Low National-Morale Among "University-Oriented Americans (UOA's)"

"More than at any time in history mankind faces a crossroads. One path leads to despair and utter hopelessness, the other to total extinction. Let us pray that we have the wisdom to choose correctly."

Woody Allen

This Introduction is necessary to warn you that Part IV is very different from what has gone before, and that the next two chapters will seem like a diversion from the material of the previous chapters.

The first three parts have been almost entirely devoted to presenting well established, clear, broad facts about the world. Part I briefly described the exciting passage we are now making between the natural worlds of poverty, in which all prior generations lived, and the human worlds of wealth in which all future generations will live. It showed the nature of modern wealth and why we can expect it to spread throughout the world. Part II showed why we should not expect the passage to a human world to be blocked by shortages of raw materials, increasing risks to life, or the destruction of our environment. It dissolves the edifice of error about the physical state of the world that has prevented so many people from seeing what is so obviously happening in history. Part III discussed some dangers to the passage to a human world—real dangers and others that are only other parts of the same edifice of error.

Part IV, in contrast, contains some newish ideas. The propositions presented in it are not well-established—although they are mostly the kind of thing you can judge yourself from your own experience. And Part IV, unlike the others, contains not facts about the world, but a theory about why a key group of people have a distorted perception of the world.

Chapter 14 describes a category that I have invented called "university-oriented Americans (UOAs)." Chapter 15 is a discussion of the familiar concept of "morale," and an application of it to "national-morale." These two chapters are building blocks for Chapter 16, which will present an hypothesis about why so much that one reads and hears on television and that is taught in the schools seems to lead to almost the opposite view than that presented in this book.

F O U R T E E N

Who Are "University-Oriented Americans"?

MANY AMERICANS HAVE RECOGNIZED that our country has been increasingly divided between "the people" and some other much smaller group. While different names have been given to the smaller group, such as "elites," or "intellectuals," or "the new class," there has been a widespread perception of some kind of separation. The 1984 election made this separation clear to many people who knew scarcely anyone who voted for Ronald Reagan, but who woke on Wednesday morning to the fact that somewhere there were enough Americans they didn't know to give Reagan a landslide victory.

So far nobody has really put his finger on who this smaller group is and how it is different from the rest of the country. As a result we don't know how to talk to or about the American people, because we don't know how to separate the two groups. The special group is mixed in with ordinary people—but they are different. About many things they think one way, while most people think another way. If you want to understand or communicate with Americans you have to divide us into the two groups. If you don't do so, you can't use polls to understand our opinions because the answers of the great majority will hide the views of the special minority—who are the most significant for policy making.

I call the smaller group "university-oriented Americans," or

"UOAs" for short, and I believe it includes about one American in ten. (End-Table 8 is an Annex to this Chapter which shows who this 10% include, in terms of particular professions and jobs.)

Strictly speaking UOAs are not a "group," because nobody knows that he or she is a UOA, and there certainly isn't any formal organization such as "United University-Oriented Americans, Inc." University-oriented Americans are an objectively defined "category" of people. The key point about UOAs is that the average UOA sees many things in significantly different ways than do other Americans. We don't usually talk about such peculiarly defined categories of people. But everyone is entitled to define categories; and it's easy to do. There are millions of categories. For example: people who live in houses with a street number lower than one hundred; people who were born on Thursdays; people with two parents who voted for Calvin Coolidge; people who eat large breakfasts. There is no doubt that each of these categories exists, almost everybody would know whether he is in any one of them. But there are no statistics about the size of such categories of people, although it may be fairly easy to estimate (e.g., the category of people born on Thursday is approximately one-seventh of the total population).

Certainly there are no statistics about the behavior of these categories of people. (That is, there are no polls or other data that show how many of the people born on a Thursday voted Republican in 1980. Although I would bet at least a nickel that it was no more than 1% different than the percentage of the rest of the country that voted Republican.)

This chapter defines a slightly complex category of Americans. The definition should be non-controversial; that is, there is no doubt that the category exists. Of course there could be controversy about whether the definitions are clear. And some people may want to argue that there is no good reason to define a category this way. But that really depends on whether I can make an interesting hypothesis about the category. (I cannot make any interesting hypothesis about the category of people who were born on Thursday because the people in that category are no different than other people.)

Here I am merely exercising my constitutional right to define a category, and giving a rough estimate of how many Americans are in the category. I am not yet saying anything about the category—UOAs—except that it exists.

Before beginning let me emphasize that, despite all the effort here to be careful and formal with definitions and measures, the category of university-oriented Americans is just a loose qualitative concept. I think there is meaning to it. I think it helps one to understand how things happen in America. But I certainly do not think that either the category of university-oriented Americans or the idea of low national morale can be dealt with in truly scientific ways.*

Category UOA includes all Americans under sixty in the following groups—plus their families:

(1) College and university faculties and administrations, and academic and research workers;

(2) People in publishing, the media, the arts and entertainment industries;

(3) People in fashion, design and decorating, advertising, public relations, and similar services;

(4) Governmental managers, health and education administrators, city and other planners;

(5) Religious workers except in the evangelical religions;

(6) Part of the following professions: law, medicine, business management, engineering, teaching, and accounting.

> Category UOA includes those people in this group of professions who are oriented toward their profession and its leaders. (The people in these professions who are less concerned with their profession and more involved with their customers, and the organizations of which they are a part, are not part of Category UOA.)

* Although I do not claim that this material is science I do claim that it is a serious attempt to think carefully and fairly. I have tried to present the material in a way that makes it possible for the reader to evaluate the ideas, and that facilitates honest debate about the issues. I have tried: to separate facts that are not in dispute from those about which there is doubt; to make my reasoning clear, so that the critical assumptions and steps are visible and can be challenged; and to make sure that relevant writings and studies by others have been taken into account and that the arguments against my positions have been raised so that readers can decide for themselves.

Let's contrast three different categories of Americans. The first category is all those who were born in the first three days of any month; the second category is all those who were born in the first thirty-six days of any year; and the third category is UOAs. Each category is about 10% of the population. Any poll taken among the first two categories would produce exactly the same result as a poll taken among the country as a whole. But I believe that many polls taken among UOAs would come to radically different conclusions than the same polls taken among the rest of the people. Of course UOAs would not all give the same answers, but the pattern of answers would be different enough so that it is reasonable to contrast UOAs and "the people" without implying that UOAs are not part of the people.

The Category UOA includes the country's "best" people. The people who work in all the industries that are in the idea business or any communication business are UOAs. Educators, publicists, media people, governmental elites, politicians who are respected leaders (not just political hacks), and the great bulk of academic experts and the clergy (except clergy of the evangelical faiths) are part of Category UOA.*

Thus virtually all the people who most Americans look to for the articulation of ideas, for thinking about the world, for study and analysis, and for teaching belong to the category of UOAs.

It is a sensitive matter to talk about how one category of Americans behaves differently than "the people," particularly since the Americans in that category haven't chosen to define themselves as a separate group. I should emphasize that by saying that UOAs are a separate category of Americans I am not at all suggesting that they are in any way illegitimate or un-American. They are part of the people, a substantial and fully legitimate part of our population.

* The definition of Category UOA is made up of objective factors such as education or professional field. So any observed differences between the attitudes of UOAs and the rest of the population are interesting new facts, not a circular effect of the definition.

How do You Tell a UOA From an Educated Person?

UOAs are about 10% of the country. I estimate, for example, that between one-fourth and one-third of the lawyers are in Category UOA. It is important to be clear about what this means. I am not saying that each lawyer—or the average lawyer—is 30% as much a UOA type as Social Science professors. Each person is either a full member of the category or not a member at all.

The test of whether a lawyer, for example, is a UOA is not whether he has low national morale or whether he understands the scarcity problem. The test is how he sees himself. If he sees himself as a person trying to make a living by providing services to his clients, and if he accepts his customers as the primary "judges" of his success, he is not a UOA. But if he primarily sees himself as a person who is practicing a profession, and admires most the leaders of his profession, especially the leading law school faculties, and tries to look at himself through their eyes when he evaluates his performance, then he is a UOA.

The distinction is similar for teachers. Many teachers see themselves primarily as doing a job, and care most about how they succeed with their students. Other teachers define themselves in more professional terms, see their future as an educational administrator or expert, and orient their development and thinking to the concepts that are circulating in the schools of education and the Board of Education. Only this latter group is part of Category UOA.

While I argue in Chapter 16 that the percent of UOAs who have low national morale is much larger than the percent of other people who have low national morale, this is not part of the definition of who is a UOA. I am not saying that educated people who have low national morale are UOAs. Only some UOAs have low national morale, and some people with low national morale are not UOAs. Not all highly educated people are UOAs, nor is it "in the nature" of UOAs to have low national morale; my hypothesis is that twenty years ago well under half of Category UOA had low national morale.

Types and Tendencies

There is another way of looking at the category of university-oriented Americans which is less statistically neat but more psychologically realistic.

Instead of saying that each person is either completely in or completely out of the category UOA, you can think of category UOA as something like a personality type, or style. Obviously if you think about it this way people can be more or less "a UOA type" just as people are more or less cultured, other-directed, old-fashioned, or what have you.

But even if we think of the category of university-oriented Americans as describing a personality or attitude *tendency* I still define it separately from low national morale. I believe that UOA types are much *more likely* to have low national morale than others are, but the two are not the same. Plenty of perfect examples of the UOA type don't have low national morale, and there are plenty of people with low national morale even though they have no more university orientation than a bowling ball.

The kind of person I have in mind as a member of Category UOA is one who directly or indirectly looks to the academic world as the highest source of truth and wisdom. The group starts with a large share of the college and university faculties and the intellectual leadership of the major professions (law, medicine, engineering, etc.), but it goes much beyond those small groups, and well beyond the ranks of those who think of themselves or are accepted by others as "intellectuals."

The following is from the Preface to Eric Hoffer's, *Working and Thinking on the Waterfront*, Harper & Row, 1969:

> It is perhaps not out of place to state here plainly what I mean by intellectuals. They are people who feel themselves members of the educated minority, with a God-given right to direct and shape events. An intellectual need not be well-educated or particularly intelligent. What counts is the feeling of being a member of an educated elite.
>
> An intellectual wants to be listened to. He wants to instruct and to be taken seriously. It is more important to him to be important than to be free, and he would rather be persecuted than ignored. Typical intellectuals feel oppressed in a democratic society where they

are left alone, to do as they please. They call it jester's license, and they envy intellectuals in Communist countries who are persecuted by governments that take intellectuals seriously.

The category of university-oriented Americans is broader than Hoffer's definition of "intellectual." Perhaps Hoffer's intellectuals can be thought of as an ambitious minority of the university-oriented category.

UOAs are the kind of people who, in case of doubt, believe arguments and facts that seem to come with the right intellectual credentials (whether the *Journal of Sociology, Time* or the senior TV pundit).

Indirect representatives of widely accepted academic thinking, such as *Time* or Dan Rather, are accepted by UOAs because of a subtle sense that at their own level of sophistication these sources have been somehow validated by the academic community.* In different degrees members of Category UOA look to recognized academic experts and to university leaders as the most admirable people, those whose views are most to be respected, whose values and styles are the highest standards—although many university-oriented people do not choose to try to live on such an elevated plane themselves.

In general, university-oriented people regard information that comes from books, or media reports of "studies," as the best information or the only serious and reliable information. Personal experience, the views of ordinary men (who haven't done or read a "study"), and common sense or simple analysis, are all seen as second class sources of understanding.

---

* This sentence may do more to destroy my credibility in the scholarly world than any other statement in the book. *Time* and CBS, and the other popular media they symbolize, are regarded with contempt by most quality academics (envious contempt in many cases) because they are seen as superficial and often wrong.

Nevertheless, my statement is subtly correct. In effect, each level of popularizer checks his views on the next level up the scale to the real academic community. So generally, at least on issues that are not new, people like Dan Rather have a sense that they are not saying things that the academic community would reject. University-oriented people can tell when the popular media and personalities are speaking as best they can within what they understand to be the mainstream of "better" thinking. And the respect that many listeners' give the senior TV pundits depends on the perception that they have this kind of validation.

There are two kinds of Americans who are not in Category UOA according to this second definition: (1) a large number who are not well-educated and who are largely unaware of and/or uninterested in the academic world, and (2) a smaller, but very sizeable group of people who are as well and highly educated as those in Category UOA. These people, who could be UOAs but whose attitude is different, do not deny the intellectual power of scholarship and science, but it is not what they value most highly. They are used to trusting their own judgement. They care more about effectiveness than style or other credentials, and their normal recourse is to experience and wisdom rather than the ideas that have filtered out from academia. They live by their understanding that the scholarly community has not yet achieved its ideal of self-correcting behavior, and of humility before the complexities and uncertainties of the world.

If people are more or less UOA types, then it is natural to assume that there is more than one factor associated with the type. We have already used three factors—age, family, and job or job-orientation. Another factor is probably location. More people in the Northeast, California, big cities, and university towns are UOA types than in other parts of the country.

For most of the discussion of Category UOA it doesn't matter whether you have in mind a specific set of people who are members of the category or have in mind a personal orientation which some people have strongly, some weakly, and some not much at all.

Don't be diverted by this attempt to make a precise example of the general idea. The whole concept of "university-oriented Americans" is intended to be suggestive not rigorous. I am only saying two things: (1) there is a category of Americans which is a small but substantial fraction of our population, and which includes all of us who have responsibility for the articulation of ideas and for thinking about big questions; and (2) on average the Americans in this category have a different set of basic views than the rest of the country.

Although I call this category "university-oriented Americans" it does not include anywhere near all Americans who have a university education. (And not all UOAs have university degrees.)

Therefore, although UOAs have more education than the average American, there is an equal size group of Americans who are not UOAs and who have as much university training as do the UOAs.

The question is whether there is such a substantial category of Americans who see things differently than the majority. If I have the center of the group reasonably correctly described, the exact size or definition of the category isn't so important. Each reader can decide whether the suggestion that such a category exists fits with his or her own observation of our country.

F I F T E E N

Morale, Low Morale, and National Morale

OST PEOPLE HAVE EXPERIENCE with how important "morale" is in the organizations they know about—whether Girl Scout troops, armies, offices, or companies. Sometimes you can almost feel a change in morale in an organization. Very high or very low morale is so obvious that people recognize it immediately.

Since morale is so important, one of the most important tests of a leader is her ability to keep her organization's morale high. The effects of difference between high morale and low morale in an organization are seen in the quality of life and relationships for the people in the organization, and in the ability of the organization to respond to challenge, stress, and danger, and to get its work done well.

Although the practical importance of morale is widely recognized, it has little academic, scholarly, or scientific standing. Psychologists and sociologists have paid relatively slight attention to it. There is no accepted, internally consistent definition in the academic literature. Mostly the word is used as a catchall for almost anything having to do with the feelings of people in organizations.

One reason for lack of scholarly attention to morale is that it is a group phenomenon and therefore it sits somewhat uncomfortably with an individualistic ethic. The whole area of group behavior that is different from individual behavior is uncomfortable. For example, it is mysterious and disquieting that a crowd will do things that almost no one in the crowd would do individually. People in crowds are in some ways less human, or at least less individual. Also, in many people's minds morale is associated mostly with groups like athletic teams and armies, and with conflict situations which most psychologists and social scientists are inclined to denigrate.

Probably the most important reason why morale has received as little sympathetic consideration as it has in the intellectual community is its relationship to authority, something with which much of the mainstream of the intellectual world is uncomfortable. Also, a concern for morale seems to suggest an interest in artificial manipulation of people and their feelings. It seems unattractive to discover how to help the leadership of an organization make its members feel good about the organization when they ought not to. Finding out how to deliberately exploit the special characteristics of people when they are in groups seems unfair or immoral.

While the concept of morale is not truly deep or solid, it deserves more respect than it is usually given. First, the word "morale" should be used in a precise way, based on the central idea of morale in its most common usage, rather than being applied to any kind of good or bad feelings of groups.

Second, we should respect the idea of morale by treating it as a natural, healthy part of human psychology, deserving sympathetic analysis. Unfortunately discussion of morale often has a disrespectful undertone, as if feelings of high morale or low morale were flighty, manipulatable, and something that diverts people from real issues and from their real interests.

If you have respect for the morale part of people's feelings, and for the way these feelings develop and what influences them, then when you want to think about how morale works your first step is to *ask how it ought to work;* what would be a sensible, mature way for people to behave? This, plus ordinary observation of people's behavior, is what I have done to construct this analysis of morale.

This chapter spells out the meaning of "morale" as that word is ordinarily used. While it doesn't have anything in it that most people don't know—except maybe the explicit idea of "national morale"—it may be helpful for those who have been influenced by writings about morale, or who are used to learning by reading and analysis rather than from ordinary experience.

HAVE YOU EVER TRIED TO EXPLAIN in writing how to tie your shoes? Most people in their ordinary relations with other people gradually learn patterns of behavior and understanding that are more complex than tying shoes—and even more difficult to articulate. Therefore those who try to understand life by academic reading and discussion have problems with the normal complexities of human relations. This section spells out one of the simpler common phenomena of ordinary human behavior, but it may seem as complicated as a description of the difficulties in tying one's shoes neatly, securely, and quickly.

Is it Singular or Plural? (or Both?)

When we try to analyze morale, the first tricky thing is that although we speak of the morale of an organization—such as the mailroom at the IBM headquarters—morale concerns feelings and an organization doesn't have feelings. The "emotions" of an organization are felt by the individuals who are members of that organization. If morale is high in the mailroom it is because Joe Jones and Jane Smith and most of the others working there have high morale.

On the other hand, since the morale of an organization can be changed by what happens to that organization, the morale that Joe and Jane feel is not primarily theirs, that is, it doesn't come mostly from within them.

The fact that the high morale of the mailroom crew is not just the sum of their individual personalities can be seen also from the fact that the same people who have high morale in the mailroom may have low morale in their bowling team (or vice versa). So clearly high morale in the mailroom doesn't come just from a collection of a bunch of high-morale people; there must be something about the mailroom.

Another peculiarity about morale is that although it is always spoken about in the singular, in fact it is always plural in several ways. The mailroom morale is really the morale of the many people who work there. And in any large organization some will have high morale while others have low.

Furthermore, each of those people doesn't have one morale, he has many, one for each organization that he or she is part of and cares about. Jane may have high morale about the mailroom, low morale about her bowling team, high morale about her church, low morale about her political party, high morale about her family, etc. She and each of her colleagues have many morales.

Of course both high morale and low morale are catching. When almost everybody in a group has low morale it is hard for the others not to share the feeling. But morale can't be completely catching or consistent, or else everyone and every organization would have to have the same morale. So there are low-morale people in high-morale organizations, and vice versa; and most people have some high and some low morale.

WHAT IS MORALE ANYWAY? Probably the best single summary is that morale is feelings related to the degree of self-respect people have about an organization they are attached to. It is a part of the emotional makeup of members of an organization.

Morale, like an ego, can never be seen or identified directly. We can see signs of it, but we can never see the thing itself. And since morale is only one piece of each person's emotions, usually not the most powerful, it doesn't always produce identifiable signs.

When the members of an organization have respect for their organization the organization has high morale. Respect is expressed by feelings about the organization's past performance, moral standing, essential competence, and future prospects.*

When an organization has high morale the members of that organization have an emotional identification with it, and consciously or unconsciously they have decided that they accept and respect the organization for what it is—despite whatever doubts and drawbacks they see. Such identification and respect is neither given nor withdrawn lightly.

---

* Where "morale" is defined as a coherent concept in the scientific literature (as it often is not), the most common definition is "a sense of shared goals between

By analogy we can also talk of "personal morale," the morale people have about themselves, apart from any organization. One difference between individual morale and organizational morale is that a person's fundamental respect for himself is indivisible. Although you can think "I am a good tennis player and a bad speller and fairly handsome but not very strong, etc.," basically you have a single feeling about yourself as a person.* If you are psychologically healthy you feel good about yourself, you accept yourself as a whole person, the bad with the good. (This doesn't have to stop you from working to improve your behavior or character. And it doesn't mean you have to think you're a good dancer if you're not.) An individual who doesn't respect or accept himself can be said to have low personal morale (which may be related to clinical depression). Individuals who respect themselves, for whatever they are, have high personal morale.

A person's basic respect for the organizations she belongs to may be more specialized. Her self-respect for any organization is based on what that organization is supposed to be, or on the particular place she gives it. You don't lose self-respect for your football team because your teammates have unsound views about foreign policy, and you don't lose self-respect for your employer because he isn't cultured, or for your glee club because it isn't run on a business-like basis. This aspect of morale is important because it means that organizations can have high morale even though they have great problems and defects, and even though their members understand the bad things about the organization. It means that the members of organizations with high morale can accept criticism and if possible work to fix the problem.

---

the individual and the organization of which the individual is a member." The definition given above is very close to this standard formulation.

* In Yiddish there is the word "mensch." Every person should be a mensch—which means something like an independent responsible person. But there is no equivalent standard that applies to all kinds of organizations.

Why High Morale Is Normal and Healthy

Everybody understands that in an individual a lack of self-respect is unhealthy. Anybody whose psychological condition is normal and healthy has a strong sense of self-respect, regardless of how small his achievements and capabilities. A healthy janitor is proud that he supports his family and doesn't grieve that he is not smart enough to be an engineer.

Similarly, when most of the members or employees or citizens of an organization have low morale it usually is a sign that the organization is somehow unhealthy. Note that I am *not* saying that the *members* are unhealthy because they have low morale about the organization; it is the organization that is unhealthy.* In fact in some situations it is normal for an organization to have low morale and one would wonder about the psychological health of its members if they didn't have low morale—for example if it were discovered that the organization had been devoted to immoral purposes and would soon be dissolved.

Low morale and high morale are not equally valid alternatives. The phrase "high morale" is like the word "health," it is what you are supposed to have. Low morale and bad health are unfortunate conditions with bad consequences—they are not preferences. High morale, like good health is the natural, normal, and desireable condition; although of course both low morale and bad health are quite common.

High morale is normal because it is normal to have respect for those one is attached to. The respect need not be foolish. It can recognize weakness, sin, danger, poor prospects, etc. But so long as the attachment is there, the respect or high morale should be there also, despite the negatives. When the respect goes, when morale falls, the organization has a big problem and needs to find the cause and/ or do something.

Of course there is no reason why a person has to have much

---

* Of course some people have low morale about all of their organizations because of their individual emotional problems. But if an organization has low morale because of the personal character of its members, not because the organization is doing something wrong, one must ask why the organization has mostly unhealthy people in it.

feeling at all about many of the organizations she is a part of. And if most members of an organization don't identify with it—like the Automobile Association—it doesn't mean that the organization has low morale; its membership morale is just weak or non-existent. This is not necessarily unhealthy for an organization, although it would be a strength if it were able to attach its members more. But where non-attachment is appropriate it is not low morale or unhealthy.

The reason that high morale is normal healthy behavior is like the reason why self-respect is normal and healthy for an individual. Generally, healthy people want to feel good about the organizations they identify themselves with. So they either stay away from or try to avoid caring about organizations they can't respect. And with the organizations to which they must be linked, they choose to pay attention to those aspects which they can respect, and to ignore more troubling features.

Generally when you come to an organization you can see its character. You know what you are getting, and you can see whether there is a basis on which you can accept what is there. If you become attached to an organization and begin to care about it, the normal healthy way to behave is to make the attachment on the basis of what that organization is. In other words you accept it for what it is, as you accept your self, and you respect it for reasons similar to those you respect yourself. All other things being equal, if an organization is composed of mostly normal healthy people they will respect that organization.*

* Why did so many marriages work out when they were arranged by parents without regard to the children's feelings about each other? It was not primarily because the parents made "good" choices. It was because within the culture even couples chosen at random would have successful marriages because the men and women expected to have to accept whatever qualities their spouse had and to make the best of the marriage. (I understand all the differences from today, and I don't have any silly illusions about the old system working perfectly, and I would not want to go back to it even if it were possible. But it is useful to be able to understand the strengths of a system even if you don't like it.)

Just as in the arranged-marriage system healthy behavior was to accept and commit to the spouse you had—which sometimes even grew into love as we think of it, so today if you decide to work for a company because of whatever practical necessities bind you, the healthy thing is to accept and commit to that organization, and not necessarily ardently or romantically, but with a limited part of your self.

For organizations there are two reasons people can feel self-respect even if the organization does badly. One is acceptance—as of oneself—"it's mine so it's alright, it is what it is." The other is perspective: "It may not be so good, but it's getting better." or "It's as good as most," etc.

Subjective Feelings Masquerading as Objective Description

Although self-respect—either individual or organizational—sounds as if it depends on objective facts (such as whether an organization has been successful or it hasn't), it really is determined by subjective feelings. Because the "facts" are inevitably comparatives. Whether a baseball team was successful last year depends upon what you compare it with. The pennant winner may be "unsuccessful" because it lost the World Series or failed to win as many games as the year before. The last place team may be "successful" because it ended the season closer to .500 than it has for ten years. So objective facts don't determine morale. The subjective choice of what comparisons to make determines what objective facts are seen and felt.

The feelings of a patriotic and moral German soldier in 1944 are a striking illustration of the relation between morale and objective facts. Such a German would have believed that his country would soon lose the war, a terrible war that it was guilty of starting. He would also have believed that his government, which was based in part upon a free election and which had a great deal of popular support, had committed one of the most horrible crimes in human history. But he would also have believed that Germany was a country that had contributed much to civilization in the past and that, after they been punished for their crimes, the talent and discipline of the German people would enable them to contribute enough to the world to eventually make up for the horrors perpetrated by the Hitler generation.

Such a German soldier would continue to have high morale as a German. That is, he would continue to have respect for the German nation, self-respect for himself as a German.* The effect

---

* Such high-morale German soldiers migh reach different conclusions about what they were morally obligated to do as loyal Germans. Some could think that their

of his realistic judgment of the evil immediate situation is to make him focus on a longer perspective. He does not need to deny the short term facts. He preserves his respect by focusing upon a time long enough for the immediate evils to be outweighed.

In fact probably most Germans did preserve high German morale throughout the war and the postwar period. (Of course many of them did so in a less commendable way than the hypothetical soldier described here.) Many people practice psychological denial of facts or their moral implications, or try to put the blame somewhere else, or use any of the many other devices that people use to shield themselves from unpleasant truths about themselves and those they care about. But one does not need to conceal even the most unpleasant truths one can imagine in order to retain high morale.

One of the most important things in evaluating morale is to remember, whenever someone says something about her organization, not just to ask whether what she is saying is true but to ask why she is paying attention to that particular fact. For example, the man who is a booster for his company refers to the fact that it is the biggest in town—and doesn't ask whether bigger is better or whether he should be comparing with other companies in the state or in the industry. Members of an organization with low morale, on the other hand, have the negatives at the top of their mind and reasons to dismiss the positives if someone happens to mention them.

People talk about morale as if it depended only on facts, as if high morale naturally follows from success and right behavior, and low morale is the inevitable result of problems and failures. Of course there is some truth to this. Certainly high morale and success often go together, as do low morale and failure; but there is a big question about which is cause and which is effect.

But perhaps more important than the question of which is cause and which is effect is the question of how success and failure

---

responsibility was to continue fighting in a lawful manner until the government was forced to surrender. Others could think that they must try to overthrow the government. And others might think that they should use sabotage of some kind—at least passive—to hasten Germany's defeat and punishment.

are defined. It is easy to talk as if everything had a label on it which said "success" or "failure," but almost always there are facts that justify either label. Which label is used tells you as much about the person who chooses the label as it does about the facts.

Thus morale is primarily subjective; it is part of the realm of feelings. Morale talks in terms of objective reality—e.g., failure, incompetence, immorality, etc.—but the choice of which standard to apply is based on feelings, and this subjective choice of standards determines the supposedly objective conclusion.

In brief, morale is the collective emotional set of the members of an organization that influences how they react to what happens in that organization.

How Changeable is Morale?

Since morale is part of a person's emotional or psychological make-up, clearly it can change from time to time. But morale is not "mood" it doesn't change from hour to hour or day to day. Mature self-respect is a deep feeling. It can tolerate ups and downs, and much failure and sin.

For example, although the people in the mailroom would feel grief if one of them were killed in an accident, ordinarily that would not produce low morale—although the mood would be pretty bad for a while because of the feelings of sadness. Or, despite their high morale, they might be worried by a real possibility that the company may move, or because of some other real danger to their organization.

If high morale is not the same as good mood, neither is it the same as optimism. If bad things are coming, high-morale people will expect them; they do not need to be foolishly optimistic.* If a serious person respects an organization she can face a lot of bad

---

* Incidentally, "optimistic" is one of the sneakiest words in common use. You can never tell what it means. Suppose I'm playing cards and I need a spade and I predict that I will draw a spade. Is that "optimistic"? In one sense it is; I want it and I predict I'll get it. But suppose only spades are left, so I am certain to get a spade? Then is it optimistic to predict a spade? Suppose I have four tries?

"Optimism" always implies a comparative which is usually unnamed. It expects "good" results, but compared to what? To last time, or to what is needed, or to what is wanted, or compared to what is likely? Which of these you mean makes all the

news for that organization. In fact it is more likely to be people with low morale who cannot face facts, who need unrealistic assessments and hopes to sustain themselves.

This perspective on the nature of morale helps to answer questions like: Will a company have low morale if it loses money? If you respect people you would expect their attitude about their employer's loss to depend on a number of factors. A single year shouldn't influence many people's fundamental attitude. For organizations whose real purpose is something other than profit, morale might be hurt worse by too much financial success than by too little. Of course if an organization ceases for a long time to do those things on which its members had based their respect for it, morale will go down. The members will lose their respect.

When this concept of morale is kept in mind it is easy to see how different morale is from: employee motivation, job satisfaction, mood, optimism, productivity, and other issues which are often related to morale but which are quite distinct.

For example a person can be satisfied with his job, and motivated to work quite hard even though he has low morale. (For example if he is very well paid and has to work hard to keep his job, but has contempt for the company.) Or the opposite, a person can have high morale about his employer but be very dissatisfied with his job, because of facts that the employer cannot do anything about. If morale is good the dissatisfied worker may work hard and well despite his dissatisfaction.

Of course most people have some drive toward making their feelings consistent with each other. So a person who is personally doing well in a job often unconsciously looks for reasons why she can respect her employer, and a person who is in a job that is not right for him often gradually grows to blame his company and lose respect for it, even if it is not at fault.

---

difference. And sometimes "optimism" means something else entirely, it means how you feel about something. The "optimist" with cancer says "I'm going to lose only one leg." The "pessimist" says "I will lose a leg." Their predictions are the same. In fact, the "optimist" may have less chance of losing his leg than the "pessimist." So what does it mean to say that he is an "optimist"? Nothing. You can't tell what the statement means. This is usually a weakness for a statement.

Understanding morale in this way it is much easier to think about how employee morale, for example, can relate to practical concerns like turnover, absenteeism, productivity, and to broader issues like job satisfaction and motivation. The various morales of employees, in the overall corporation and in its sub-groups, are part of the environment that influences motivation, and the other concerns listed above. An organization that is trying to find ways to influence the motivation of its members is likelier to find it easier if the members have self-respect for the organization. But rarely is good morale sufficient and often it isn't necessary. (Later we will talk a little more about the effects of low morale.)

Because most social science does not seriously try to handle the complexity and subtlety of ordinary experience, many of the academic writings about morale have had trouble with the question of whether a person's morale in a large organization is determined by the small unit or by the organization as a whole. The obvious answer is "both." People's morale about the small unit is often separate from their morale about the overall organization. A soldier can have high morale in his company, low morale about his division, and high morale about the army. (Although there is some drive toward consistency.)[19]

Low Morale

As we have seen, an organization's low morale is a part of the psychology of its members. It is usually expressed by seemingly objective statements reflecting on the success, morality, and/or competence of the organization. And it has characteristic influences on the behavior of the members of the organization. These influences produce the familiar experience with low morale: back-biting, mediocre or poor performance, unhappiness, and hysterical or no response to the organization's problems. While in high-morale groups one sees loyalty, rising to the occasion, and creativity.

Of course the bane of social scientists is that people are complex and contradictory. They don't always say what they feel or mean what they say. Attitudes and expressions are often socially prescribed. The observer who doesn't know about the convention, and believes such prescribed expressions, necessarily reaches wrong conclusions. For example, in many communities workers are not supposed to say they like their jobs; any more than kids are supposed to say they like school. Any coal miner who says he is proud to be a miner because of the difficulty and danger of the job, and because his hard work and skill produces something that people need, would be laughed out of his favorite beer joint. His upbringing requires him to complain about his work. His real feelings can only be determined by looking at his actions, not his words. So it is difficult to find out about morale by asking people questions, unless you understand them.

People gripe in high-morale organizations and in low-morale organizations. But in low-morale organizations people will be genuinely distressed about the slightest unpleasantness or the most unavoidable defect in arrangements. The color on the walls of the beautiful new office building will be insufferable to a low-morale group and they will be inexpressibly bitter that everybody couldn't have the vacation schedule he preferred. While the high-morale company works happily in crowded and threadbare offices which close so that everybody gets his vacation the same two weeks, and nobody has any choice.

The members of an organization that has low morale will believe that the organization has been unsuccessful, that its moral standing is weak, that it does not have the essential competence to do what it has to do, and that its prospects for the future are poor. Note the direction; I am saying that these members believe the organization's moral standing is weak, etc., because they have low morale, not that they have low morale because the organization's moral standing is weak, etc. (In most cases the moral standing depends on what tests you decide to apply.)

Almost everybody has had the experience of coming into contact with a low-morale organization and knows what it feels like. Here are some of the kinds of behavior that are characteristic of low morale organizations.

(1) Divisive spirit among the members of the organization.
This is expressed in excessive back-biting, criticism, and buck-passing, and in excessive reluctance to compromise and inability to work out practical understandings.

(2) Unhappiness about undesirable conditions.
People in low-morale organizations are both hypercritical and extremely intolerant of things that aren't right. This genuine distress about real or imagined complaints in low-morale groups is to be distinguished from the "griping" which is a social convention in many high-morale organizations. (If you want a formula that will let you tell "griping" from "low morale" you must be a social scientist, and you shouldn't be a manager or a leader.)

(3) Inappropriate responses to challenges or dangers to the organization, such as:
Fear, paralysis, and increased internal conflict. Also useless or erratic measures.

(4) Lack of concern for protecting the organization's interest and safety.
This includes an insensitivity to insults and dangers, a vulnerability to pressure, and a defensive manner which makes accusations believable.

(5) An excessively pessimistic evaluation of facts or selection of which facts to pay attention to.

(6) Often an excessive optimism about radical solutions, which are, in fact hopeless.
"Crackpot solutions" are attractive to people with low morale because they don't mind risking what they don't respect, and because they don't believe that good solutions will be found.

(7) Habit of evaluating success and failure on the basis of unreasonable goals and measures.

(8) Widespread personal unhappiness and lack of pride.

National Morale

A country is an organization; so I use the phrase "national morale" to mean the same thing for the country as "morale" means for any other organization. Our country's morale is the sum of the "national morale" of its inhabitants. And each individual's national morale is the fundamental self-respect he has for his country.

But morale works somewhat differently in large organizations, like the country, than it does in face-to-face groups; and somewhat differently in each kind of large organization, such as corporations, national political parties, religions, etc.

One would expect national morale to have special features, because of the strength of nationalism and patriotism, because most people have little choice about what nation they are part of, and because almost everybody is a citizen of one and only one country.

The discussion here about national morale applies specifically to the United States. The relationship among individual, nation, ethnic group, government, and state in our country is different from that in most of the world. I have not tried to take into account how the situation in other countries would differ from the discussion here of national morale in the United States.

I referred to American national morale as the "sum of the national morales" of Americans, but this is obviously an over-simplification. Let's try to go deeper.

The 240 million Americans have widely different degrees of self-respect for the United States. Some Americans have much less interest in the country than do others (that is, some are less political and more private people).

In connection with their fundamental feelings of self-respect for their country, different Americans define America in different ways. Some attach their national morale primarily to the United States government, or even to the actions of the current administration. Others identify more with the American people as a whole—what they do privately and individually more than what they do collectively. And the national morale of other Americans is attached more to our constitution and system of government, broadly defined.

For this reason it is quite common for Americans to have very negative feelings about the government's policies and actions and still to have high national morale. This discussion of low national morale does not in any way imply that someone who criticizes the government, or part of the country, is unpatriotic or has lost respect for the country, or is un-American.

Also, it is not true that it is unpatriotic to have low national morale. A person can have low national-morale and still be patriotic. It is quite possible to develop feelings of lack of respect for the country, and pessimism about much of its future, while you still love it and are willing to sacrifice for it.

To try to talk about national morale with even a little precision you have to talk in terms of (1) fractions of the population, and (2) sub-groups within the population.

For the country as a whole one would say that national morale is normally high if two-thirds or three-quarters of the people have high national morale (or don't have much national morale at all, neither high nor low). I would guess that it has never been true that 90% of Americans had high national morale at any one time. But the concept is so vague, and relevant data so non-existent, that it is not clear that such a statement is meaningful.

Often particular segments of the population will have a lot of low national morale for some special reason. Some examples are: Southerners after the civil war, and German-born or Germany-identifying Americans during World Wars I and II. But sometimes when a group has special troubles, such as the workers in a dying industry, their national morale may go up because of their need to believe in something larger. Apparently many slaves developed strong American patriotism and high national morale even while enslaved.* Many Japanese-Americans retained their national morale through three years of unjust imprisonment during World War II. And most unemployed workers during the depression did not lose their basic faith in the country. Mass unemployment was seen by many as some powerful disease sweeping over the world that neither the United States nor any other government had any power to prevent.

---

* But generally a large share of what some scholars call the "under-class" have low national morale at all times.

The Hypothesis of Low National Morale Among UOAs

(and the Implications Thereof)

I N 1983, I TAUGHT A GRADUATE SEMINAR at New York University which I started by giving a quiz composed of the following five true-false questions:

"1. The overall physical condition of the Earth is getting worse as more and more people use it more and more intensively. Consider the possibility of:

—raw material scarcity

—pollution

—dangers to health (chemicals, nuclear wastes, etc.)

2. As raw materials are consumed at ever-increasing rates, the world is eventually doomed to have great raw material scarcity (and/or pollution problems).

3. Current world population trends threaten to exceed the Earth's carrying capacity in the next few centuries. If they continue there would be ten times the current population in only a few centuries and there would be a shortage of living space.

4. Already the amount of arable land is shrinking and losing quality as farmland is converted to urban use and to roads, and as topsoil is eroded.

5. Therefore, a basic long term problem for mankind will be how to adjust to increasing scarcity."

The questions were written to express what I understood to be prevailing misunderstandings. As we have seen in Parts II and III all the statements are demonstrably false. But the average number of "true" answers from the students was more than three and a half. (I think that more "trues" would have been given if the students hadn't doubted that true could be the correct answer to all the questions.)

After some weeks of discussing these issues—and reading some of the material I provided—all the students wanted to talk about was why they, and everybody they knew, had such an erroneous view of the world—without even realizing that their ideas were controversial, much less wrong.

While writing this book, like most authors, I often became discouraged—but my discouragement involved an unusual paradox. Half the time I was discouraged because almost everything in the book is so well-known and obvious that it was hard to believe that it was worthwhile writing a new book about it. The other half of the time I was discouraged because I read and heard so much with completely the opposite view that it was hard to believe that anyone would pay attention to a book with this message, or that I could convince anyone.

The Edifice of Error

In short, there is an edifice of error concerning the physical state of the world. Most people whose ideas come from what they read, or see on television, or are taught in school, live in the same edifice of error as did my students. This edifice was built and grew strong during a time when the truth was readily available—in academic forms, and more importantly, by looking at the world and thinking about the implications of the facts that people knew.

So we need to ask: How did such an edifice of error come to be constructed? Why does it still stand, so effectively blocking the view of the real world for many Americans? Why is the edifice of error still the reigning wisdom in so much of our society when correct information is available? Why will the ideas in this book be a shock to many readers? Why will some people find it very hard to believe what is said in this book?

My answer to these questions is the hypothesis that the group of people that operates the media and writes the textbooks for our schools has low national morale—and because of this emotional condition they are ready to believe bad things about the United States, and don't notice or believe evidence that goes the other way, or else quickly forget it.*

For people who have an emotional investment in their lack of respect for the United States, it is impossible to accept that what they conceive to be the American way—technological advance and mass consumption—could be leading to the liberation of people from domination by the forces of nature that have impoverished and constrained man since our creation. Their feelings are much more compatible with the idea that the American way is advancing the world toward disaster, and that our future survival requires that we make profound changes in the way we live—and most important, in how we make decisions.

The UOAs' low morale about the United States leads them to be afraid that the edifice of error is correct, because if it is, the moral position of the United States would be untenable—which is what they suspect. (If their fears are correct it would be as if we were on a huge lifeboat—"spaceship Earth"—where soon children would be dying of thirst, and we were using the only water available to take long leisurely showers.) On the other hand, the correct view of the world aligns our country with history, and implies something that those with low national morale can't believe—that we are leading the way on the passage to a human world.

The Precise Hypothesis

But before we consider this answer let me further spell out the hypothesis more precisely. The hypothesis is that in the last few decades a very high percent of the category of UOAs have had low

---

*For some people low national morale has expanded to become low species morale. (See "The Decline of Man," *Commentary*, November, 1986.)

national morale. I believe that the low national morale in the community responsible for ideas in America is a major cause and result of the edifice of error and of our general failure to recognize what is happening in history.

Specifically the hypothesis here is that among UOAs low national morale may be nearly three times as common as it is in the rest of the country. Probably some two-thirds to three-quarters of UOAs have low national morale now. The hypothesis is that among UOAs low national morale has increased over the last generation from well under a majority to well over a majority; although only a quarter or so of the rest of the population have low national morale—not much more than forty years ago. During the time when the national morale of the majority of UOAs was changing from high to low, the number of UOAs has been increasing much faster than the general population. There now must be well over twenty million UOAs, twice as large a fraction of the population as forty years ago. (End-Table 8 shows some hypothetical numbers to illustrate these suppositions.)

In recent years the jobs that UOAs hold have become more important than they used to be. In politics you see the growing importance of media and staff as compared to other politicians and the people. In business you see a growing importance of staffs and consultants—experts on various relations, systems analysts, planners—and of professional managers, at the expense of line managers, salesmen, and company men. So, as a result of both growing numbers and growing importance, the whole role of UOAs in our country is very different than it was.

Furthermore, when there were many fewer UOAs and they lived amidst ordinary Americans, and were shaped, influenced, and constrained by them, UOAs' ideas were constantly bumping up against the reality of mainstream thinking. The great increase in the number of UOAs means that now many UOAs live mostly among other UOAs, separate from the rest of the country. Almost everybody they know and respect are also UOAs. So the opinions and ideas that UOAs hear from other UOAs seem to them like the voice of the whole country. Most UOAs don't realize how much of their thinking is not shared by a large part of the population, including many who are as well educated as they are.

Of course the concept of low national morale is too vague to support real statistical analysis. Nobody can measure who has low national morale, so nobody can count the number of low-morale people in any group. But my hypothesis is that the national morale in Category UOA is so low that we need to think of it almost as a social pathology. (Which is definitely not to say that the individuals who have low national morale are sick; it is the country that has a malady when such a significant group of its citizens have low national morale. Nor does the statement that most UOAs have low national morale imply that they are not patriotic.)

AMONG THE TWENTY-FOUR MILLION or so UOAs, most of whom have low national morale, there is a very much smaller group of Americans who hate their own country. Hating your own country is very different from having low national morale, although of course the two different feelings often express themselves with the same ideas about history and policy. But it is unfair and unwise to accuse most of the Americans who have lost self-respect for their country of hating it. Neither they nor others will feel the truth of such a charge—and indeed it is untrue.

Normally the small number of Americans who hate their country don't constitute a problem. Other people usually recognize their hatred and therefore reject what they say. However a person who has low national morale is less likely to be put off by someone who hates the United States. (A common symptom of low morale is reduced sensitivity to insults and dangers to the organization.) Therefore when low national morale is common the small number of Americans who hate America are much more influential than in normal times.

OF COURSE THERE ARE MILLIONS of UOAs who have high national morale. And most of the UOAs with low national morale, don't go around with drooping chins; a normal share of them have high personal morale. Presumably they have high morale in their other affiliations—often including political organizations they work for partly because of their lack of self-respect as Americans.

Nevertheless the kind of errors that are a characteristic result of low morale permeate much of our national discussion because that discussion is conducted primarily among the university-oriented 10% of our population. And because virtually all the people who most Americans look to for the articulation of ideas and the reporting and analysis of world events belong to the category of people among whom low national morale is dominant.

Other Footprints of Low National Morale Among UOAs— Foreign Policy

If the hypothesis about low national morale among UOAs is correct, and if it is significant enough to be an important part of the explanation for the edifice of error about the physical world, it must also have an effect on other issues too. I believe it does. Here are some other ways in which I believe the low national morale of UOAs has gravely distorted our understanding of the world:

Our discussion of most foreign policy has been unreal for many years because it refuses fully to face one of the most fundamental features of the international landscape: the profound difference between the United States and the Soviet Union, and the danger presented by the nature of the Soviet regime and the imperatives of its character and situation.

Of course almost all Americans recognize that the Soviet Union is less democratic than we and a terrible regime under which to live. An anti-Soviet political consensus is the principal justification for our vast defense expenditures. But among UOAs this consensus has somewhat the character of a moral convention, one that is observed in public, but not internalized.

The public discussion, which is largely conducted by the UOA minority, has subtly begun to treat the Soviet threat as a "convention" not a reality. It normally excludes the emotional and logical effects of really believing in the Soviet threat—or in the character of the Soviet regime. For example, the national defense program is talked about as if it were a pure waste of resources, and the Department of Defense is regarded as just another special interest group that should "bear its share" of the sacrifice required to reduce the deficit. The United States discussion of conflicts in places like Nicaragua or Mozambique shows much more suspicion of the United States position and motives than of groups allied with the Soviet Union. Nothing in our discussion of foreign policy gives the sense that the United States could lose anything important, such as our freedom, because of a failure of our foreign and defense policy. (Of course this adolescent-like sense of invulnerability can also come from high morale or simple innocence.)

Sound foreign policy obviously requires much more than recognizing the danger presented by the Soviet Union; that recognition is only the beginning. But almost all policies must be created to live within the "ocean" of conflict with the Soviets, and our discussion doesn't recognize that the water is there. Instead of being able to talk realistically about difficult choices and gradually learn from mistakes and refine our approaches, we have not yet reached agreement that the Earth is round. The result is that the public discussion of foreign policy is "Alice-in-Wonderland"; removed from reality, sterile, destructive, and dangerously manipulatable.

Other Footprints of Low National Morale Among UOAs— Domestic Policy

In domestic policy there is a weak parallel to the blindness of our foreign policy debate to the nature of the Soviet danger and to their fundamental differences from us. The great domestic fact that we have only recently begun to be able to face is that a major part of the black community needs to improve its performance—that is, the culture of this community must change so that it influences its members in ways more appropriate to their own long term interests. Issues related to these points are central to any effort to help blacks.

This formerly "unmentionable" is very different than the Soviet danger and evil. The black lower class community is not evil. Unlike the Soviet Union, it has not caused tens of millions of deaths; it is not intentionally taking actions that threaten our freedom; and it does not see the United States as its enemy.

The two great challenges in creating a program to provide help to poor people are how to do it without building dependency among those helped; and how to keep up the motivation of, and avoid being unfair to, those who by great struggle have kept themselves slightly above the line of needing such help. The hardest parts of creating a program to combat discrimination are to prevent it from weakening the motivation of people who need to struggle to improve themselves, to prevent the reduction of the value of the credentials they earn, and to keep it from being so unjust and destructive to the rest of society that it does more harm than good. This means that the key to the effectiveness of many social programs is the way that they interact with the black culture. To succeed we have to pay attention to that issue, and it is a very difficult one.

But for years we were not even able to talk about the problems that the black lower class community causes itself, much less take them into account in designing policy. New York Senator Daniel Patrick Moynihan's sympathetic attempt to address part of the issue twenty years ago, in his memorandum on problems in the black family, was used against him for years, and the charge of "blaming the victim" still stifles discourse. The recent tentative beginning of such a discussion only emphasizes how much of a void there has been in our national policy debate for twenty years.

Because the single most important, most subtle, and difficult part of the problem was for years effectively excluded from consideration, our discussion of issues related to poverty and race relations has been nearly as sterile and incompetent as our discussion of foreign policy. Just as in foreign policy, the ocean within which any program must operate is ignored when the programs are designed.*

---

* To make the parallelism clearer, I have emphasized the issue of black weaknesses, but I fully recognize that the following statements are equally true. They in no way contradict what is said above about black responsibility for their own future progress:

— Much of the blacks' problem is the result of injustice at the hands of whites both before and after slavery.

— There is still a great deal of discrimination and prejudice against blacks.

— Blacks are not an inferior people. (I would not make a remark as seemingly patronizing as this, or as the next one, except to head off the false charge that I think the opposite.)

— Black culture is legitimate and has many virtues. (The problem is that it also has features that make it maladaptive to the needs of blacks today.)

IT IS EASY TO DISTORT what I am saying, or to take it as racism, although it does not go beyond that of such an eminent black scholar as Professor Glenn Loury of Harvard, who recently wrote that: "Much of contemporary racial inequality will not go away until failures of family and community, so painfully evident in our inner cities today, are directly addressed. . . . But coming to grips with the social pathologies of the ghetto will require an understanding that, whatever culpability white Americans may have for the history of racism, the responsibility for altering attitudes, values, and norms prevalent in black communities lies inescapably with blacks themselves."*

Even without distortion this message is a difficult and delicate one. Ideally these ideas should be kept to oneself; it rarely is helpful to tell people about your diagnosis of their social problems, however sympathetic and necessary that diagnosis is.

Also, it is only fair to add that low national morale among whites has had a lot to do with some of the unfortunate aspects of the black community. This is symbolized in the change during the last generation in the name used to refer to blacks. In 1960, the great majority of blacks preferred to be referred to as "colored people," or "Negroes." The word "black" had pejorative connotations and was used mostly by Southerners who did not believe in equality. The black radicals, as part of a posture of rebellion, challenge, and provocative pride, began using the term "blacks." These radicals, mostly young, were in a struggle for power with the traditional leadership of the black community. The young radicals, for whom

— The general community should be active both to control discrimination against blacks now and to help them to overcome the effects of past discrimination and of other problems.

— The weaknesses of the black lower class community that we must recognize in order to deal with social policy are not racial (that is, they are not caused by race nor are they shared by all blacks);

— Nor are these weaknesses entirely the fault of blacks.

* Prof. Glenn Loury, in The Public Interest, Summer, 1985. His article summarizes much of the evidence and debate. And Professor Thomas Sowell, and other experts, both black and white, have presented evidence along the same lines.

a principal symbol was the use of the term "blacks," were challenging not only the political and traditional organizational leadership of their community, but also those to whom that community had given the most respect, ministers, family heads, etc. The victory of the term "blacks" was primarily the result of its acceptance by the key minority of whites; and this victory accompanied and symbolized, if it did not help produce, an increase in the power of radicals within the black community.

The last, more radical, generation of black leadership has badly served the interests of that community, and it was brought to power partly because the UOA minority of whites thought they were helping blacks by recognizing the young black radicals as the real black leaders. The result has been that the necessary attention to the problem of the behavior of the black lower class has largely been postponed for a generation, at untold cost to members of that group. (Although at least one of the radicals, Jesse Jackson, has sometimes campaigned among young blacks with the message that they need to work harder to make something of themselves.)

The great need of the black lower-class community is to find the strength and discipline needed to be effective in a modern society. This is a terrible task, and no one should belittle the effort and courage and character required. Many blacks have succeeded, their task made harder and their accomplishments denigrated by our reluctance to recognize the weaknesses of lower-class black culture.

To illustrate with a horrible analogy—imagine a mother who in a drunken rage does something to her small son that results in his losing an arm. Afterward she feels both the natural sympathy of a mother for a handicapped child plus a terrible guilt for what she did to him. But she will be doubling that handicap if she lets him use her guilt to exploit the handicap—instead of holding him to strict standards so that he is forced to overcome and compensate for his handicap as much as physically possible.

What is needed to help a group find the strength to improve itself? It needs a reality that demands performance, and it needs authority that rejects excuses. For a generation now many Americans, in the name of helping blacks, have worked to take away these two crucial supports for black growth and development. The urban

262

lower-class black community needs "tough love," and our low national morale has led us to provide only guilt and sentimentality.

Summary—Low National Morale and Policy.

What do these two paralyzing gaps in our public policy discussion—concerning the Soviet role in world conficts and the problems caused by black lower-class culture—have in common with each other, and with the edifice of error exposed in this book? And how are they related to the alleged low national morale among a special minority of Americans? One policy gap comes from a failure to fully accept: that the United States is basically right and the Soviet Union basically wrong, that our system and government are morally superior to theirs, and that the conflict is basically their fault. The other gap comes from a failure to fully accept: that much of black culture is inadequate, inappropriate and harmful to blacks; that "middle class morality" and standard English is clearly preferable to "black culture"; that a key component of the task of solving the problem of the blacks is the improvement of the behavior that they choose for themselves; in brief, that the most critical obstacles to black progress now are within the black community.

The parallel is that in both foreign and domestic policy our failure is that we do not recognize our own moral and practical merit and do not fully accept the extent to which the basic problem is inherently in "the other guy." And the edifice of error comes from our failure to recognize the scope of the success of our economic system.

Realistic consideration of policy requires that we recognize and accept, understand and be confident about our strengths and virtues. Our policy has been poisoned by our inability to do so. (Of course we should, at the same time, recognize and try to do something about our weaknesses, failures, and evils.)

It takes normally high morale (or arrogance and stupidity) to build a discussion of policy on the premise of one's own superiority. We all have a form of this problem in raising our children. As everyone knows, children are in some ways morally superior to adults. They are also more charming, lively, and creative. Nevertheless they have some bad values and some gross misunderstandings that it is their parents' job to compensate and correct. Despite the child's persuasiveness and intensity of feelings, despite his apparent confidence that he is right and his father and mother wrong, unjust, and old-fashioned; his parents' responsibility is to have confidence in their experience, judgement, and values. If parents do not have this confidence, and cannot successfully pretend to have it, then their children will be cheated of the parental guidance they are entitled to and they are likely to suffer as a result.

Of course neither Soviets nor blacks are like children. Nevertheless, the United States cannot intelligently go about making policy unless we have a fundamental confidence in our basic values and our understanding of the facts.

Such confidence is not inconsistent with adherence to Cromwell's great cry: "I beseech you, in the bowels of Christ, think it possible that you may be mistaken." But people who have low national morale cannot have a mature and serene confidence in their nation's basic position, combined with a sympathetic understanding of the justice of others' and a recognition of their country's fallibility and limits. In this way the low national morale of a key minority of Americans has made it impossible to even approach a reasonable discussion of many policy issues.

An Approach to Checking on the Prevalence of Low National Morale

Column A is a recapitulation of some low national morale ideas, stated in simplified form. Column B is a set of alternative views which I hope I have demonstrated are more correct.

COLUMN A	COLUMN B
Some Low-Morale Ideas	**Correct, High-Morale Ideas**
1. The world is divided into rich nations and poor nations.	The world is moving quickly from a time when most, but not all nations were poor to a time when all nations will be rich. Some nations are moving faster through the transition than others.
2. World population is growing faster than ever and is out of control.	The rate of growth of world population reached its peak two decades ago. Population will "level off" at a level which will not cause harmful crowding and for which there are ample resources.
3. The United States is using a disproportionate share of the world's resources, very wastefully, and eventually these resources will be used up with disastrous consequences for mankind.	Since the world is very unlikely to run out of resources for many millennia, at least, nobody is hurt by our use of resources. Rather, our use of resources helps speed up the economic growth of poor countries, and increases the ability to get resources for everyone.
4. The United States has exploited and is exploiting poor nations and providing very little help to them. Most poor nations do not have the resources necessary to become rich and modern.	All countries having extensive economic relations with the United States have benefited from those relations. All poor nations have enough resources to become rich, because wealth comes mostly from things other than resources. The rate at which poor nations become rich is primarily determined by how well they adopt political and economic systems and personal and cultural behavior patterns that are compatible with economic efficiency. The United States' example is a powerful help in doing this.

5. Modern technology is very dangerous and getting harder to control. It is at least a close question whether the harm from new technology outweighs the benefits it may produce, apart from wasteful new gadgets.

Modern technology is a major reason why dangers to human health and life have decreased so rapidly. Future technology is part of the reason these dangers will continue to decrease until almost everybody lives a full human life-span. (This is partly lifesaving technology and partly technology to create wealth so that people have enough food and good living conditions.)

6. People and groups working for profit cannot be trusted.

People and groups working for profit are about as trustworthy as those working for other motives—not very. People working for profit have been responsible for at least their share of progress and human welfare.

7. Since our nation is organized on the basis of self-interest and profit-making, it is not idealistic, and our idealistic feelings must be expressed by support for something else other than the country.

Since our country has done—and can do—a tremendous amount of good for the world it is eminently suited to be a vehicle to express idealism—for people who care about real results, that is, about actually doing good for people

8. Our nation contributes little to the right kind of human progress. The Third World needs fairer income distribution; they are not adapted to or ready for democracy, which is inefficient for development; and our democracy has little meaning for them.

In addition to our technical and economic contributions to progress in the world, our democracy has been and can continue to be a great force for human welfare and freedom. Many, if not all, countries aspire to some form of democracy—often quite different from ours, but nevertheless taking inspiration from the United States and the results of what we have done. While it will take generations before most of the world is free, we can continue to be

a major help to that process, and
believe in the eventual expansion of
freedom in the world.

If you have any question about why Column A is labeled
"low-morale ideas," think about what that column says to us as a
country. It says that what we thought were our national triumphs
(abundance, efficient mass production, mass consumption, technological progress, and democracy) are part of the world's problem—
scarcity—not part of the solution. It says we are selfish, not idealistic.
It says we have no mission for the future, except to change
ourselves—fundamentally and impossibly. It says the world is going
to get worse. In brief, our past is sin and harm, our present is selfish
and destructive, the future is worse and we have no national goals
that we can idealistically care about. That is as fundamental a low-
morale message as there can be. People who believe that about their
country must have low national morale.

I hope the previous chapters have shown how false the first
five points in Column A are. The last three items cannot be so
conclusively established, although I believe that if the ideas are
defined precisely enough the evidence is almost equally as strong
as for the first five points.

Two From Column A and Five From Column B

Some of the statements in Column A are misleadingly or incom-
pletely true. If Column B were generally understood and accepted,
some version of much of Column A would be worth talking about
too. But if you look at what our schools are teaching, researchers
are studying, the "better" periodicals are writing about, what
President Carter chose to emphasize in the *Global 2000 Report* and
in his speeches, the main thrust of discussion among UOAs, and
most of what is shown on television—they all are mostly ideas and
data that tend to buttress Column A, and tend to deny or ignore
Column B.

Much of Column B is not known by most people. It is not
talked about. It is mostly not taught. There are not hundreds of Ph.D.
theses written to provide bits of supporting data for Column B.

Columns A and B are at least nearly equally reasonable approaches to the truth (and I think we have gone a long way toward establishing that Column B is clearly more correct overall). But, since Column A is against us, what could be the reason for disproportionate emphasis on the points in that column, and the persistance of belief in those parts of it that have been demonstrated to be wrong? Excessive emphasis on Column A cannot be explained by random truthseeking behavior and normal differences of opinion. It must be the result of something special—like low national morale. When a group unrealistically accepts views that are against its country it is reasonable to suspect that they have low national morale.

Therefore these two columns can be used in the following way as a diagnostic test of low national morale. First, ask a random sample of the population which column is more correct. The percent saying that Column B is more correct can be taken as a baseline. Then ask a group of UOAs the same question. To the extent that the small group has a higher percent of people who say that Column A is more correct than Column B, that group has low national morale. The extent of belief in, and emphasis on, Column A in our public discussion is strong evidence that low national morale is a significant factor among those responsible for that public discussion. (See End-Table 9 for a similar diagnostic test focusing on environmental issues.)

While it seems clear that there is a large group of people and much literature which presents Column A almost exclusively and Column B barely at all, the hard question is how deeply these ideas affect people's morale, not just their superficial beliefs? Although I said that anyone who believes those ideas must have low morale about the country, fortunately that is an exaggeration. People are not so consistent; and many are not really affected by ideas. Therefore it is possible for people to have low-morale ideas without having low morale. That is, they are able to work loyally, creatively, and effectively, respond positively to challenges, and feel good, even though they think they believe all those terrible things. The question is: How many people really do have low morale, and how does it affect their behavior and the country's welfare?

Implications of UOA Low National Morale

There are some pitfalls that we need to avoid when we think about how to respond to the problem of low national morale. For example:

1. People who pursue happiness rarely achieve it; and morale has the same problem. Mostly high national morale is a by-product of a country going about things in a reasonably competent and moral way, in relation to its culture. Groups that spend a lot of thought and resources building their own morale usually are making a mistake. Thinking about your morale is usually a waste of time and a symptom of something wrong. Nevertheless, because the unconscious attack on American morale is so pervasive and overwhelming, we must overcome our healthy reluctance to examine our morale.

2. A concern for our national morale seems to imply that our pride must be buttressed and that we shouldn't spend too much time criticizing ourselves. This is a ready-made excuse for rejecting all criticisms and never fixing our mistakes or righting the wrongs we do. But we shouldn't use such an excuse, even though concern for morale like anything else, can be carried to excess.

3. It is very difficult to make testable propositions about morale and it is hard to find data to use to discipline the discussion. Even poll data related to morale are difficult to evaluate for several reasons. Healthy people resist low-morale ideas. They don't pass them on. They don't explicitly draw their implications. If you ask them they may deny either the ideas or the implications. But often they are afraid—that is they really believe—that such ideas are true. That "realization" undermines their morale. But such fears, or unaccepted beliefs, are difficult to detect, and would not show on some polls.

Similarly, healthy people like to express high-morale ideas. They keep saying things—Fourth-of-July platitudes—long after they have stopped really believing or caring. But statements without belief do not sustain morale, they only confuse the data seeker and prevent the honest discussion that might relieve the fears and give a restored basis for high morale. That is part of the reason why apparently strong groups sometimes collapse all of a sudden when faced with a challenge. The ideas and beliefs which had been the foundations of morale had been undermined for years, and when pressure came the structure collapsed. The classic expression is *ancien regime* morale, which is what made it possible for the French Revolution of 1789 to overthrow the monarchy. The regime's supporters no longer believed in it, so they were not able to muster the will to defend it effectively.

Estimates can also be confused in the other direction by people who talk as if they believe in low-morale ideas, but who are not affected by the implications. The ideas are just talk; the high morale comes from real feelings and is dominant. And why worry about consistency?

WHAT DO I ADD TO THE DISCUSSION when I say that a certain idea is a "low-morale idea"? Isn't the important thing about an idea whether it is right or wrong? What difference does it make whether it is associated with low morale? There are at least three reasons why it is necessary to go beyond debate on the merits and to decide whether or not low national morale is an important factor.

1. The overall balance or cumulative weight of ideas is important. Since many low-morale ideas are correct, it is the absence of balancing high-morale ideas that is the real problem. The lack of discussion of high-morale ideas may be explained, not by the absence of high-morale truths, but by low morale among the discussers. In the face of this it is necessary to be aware of the need to restore a reasonable balance.

2. Many people find it hard to believe that "everybody is wrong" about something, so they cannot be convinced to give up widely accepted error unless they have some theory to explain why "everybody" has been taken in. Low morale is an explanation that may help people to resist the ideas of the intellectual mob.

3. It is hard to convince people they are wrong when their errors are fed by low-morale feelings. A straight answer on the merits often won't work by itself. Understanding the effect of low morale may make it easier to discuss issues more effectively.

Conclusion

There is a two-way connection between two parts of this book—low national morale and the edifice of error. In one direction the idea of low national morale supports the argument against the edifice of error because it explains how such a structure of ideas could be widely accepted even though they are wrong.

Going the other way, the edifice of error can be used to support the hypothesis of low national morale—by giving a real example of the effect of low national morale. Standing by itself the hypothesis is vague and speculative; but pointing to the edifice of error gives it reality. Does anyone have a better explanation for how such an edifice could have been built and sustained—against so much evidence—for so long? (And, as suggested in this chapter, there are similar profound distortions in our public discussion of foreign policy and a major area of domestic policy.) While the arguments about low national morale are theoretical and undocumented, the edifice of error is hard evidence that something is wrong.

I AM OFTEN ASKED what is the cause of UOAs' low national morale. I refuse to answer—even though sometimes the implication of the question is the rather silly idea that if I can't say where the low morale came from, perhaps it doesn't really exist.

Even though there is a good reason to want to know the cause of low national morale—namely to prevent or reduce it—I will not even speculate about possible causes. There will be enough trouble just from describing such an important and dangerous factor in our national life, without speculating about where it came from. Someone else can take on the task of figuring out the cause and assigning responsibility.

I think we have to deal with the low national morale that exists—whatever its cause—because I do not think it is possible to make it go away. This is one problem—like the common cold—where you have to deal with symptoms and not worry about root causes.

Much of what is needed to respond to low national morale

among UOAs can be done by individuals. Each person can become aware of the low-morale distortion of our public discussion and learn to filter out the bias and to build a more realistic balance in his or her own thinking. This is a tough prescription. It means that people have to think for themselves about overall perspective, rather than taking it in the usual way—a subconscious automatic weighting of all that one reads and hears.

Also, people have to learn to look for the minority views, and to be prepared to believe that their own common sense and judgement is right, even when it is contradicted by many people with strong credentials, and by what seems to be a consensus of experts. To the extent that we each influence others we should be aware of the need to avoid always giving the low-morale perspective, and to look for balancing high-morale ideas.

National decision-makers have to lead the bureaucracy away from its tendency to low-morale perspectives and policies. Leaders need to take the initiative to get high-morale ideas considered and presented to the public.

Where the government is presenting material to the public— e.g., in schools, or in public radio and television—it is important to be on the lookout for false low-morale ideas, and to make an effort to introduce enough high-morale information and perspective to provide a reasonable balance.

This is a circular process. People with low morale produce low-morale ideas; and low-morale ideas tend to lower people's morale. Young people with healthy morale about their country can grow up being provided with virtually none of the information necessary to support a sound high-morale understanding of the world. This makes it hard for them to sustain their national morale. And in some cases the low-morale ideas produce more low-morale people.

Basically our response to low national morale must be to be alert to the symptoms and to protect and strengthen those who do not have low national morale. The primary job is to prevent those who have low national morale from contaminating the rest of us— particularly by use of unfair means, or with government funds.

PART V

Conclusions

S E V E N T E E N

A Glimpse at the Future

WE HAVE BEEN DESCRIBING THE GENERAL PROCESS by which the whole world is becoming wealthy; now let's get more specific. In this chapter we will try to describe the world as it might be in the year when the passage to a human world has just been completed.

The definition of "wealthy" is so loose that it is more reasonable to speak of the decade in which a country, or the world, crosses the threshold to wealth. Therefore it would not be an extreme coincidence for China and India to become wealthy at more-or-less the same time.* When they do there will be no doubt that we will have moved into a wealthy world.

That will be a great moment. Through the great sweep of history all human societies were poor. Almost suddenly we will be living in a new, human world—a world that none of our ancestors, even the founding fathers of a country as young as the United States, ever knew or even dreamed of. And like great moments in our own lives (our 21st birthday, our marriage, the birth of our first child) it will be notable both for the fact that ever afterwards things will be profoundly different, and for the fact that life will go on much as before.

The purpose of presenting the hypothetical world described here is not to predict the future. While the label "2064" is attached

---

* As noted in Chapter Four, some people think that China will surely become wealthy before India, and others think that India will surely become wealthy before China. Partly to avoid such questions we will assume that neither India nor China will become wealthy before the other.

to the tables in this chapter (and those in Appendix A*), I do not mean to predict that the world in the year 2064 will be as sketched here. The idea is to take whatever year it is when the GNP per capita of China and India reaches $3,000, and to look at what things might be like in that year—the year in which the passage to a human world will be completed. In presenting this description, I am more concerned about the shape of the world economy at that time than I am about exactly when it will actually occur. In order to do calculations it is necessary to pick a single year, and I have chosen 2064, eighty years after our base year of 1984.** All in all, 2064 is one of many plausible years for the completion of the passage to a human world—but the precise date shouldn't be taken too seriously.

Of course we cannot know most of what the future will bring. But since we can be sure that it will bring change, we don't have to be very good at predicting to describe the future more accurately than extending forward the picture in our mind of how the world is today. There are a thousand variants of the world described here; and, as far as anyone can know, each of them is equally likely. But all of the variants are more different from the world today than they are from each other.

One way to get a feel for how things will be in 2064—or whatever year it is when the passage to a wealthy world has been completed—is to look at lists of the biggest and richest countries. Let's start with the countries that have the most people.

Of course the specific numbers in Table 15 are uncertain (even though they are only given to the nearest fifty million people),

---

* Appendix A and End-Table 10 contain the detailed Tables from which the summary Tables in this chapter are taken. They are based on hypothetical projections for each of the thirty-eight countries with over fifty million people in 2064, and for fifteen groups of smaller countries from the geographic areas. (The groups are listed in End-Table 11.)

Appendix A and End-Table 10 also show the same information for the year 2024, the half-way point between 1984 and 2064—using the assumption that the growth rate for each country's GNP per capita is the same during the two forty-year periods (1984 to 2024, and 2024 to 2064).

** In fact India and China might reach $3,000 per capita in 2054, or not until 2104.

but there is very little doubt about the general shape of this list. China and India will definitely be more or less equal—and each will be about three times bigger than the next largest country. Together India and China will almost certainly have approximately one-third of the world's total population.

TABLE 15
The Nine Biggest Countries in 2064
(by population)

	mil.	% of world
China	1600	16%
India	1600	16%
Nigeria	500	5%
Soviet Union	400	4%
Indonesia	350	3%
Pakistan	350	3%
Bangladesh	300	3%
Brazil	300	3%
United States	300	3%
Nine Biggest	**5,700**	**57%**

No one can be sure that Nigeria will rank third and have five hundred million people, but we can say with confidence that Nigeria and the other six countries listed above will each have populations much larger than any other country—probably by one hundred million or more. So these nine countries will almost definitely be the largest countries by far, with well over half of the total world population among them.

The most noticeable thing about this list is how large the numbers are. The same countries would be on the list today (except for Pakistan, which will join the list by passing Japan soon), but the order will have changed somewhat by 2064—with Nigeria moving from ninth to third, and India catching up with China in first place. Notice that no European country is in the group. (While the Soviet Union is partly in Europe, only a minority of its population will be European in 2064.) The biggest uncertainty may not be about the birth rates of people, but about the birth and death rates of countries. See Endnote 19.

It is not possible to predict average income levels with as much confidence as population. Here is what the list of the wealthiest countries would be if—by some amazing coincidence—the hypothetical growth rates shown in End-Table 10 turn out to be correct:

TABLE 16
The Eight Richest Big Countries in 2064

(only countries with over fifty million people)

	GNP per capita	Assumed Growth Rate
Japan	$75,000	2.5%
Korea*	60,000	4.5%
United States	50,000	1.5%
Germany*	45,000	1.9%
France	40,000	1.8%
Italy	40,000	2.3%
United Kingdom	30,000	1.6%
Soviet Union	20,000	1.7%

* All tables for 2064 and 2024 give combined figures for both parts of Germany, Korea, and China, as if they had been reunited. The figures are combined partly because I am reluctant to speak as if these divisions are permanent — and partly to express the idea that such projections shouldn't be treated too seriously — so why not be hopeful and show Korea and the other countries reunited?

The main things that Table 16 shows happening during the next eighty years are that Korea joins the top group (replacing Spain), and that Korea and Japan rise in comparison to the others. Both of these changes seem reasonably likely because of the extraordinary record of Japan and Korea over the last thirty years—and because their competitive feelings about each other are likely to make them reluctant to stop growing. (The variation in the estimates for the United States and the European countries is almost completely arbitrary.)

While the precise numbers shown on this list are almost arbitrary,* the general shape of the list is surprisingly free of doubt. If you said: There is a seven-way tie for first place and the Soviet Union is eighth. you could be pretty confident that you would have the right countries in the right order, because no other large country is likely to be a contender for the list of richest countries in 2064. And the Soviet Union is very unlikely to be as rich as any of the top seven, or to be lower than eighth. (There are about four major contenders for ninth place—Argentina, Brazil, Mexico, and South Africa.)

The income *level* of the wealthy countries as a group is as uncertain as the order of the various countries. The numbers shown here assume that these countries grow substantially more slowly over the next eighty years than they did during the last twenty or thirty years. It would only take an average growth rate of 2.6% (instead of the 2.2% assumed) for them to have about $70,000 instead of about $50,000 GNP per capita in 2064.

If we combine the biggest countries and the richest countries we get the list of the biggest economies for 2064, ranked by GNP, which is shown on Table. 17.

We can be fairly sure about the general shape of this list, too. The United States is almost certain to continue at the top—with Japan, and the Soviet Union next because they are the only other countries that combine high average income with large population.

Because their populations are so large, China and India will definitely be on the list, even though, by hypothesis, this list

* Here are some alternative lists that are almost equally plausible:

Japan	$90,000	Italy	$70,000
United States	75,000	United States	70,000
Korea	60,000	Japan	70,000
United Kingdom	60,000	Germany	60,000
France	60,000	France	60,000
Germany	40,000	United Kingdom	60,000
Soviet Union	30,000	Korea	40,000
Italy	20,000	Soviet Union	40,000

And there are many other possibilities. The United States doesn't have to be second; it could be first, or sixth. (Of course, in addition, at least as much variation is possible among the smaller countries, which are not shown separately in the Tables, and some of which may be richer than the richest of the big countries.)

describes the year that they first become wealthy, and their average income level will still be fifteen to thirty times lower than the wealthiest countries. Korea* will have an economy about as large as China's and India's so long as: either it is reunited or it has almost as high a growth rate as I have specified (over 4%). All the other countries are likely to have economies that are no more than half the size of China's and India's.**

TABLE 17
The Seven Biggest Economies in 2064

	GNP bil. $	% of world
United States	$14,000	16%
Japan	10,000	11%
Soviet Union	8,000	9%
Korea	7,000	8%
China	5,000	6%
India	5,000	6%
Germany*	3,500	4%
Top seven	**$52,000**	**58%**

* Germany would not be on the list of biggest economies if they were not united by then — they would be more nearly comparable to France, the United Kingdom, and Italy.

To add to the statistical description of the hypothetical world of 2064, it may be helpful to contrast it with the reality of 1984. Table 18 is in the same form as Table 4 on page 44. The latter shows the world as it is today in mid-passage, while Table 18 shows the world right after completing the passage to a human world.

---

* In 2064 the population of a united Korea would be about 110 million; South Korea by itself would be more like 70 million.

** Appendix A also includes a fairly reliable list of all of the only eighteen countries that can stand out because of their size and/or wealth in 2064. The list includes all countries on one or the other list of "tops"—plus the close contenders.
   The way things work out, it is not too likely that any other country will get on such a list, or that any of these eighteen would fall off.
   Of course size isn't everything. some countries are important despite being small—Israel, for example. And there will be many small countries with high average income levels, as wll as other significant accomplishments.

TABLE 18
A Possible Distribution of Wealth
in the World, 2064

(Comparable to 1984 Distribution in Chapter 4)

Category of Country	No. of Countries	Population
1. Already Wealthy *(over $3,000)*	89	8 billion
A. *Very, Very Wealthy* (over $24,000/person)	26	1 billion
B. *Very Wealthy* ($12,000-$24,000)	16	1 billion
C. *Middle Class Wealthy* ($6,000-$12,000)	18	1 billion
D. *Newly Wealthy* ($3,000-$6,000)	29	5 billion
2. Nearly Wealthy *($1,500-$3,000)*	16	1 billion
3. Last-to-Become Wealthy *(under $1,500)*	19	1 billion
All Countries	**124**	**10 billion**

See Appendix A for details, including specific assumptions for all countries with population over 50 million.

We can also look at changing income levels, with our hypothetical world of 2064 contrasted to the world of 1984.

Table 19 says that in 1984 the poorest two-thirds of the population produced only about 14% of the total income of the world, while in 2064 the poorest 70% of the population will produce about 22% of the world's income.*

The distribution of wealth eighty years from now really depends on two questions, only one of which can be answered with confidence—along the lines of Table 18, which shows half the people living in Newly Wealthy countries. In these countries the typical lower class family income would be, say, $2,500-$4,000. Of course this is by no means wealthy according to our standards, but

---

* But if growth in the United States and the other wealthy countries doesn't slow down, the share of the poorest 70% of the people in 2064 might be more like 18% of the income.

it is wealthy by the standards of most people today and of most people in history. (Those countries would be at about the economic level of the United States in 1910 or 1920—but with more medical

TABLE 19
Changing Income Levels in the World

1984	Pop. (bil.)	GNP (tril.)	GNP per capita
23 Very Wealthy Countries	.7	$ 8.4	$12,000
9 Middle Class Wealthy Countries	.4	$ 1.9	$ 5,000
Sub-Total: Wealthy Countries	**1.1**	**$10.3**	**$ 9,000**
22 Nearly Wealthy Countries	.6	$ 1.3	$ 2,300
30 Well Begun Countries	.5	$ .9	$ 900
45 Barely Started Countries	2.6	$ .9	$ 400
Sub-Total: Not Yet Wealthy Countries	**3.7**	**$ 3.1**	**$ 800**
All Countries*	**4.7**	**$12.7**	**$ 2,700**

2064			
26 Very, Very Wealthy Countries	1	$50	$50,000
16 Very Wealthy Countries	1	$16	$16,000
18 Middle Class Wealthy Countries	1	$ 8	$ 8,000
29 Newly Wealthy Countries	5	$17	3,000
Sub-Total: Wealthy Countries	**8**	**$91**	**$11,000**
16 Nearly Wealthy Countries	1	$ 2	$ 2,000
19 Last-to-Become Wealthy Countries	1	$ 1	$ 1,000
Sub-Total: Not Yet Wealthy Countries	**2**	**$ 3**	**$ 2,000**
All Countries*	**10**	**$94**	**$ 9,000**

*Only countries with population over one million.

knowledge.) More important, this level of income is sufficient to provide adequate food, clothing, shelter, medical care, and education for all the people, even if the upper classes get the lion's share of the income.

Most of the other half of the world would be richer than the half that is in the Newly Wealthy group. Probably about a third of the world's population will be scattered more or less evenly from slightly richer to very, very rich.

Some of the almost one-fifth of the world's population that is likely to lag behind India and China will be just short of the threshold of wealth when those countries cross the line. But it is possible that there will be a group of countries—maybe with as many as a billion people—which eighty years from now will still have not yet gone very far towards learning to become productive.

The broad features of this pattern are almost inevitable. That is, a graph showing the distribution of income in the world the year that India becomes wealthy, almost certainly has to look like a snake that has swallowed a pig. About half the people will be in the fat part of the snake, and the rest spread evenly from poor to very, very rich.

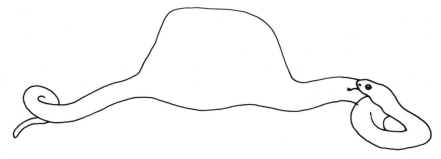

What is unpredictable is how rich the rich part of the world will be; that is, how much money will be in the part of the snake in front of the big bulge.

We know that the Newly Wealthy half of the world's population will have a total GNP of about eighteen trillion dollars. (Because it will be about half the world—five billion people—and by definition its average income will be a little over $3,000 per capita.) We also know that the Not Yet Wealthy 20% or so will have only three trillion dollars a year (if they had much more they would be wealthy too). But, although we can be pretty confident that the bottom 70% of the world will have an income pretty close to twenty trillion dollars per year, there is no way to predict whether the wealthiest 30% will be making fifty or one hundred trillion dollars per year. Either extreme is quite possible.

For our historical concern it doesn't make much difference whether the top 30% have fifty or one hundred trillion dollars of income. The key thing for history is that most of the world will no longer be living in traditional poverty. However, the amount of wealth in the richer groups does make a difference if you want to know what products will be sold, and how much, and where.

The big bulge is relatively easy to predict. We can have some feel from our national experience about the kind of things those people will want to buy and how they will live. We know where most of them will live—four out of five will be in Asia, mostly in only six countries, each of which will have a population over one hundred million. It is much harder to predict what the richer part of the world will be like, and whether it will have over 80% of all the money or "only" 70% (i.e., $100 out of $120 trillion, or $50 out of $70 trillion). The passage is more likely to be completed quickly if the rich countries are growing well—and if they do, the top 20% of the world's population is likely to be producing and consuming at least seventy trillion dollars per year when India and China cross the threshold to wealth.

Perhaps you may have noticed that I haven't said a word throughout this book about when the countries which are not yet wealthy will catch up with the countries that are already wealthy. There are several reasons for this. First, it is impossible to know when they will "catch up." Second, it isn't clear that catching up is a very meaningful idea.

Perhaps most countries will stop getting richer when they reach GNP per capita levels of, say, $30,000 (twice the current US level). If so, that would mean that they had chosen to use their efforts for something other than increasing wealth, or that they had decided to give preference to other values that conflict with further increases in productivity or wealth. If something like that happens and the already-rich countries stop growing pretty soon, then the countries that are not yet rich are likely to catch up before very long. (At 2% per year India and China would grow from $3,000 to $30,000 by 2180.)

On the other hand, it is also quite possible that countries will continue to grow wealthier even after they have become very very wealthy. What would it mean if two hundred years from now Japan's per capita income is $120,000 and India's is $30,000? We have never seen a country with a per capita income even as big as $30,000 per year. It is very hard to have any sense of the meaning of the difference between $30,000 and $120,000. Would you say that India had "failed to catch up"—because instead of being $10,000 behind Japan as it is today, it would be $90,000 behind Japan? (Would someone even dare to say that India was nine times worse off, because it was "nine times further behind"?) I will leave the conundrums of relativity to someone else.

My feeling is that some day economic growth will more or less come to an end. And when that happens I would guess that the wealthiest countries will be somewhere between four and ten times wealthier than the least wealthy countries; and that some of the countries which are still poor today are likely to be among the wealthiest countries at that time. The differences in wealth will then—like the differences among individuals—partly reflect differences in talent and industry, and partly differences in the desire for wealth.

The last piece of this statistical picture is geographic. Tables 20 and 21 show the changes over eighty years in how people and money are spread among the continents.

What happens here is dramatic. Europe, the United States, and the Soviet Union together go from 22% of the world population to 13%. On the other hand, Africa goes from 11% to 23% and South & West Asia increases from 9% to 14%. China declines from 22% to 16%. The human center of gravity of the world is moving.

Table 21 shows that the money will not move around in quite the same directions as people do. But the change in the world is just as dramatic. The big story is the rise of the Pacific and East Asia region—from 14% to 23% of the world economy. The big decline, again, is in the share of Europe, the United States and the Soviet Union—from 65% to 45%; from almost two thirds to less than half. Africa, Latin America, and India increase their share, but remain small parts of the world economy. China remains at 5%. Clearly the economic action is going to be in eastern Asia and the Pacific.

TABLE 20
The Changing Distribution of People in the World

	1984		2064	
	mil.	% of world	mil.	% of world
Europe	520	11%	600	6%
United States	240	5%	300	3%
Soviet Union	275	6%	400	4%
Pac. & E. Asia	560	12%	1100	11%
China	1050	22%	1600	16%
S. & W. Asia	420	9%	1400	14%
India	750	16%	1600	16%
Africa	540	11%	2300	23%
Latin America	390	8%	900	9%
Total World	**4,700**		**10,000**	

(Pacific & East Asia includes countries as far West as Malaysia, Thailand and Indonesia, and South to Australia and New Zealand. South and West Asia extends from Burma on the East through the rest of Asia and the Middle East including Turkey. Latin America includes all of the Western Hemisphere except the United States and Canada, which is included with Europe.)

What Will We See When We Get There?

When we get away from financial statistics, perhaps the most striking feature of the world when it emerges from the current passage will be the number of students and teachers. On an ordinary Monday eighty years from now close to two billion people will be in school—

TABLE 21
The Changing Distribution of Wealth in the World

	1984		2064	
	GNP bil.	% of world	GNP bil.	% of world
Europe	$ 3,700	28%	$18,000	20%
United States	3,600	27%	14,000	16%
Soviet Union	1,400	10%	8,000	9%
Pac. & E. Asia	1,900	14%	21,000	23%
China	700	5%	5,000	5%
S. & W. Asia	600	4%	6,000	6%
India	400	3%	5,000	5%
Africa	400	3%	7,000	8%
Latin America	700	5%	7,000	8%
Total World	**$13,400**		**$94,000**	

as students or teachers—from kindergarten to graduate school or adult education.

Consider also that all the science produced up to now has come during a time when there were—on average—less than a million scientists. Eighty years from now there will be tens of millions of scientists. There will be perhaps fifty times as much scientific effort expended in the third quarter of the next century as there was in the third quarter of this century. And the scientists carrying out this effort will have more and better intellectual tools and physical equipment than the scientists whose results we are seeing today. And they will be working from a base of knowledge that has multiplied even more than their numbers or the power of their tools.

There will also be a dramatic change at the other end of the scale of education. Today only a billion or so people are literate enough to read newspapers and books regularly. By 2064 that group will be eight times larger. It is staggering to contemplate the amount of books, papers, and magazines that will be consumed every week in that world.

But what is most exciting, challenging, and different: in the worlds of the future most people will be part of world civilization. I'm not so unrealistic as to believe that the immense increase in education will mean that by 2064 the world will be occupied by 10 billion philosopher-kings. Most people will be content with a quiet, provincial life earning a bare living and trying to raise a family— without paying much attention to the rest of the world. But almost every person will have the potential to take it into his or her head to move to a broader stage and to be an actor anywhere in world civilization. People in the modern world, even if they seem to be completely parochial, will be influenced by—and themselves influence in small ways—the broader world.

This is very different from the way things are today, and were throughout history. Up until now, most people have been in the world but not really part of the world—that is they had no influence on it, and for most purposes did not need to be taken account of by anyone except their neighbors. Most people have always been part of ignorant and largely powerless masses, shackled not only by lack of resources and qualifications, but also by traditions and by their view of what was possible and appropriate for them to do. In 2064 the great mass of people will have enough resources and education to know, to communicate, and potentially to participate—certainly to listen and to buy.

As a result, business, politics, art, and entertainment will be performing for immense and worldwide audiences. And so many people will be affected by events throughout the world that in 2064 it will be routine for television news stories to be seen by several billion people on the same day. Business events and scientific developments will be looked at within the week by millions of people around the world trying to keep track of developments to which they must react.

While the most important changes between 1984 and 2064 concern people, things will also have changed a lot. There will be close to two billion automobiles—instead of 350 million, with more than one-third in the United States. The number of miles of paved roads in the world will also have at least doubled from ten million—one-third in the United States—to twenty million—only 15% in the United States.

But cars and roads won't have grown as fast as air travel. Millions of people will be taking planes every day in 2064, although it is impossible to predict what the planes will look like, how fast they will fly, or if they will be on time.

With almost ten billion people living in economies that altogether produce nearly one hundred trillion dollars a year, the volume of international trade will dwarf our experience. Now, some one billion tons a year of freight is shipped across international borders, mostly on the 20,000 ocean freighters and tankers of the world's merchant marine fleet. Eighty years from now the fleet will be carrying ten times as much cargo. And the business of arranging for all of that movement—paying the charges, settling the insurance claims, keeping records, etc.—will have also multiplied in both volume and complexity.

But not everything will increase by leaps and bounds between now and 2064. One of the things that will not increase very much over the next eighty years is the number of farmers. (And in the following eighty years it will decline substantially.) Although there will be twice as many people to feed—most of them with enough money so that they can buy as much food as they want—it won't take many more farmers than we have today to produce all that food—because the number of tractors, harvesters, and other pieces of mechanical farming equipment, and the amount of fertilizer and other goods and services needed for modern agriculture, will have multiplied.

LET'S BREAK UP THE PROBLEM of thinking about how people will live in the future into several parts. First, many countries will move up the scale of wealth—for example, from $1,000 to $5,000, or from $3,000 to $15,000. Second, each income level will be operating in a new world, with different technology and market conditions. Third, some countries will not only have technology that doesn't exist today, but will also be richer than any country has ever been before—that is, they will be in doubly unknown territory.

It is not too hard to imagine much of what happens to countries when their per capita income grows from $1,000 per year to $10,000 per year—because there are countries whose average income now is about $1,000, like Botswana or Peru, while there are other countries like France and Japan with a GNP per person in the $10,000 range. We can look at these countries and gain a sense of how a country changes when it goes from $1,000 per capita to $10,000 per capita. Of course France is not like Japan. But it is more like Japan than Thailand is, because France and Japan have roughly comparable average income levels.

But we have two harder problems of visualizing the future. We first have to ask how similar will a country that has $4,000 of GNP per capita in 1984 be to a country that has $4,000 per capita in the year 2064. Will they be as similar as France and Japan? (The technological possibilities will obviously be unpredictably different.) The second, much more difficult task is thinking about what life will be like in countries that are four or five times richer than the richest countries are today. That is uncharted water, even without the new technological possibilities that the next few generations will bring.

But we shouldn't be preoccupied with such exotic and unanswerable questions. We should resist the temptation, as we become much wealthier, to let our perspective change so much that we lose sight of the profound importance of the threshold between historic wealth and poverty.*

One of the main points of this book is to emphasize the difference between poverty and wealth when they are defined in real and historic terms. Crossing the threshold to wealth means: healthy living conditions, long life, education, an integrated complex economy, few farmers, industrial and office work. All of these are built into the nature of modern economies and the process of becoming wealthy. Thus they aren't hard to predict. And it is clear that all of these changes have a big effect on human life. Within the last century a quarter of the world has crossed this threshold, so we have seen the variety of effects it has had on many different societies and cultures.

While I'm not prepared to say how people will feel about various levels of income eighty years from now, I believe that we can be confident that the historic threshold we have been emphasizing will continue to be important. It powerfully affects the fundamental influences on human life. Undoubtedly, in 2064 people will be talking about all kinds of fascinating and troubling problems facing the world. They may not even notice when India and China—and thus the world—crosses the threshold to enter the modern wealthy world. But for someone with an historic perspective the importance of that moment will not be reduced by the lack of attention paid to it.

So this book does not try to predict the unpredictable. All it does is to doggedly emphasize the virtual inevitability of a few obvious and important developments, which people often lose sight of for a variety of reasons—including that they are so obvious.

---

* A person whose income is $40,000/year is very conscious of the differences at that level of income. But anything more than twice as poor or twice as rich tends to blur together. It is hard for a person making $50,000 to understand why someone would care about increasing his income from $200,000 to $300,000, or to feel the joy of someone who increases his income from $5,000 to $8,000—since that person still seems unimaginably poor.

Some Implications

What can someone carry away from this attempt to analyze the many unusual questions raised by trying to think seriously about the long-term future?

The first thing is the value of the three hundred year time perspective. When one looks at the world with the perspective of centuries—comparing the world today with the situation one hundred and fifty years in the past and one hundred and fifty years in the future—it is impossible to miss seeing the transformation in human life that is taking place. Not seeing the movement that is taking place on the scale of a few centuries means missing something exciting—and important to the understanding of current events.*

The second is to remember how unimportant raw materials are. It doesn't matter that they weigh a lot and that we have to have them. Anything that is reliably available isn't important (even if it is essential—like salt). That is, we don't have to let concern about such things influence our basic policies—although sooner or later we have to take care of even such "unimportant essentials."

Although money seems superficial and artificial—as well as crass—it is the right measure of importance. It tells us how much effort we have to make to get something. The fact that most of our income goes—directly or indirectly—to pay for people's work tells us that increasingly people are what count economically (as they do in our moral value system). The fact that, apart from food and fuel, we spend only a few hundred dollars a year on raw materials tells us that we shouldn't be paying much attention to them—tells us that, while problems about raw materials can present great challenges to those of us who have the job of securing them, they cannot be truly major issues for most people.

The surprisingly low significance of raw materials in our lives hints at another important change—which might be the third

---

* We are familiar with the fact that to the geologist the mountains and continents that seem so fixed are in constant motion. (And that to a physicist glass is a liquid that is flowing—but slowly.) Each subject has its appropriate time scale. If we limit ourselves to the time scale of our experience and feelings—a few decades—we will miss much of the movement that is taking place in our environment.

residue of our discussion. Traditional views about what is important for wealth and power are outdated. Physical assets like land and gold, even steel mills and shipyards, are less and less significant. Modern wealth is increasingly based on ideas and organization. People and intangibles are the fundamental and crucial resources, not fields and factories.

And when you begin to think in those terms, it is natural to see the economic development of those countries which are still poor as basically a learning process in which societies change enough to permit modern productivity.

The passage to a human world perspective makes things much less grim and distressing for the idealistic person who thinks about the world. The poverty that exists is still a challenge and a call to action. But it doesn't call primarily for action against ourselves, nor demand feelings of guilt. Poverty is natural; we did not cause it. Our wealth doesn't deprive the poor countries or stand in their way, it makes it easier for them to follow the track we are making. We're part of the solution, not the problem.

Moreover, the task of ending traditional poverty is the opposite of hopeless. We can work at it with the warming certainty of eventual success. It does require the patience that should come from a realistic time perspective. But patience does not mean losing the sense of urgency demanded by the human needs of people who have only one life and do not have the option of waiting until the passage is completed before they live it.

A FINAL COMMENT

We've come a long way together in these three hundred or so pages—through a great variety of peculiar analogies, arguments, statistics, and theories. Where does it leave us?

Most of all I hope that it leaves you feeling some of the pleasure and excitement I feel about what is happening in history. To think about the cramped and dismal lives led by all of our ancestors, dominated by nature's grim and grimy mysterious forces. And then to look forward to all the future generations, who will be freed from the stringencies and fears of nature by the resources we are now creating. And to realize that we are living in the hinge of history—participating in a brief period of dramatic change in human fortunes—the instant in the long history of human beings on Earth when the character of human life and of the world is being forever changed.

In the United States we have the added privilege of participating in this drama in the country that, more than any other, has been the engine and symbol of the passage to a human world. We are the great experiment in human learning and human freedom. Throughout the world we are seen to be at the heart of the two great processes working in the world today—the creation of wealth and the spread of freedom and democracy.

In this book we have focused on the more prosaic process, the creation and spread of wealth. But the United States has even more responsibility for innovation and leadership in the second process—spreading human freedom and popular self-government.

What we have learned here about how much wealth comes from unlocking people's creative energies should suggest that the human imagination and effort that produces wealth will flourish most where people are free. Which means that our freedom, and that which we have helped others to achieve, is not only a value itself but may be our biggest contribution to the spread of wealth around the world.

The success this book has described is threatened by others who are concerned with protecting their totalitarian systems, but it may be even more threatened by ourselves—when we lose sight of the historic perspective and do foolish things because of an unrealistic sense of failure and hopelessness. Lack of perspective can lead to a sense of despair in the face of success. Not only can it make life less enjoyable; it can also sap our energies, and deprive us of the morale and motivation we need to meet the challenges that face us.

The passage perspective will be seen by many as a source of pride and hope. I hope that it will also be a source for the will we need to protect what has already been accomplished and the determination to complete the task.

A P P E N D I C E S

Appendix A: Numerical Description of a Hypothetical World of 2064

IF YOU WANT PEOPLE TO UNDERSTAND a time or a place, it is much more effective to write a story than to give a general description. People are interested in stories—and it is easier to discuss issues presented by a story than issues presented abstractly.

A set of hypothetical numbers works somewhat like a story to make concrete what the world may be like in the future. But there is more risk of misunderstanding when one uses hypothetical numbers than when one uses a story, because some people seem to think that when you give a number you are implying that it represents something real that somebody counted. But, of course, the numbers in this Appendix don't reflect that kind of reality or precision.

The advantages of hypothetical numbers are different for the person who makes them up and for the person who reads them. To the reader they give a detail and specificity that make it easier to come to grips with ideas than broad general statements do—which is the advantage that a story has over theoretical descriptions. But, just as you have to remember that a story may be false, you have to remember that hypothetical numbers are only hypothetical. No one can give real numbers for the future.* As with a story there are two different potential problems to watch 'out for with hypothetical numbers. First, they may be wrong in the sense of being impossible. Second, they may be untypical and thus misleading.

The other advantage of using hypothetical numbers for the person who makes them up, is that the need to make sure they add up correctly in a number of ways provides a discipline for thinking. By working with actual numbers, and the need to make them plausible and consistant with one another, one can get a sense of the web of relationships that tie a world together.

This Appendix has three kinds of numbers about the years 2064 and 2024 (and, for comparison, about 1984): population, GNP, and GNP per capita. End-Table 10 gives each of these numbers, for each year, for each country which will have at least fifty million people by 2064—and also for fifteen regional groups of small countries, which include all other countries which have over a million population in 1984. The thirty-eight countries listed individually have almost 87% of the total population of the world. (End-Table 11 lists the countries in each regional group.)

* In fact it's not often that one can give real numbers for anything interresting in the present or the past either.

295

TABLE 22

Geographic Changes in the Distribution of People
1984-2064

	1984		2024		2064	
	mil.	frac. of world	mil.	frac. of world	mil.	frac. of world
France	55	.01	60	.01	65	.01
Germany (united)	80	.02	70	.01	70	.01
Italy	55	.01	55	.01	55	.01
United Kingdom	55	.01	60	.01	60	.01
20 small countries	270	.06	300	.04	320	.03
Total Europe	**520**	**.11**	**550**	**.07**	**570**	**.06**
United States	**240**	**.05**	**280**	**.04**	**290**	**.03**
Soviet Union	**275**	**.06**	**340**	**.04**	**375**	**.04**
Indonesia	160	.03	300	.04	360	.04
Japan	120	.03	125	.02	130	.01
Korea (united)	60	.01	100	.01	110	.01
Philippines	55	.01	100	.01	130	.01
Thailand	50	.01	85	.01	100	.01
Vietnam	60	.01	125	.02	160	.02
9 small countries	60	.01	90	.01	125	.01
Tot: Pac. & E. Asia	**565**	**.12**	**900**	**.11**	**1100**	**.11**
China (united)	**1000**	**.21**	**1100**	**.14**	**1600**	**.16**
Afghanistan	25	.00	40	.01	60	.01
Bangladesh	100	.02	200	.03	300	.03
Burma	35	.01	65	.01	85	.01
Iran	45	.01	110	.01	155	.02
Iraq	15	.00	45	.01	70	.01
Nepal	15	.00	45	.01	75	.01
Pakistan	90	.02	200	.03	340	.03
Turkey	50	.01	90	.01	110	.01
13 small countries	60	.01	140	.02	210	.02
Tot: S. & W. Asia	**465**	**.10**	**1000**	**.13**	**1400**	**.14**
India	**750**	**.16**	**1250**	**.16**	**1600**	**.16**

	1984		2024		2064	
	mil.	**frac. of world**	**mil.**	**frac. of world**	**mil.**	**frac. of world**
Algeria	20	.00	50	.01	75	.01
Egypt	45	.01	95	.01	125	.01
Ethiopia	40	.01	105	.01	190	.02
Ghana	10	.00	30	.00	50	.01
Kenya	20	.00	60	.01	100	.01
Morocco	20	.00	45	.01	60	.01
Mozambique	15	.00	35	.00	60	.01
Nigeria	95	.02	290	.04	500	.05
South Africa	30	.01	65	.01	90	.01
Sudan	20	.00	60	.01	95	.01
Tanzania	20	.00	70	.01	120	.01
Uganda	15	.00	40	.01	75	.01
Zaire	30	.01	80	.01	125	.01
31 small countries	145	.03	290	.04	490	.05
Total: Africa	**525**	**.11**	**1300**	**.16**	**2200**	**.22**
Argentina	30	.01	45	.01	50	.01
Brazil	135	.03	240	.03	290	.03
Colombia	30	.01	50	.01	60	.01
Mexico	75	.02	145	.02	190	.02
18 small countries	115	.02	190	.02	280	.03
Total: Latin America	**385**	**.08**	**700**	**.09**	**900**	**.09**
TOTAL: WORLD	**4700**		**7900**		**10000**	

Population and GNP per capita are projected separately, and the GNP numbers for each country or group come from multiplying that country's population by its GNP per capita.

The population projections are based on those of the World Bank that have been discussed before. The population projection for any country has to be very uncertain because it depends on the future behavior of the people of that country, principally on how many children the average woman has during her lifetime. Other organizations, such as the Population Reference Bureau, have made different sets of projections. Since the different projections that have been made don't represent significant differences of approach, and since they come to approximately the same results for the world as a whole, there is no strong reason for preferring one set over another.

The GNP per capita projections are built on the World Bank estimates of GNP per capita in 1984. To partially reflect the difference in purchasing power parities described in End-Table 5, I have made an adjustment for all countries that have GNP per capita below $900. This adjustment doubled all GNP per capitas below $300, and made gradually smaller increases for GNP per capitas up to $860 (15%).

TABLE 23

Geographic Changes in the Distribution of Wealth 1984-2064

	1984		2024		2064	
	GNP bil.	frac. of world	GNP bil.	frac. of world	GNP bil.	frac. of world
France	550	.04	1200	.03	2600	.03
Germany *(united)*	800	.06	1700	.05	3500	.04
Italy	350	.03	900	.02	2300	.02
United Kingdom	500	.04	900	.02	1800	.02
20 small countries	1600	.12	3500	.09	7500	.08
Europe: GNP	**3800**	**.28**	**9000**	**.24**	**18000**	**.19**
GNP per capita	*$7,300*		*$16,000*		*$32,000*	
United States: GNP	**3600**	**.27**	**7900**	**.21**	**14400**	**.15**
GNP per capita	*$15,000*		*$27,000*		*$50,000*	
Soviet Union: GNP	**1400**	**.10**	**3300**	**.09**	**7500**	**.08**
GNP per capita	*$5,000*		*$10,000*		*$20,000*	
Indonesia	130	.01	600	.02	1800	.02
Japan	1300	.10	3600	.10	9700	.10
Korea (united)	100	.01	1000	.03	6000	.06
Philippines	50	.00	180	.00	500	.01
Thailand	50	.00	170	.00	400	.00
Vietnam	20	.00	110	.00	300	.00
9 small countries	300	.02	1000	.03	2900	.03
Pac. & E. Asia: GNP	**2000**	**.14**	**6700**	**.18**	**22000**	**.24**
GNP per capita	*$3,600*		*$8,000*		*$20,000*	
China: GNP	**600**	**.02**	**2000**	**.05**	**4800**	**.05**
GNP per capita	*$620*		*$1,300*		*$3,000*	

	1984 GNP bil.	1984 frac. of world	2024 GNP bil.	2024 frac. of world	2064 GNP bil.	2064 frac. of world
Afghanistan	4	.00	25	.00	50	.00
Bangladesh	25	.00	145	.00	600	.01
Burma	10	.00	60	.00	150	.00
Iran	120	.01	450	.01	900	.01
Iraq	45	.00	150	.00	250	.00
Nepal	6	.00	25	.00	120	.00
Pakistan	65	.00	350	.01	1400	.02
Turkey	60	.00	250	.01	800	.01
13 small countries	245	.02	850	.02	2000	.02
S. & W. Asia: GNP	**600**	**.04**	**2400**	**.06**	**6300**	**.07**
GNP per capita	*$1,400*		*$2,400*		*$4,500*	
India	**400**	**.01**	**1600**	**.04**	**4800**	**.05**
GNP per capita	*$520*		*$1,200*		*$3,000*	
Algeria	50	.00	250	.01	700	.01
Egypt	40	.00	150	.00	400	.00
Ethiopia	8	.00	45	.00	200	.00
Ghana	8	.00	40	.00	100	.00
Kenya	12	.00	80	.00	300	.00
Morocco	18	.00	100	.00	300	.00
Mozambique	6	.00	25	.00	100	.00
Nigeria	85	.01	450	.01	1500	.02
South Africa	75	.01	400	.01	1300	.01
Sudan	16	.00	90	.00	300	.00
Tanzania	10	.00	60	.00	200	.00
Uganda	6	.00	30	.00	100	.00
Zaire	8	.00	60	.00	200	.00
27 small countries	120	.01	670	.02	2400	.03
Africa: GNP	**460**	**.03**	**2500**	**.07**	**8100**	**.09**
GNP per capita	*$850*		*$1,900*		*$3,500*	
Argentina	75	.01	250	.01	700	.01
Brazil	250	.02	900	.02	2300	.02
Colombia	40	.00	150	.00	400	.00
Mexico	90	.01	200	.01	2300	.01
18 small countries	170	.01	570	.02	1600	.02
Latin America: GNP	**625**	**.05**	**2100**	**.06**	**7300**	**.06**
GNP per capita	*$1,600*		*$3,500*		*$8,000*	
TOTAL WORLD: GNP	**$13,500**		**$37,000**		**$93,000**	
GNP per Capita	**$3,000**		**$5,000**		**$9,000**	

The heart of the scenario presented here is the growth rates of GNP per capita, for the years 1984 to 2064, for each country and group. (These assumed growth rates are shown in End-Table 10 next to the actual growth rates estimated by the World Bank for the period 1965-1984.) The key rates are those chosen to make the GNP per capita of China and India reach $3,000 in 2064—because I believe that 2064 is a plausible year for those two countries to cross the threshold to wealth. (In view of regional sensitivities Pakistan's growth rate was set so that Pakistan would also reach $3,000 per capita in 2064.)

TABLE 24

Summary of the Spread of Wealth by Region

	1984		2024		2064	
	GNP/ cap.	pop.	GNP/ cap.	pop.	GNP/ cap.	pop.
1. Newly Wealthy Regions						
Pac/EAsia	$ 3,600	560				
Soviet Union	5,000	560				
Latin America			$ 3,500	390		
S&W Asia					$ 4,500	1,400
Africa					3,500	2,300
India					3,000	1,600
China					3,000	1,600
		840		390		6,900
2. Middle Class Wealthy						
Europe	$ 7,300	520				
Pac & EAsia			$ 8,000	900		
Soviet Union			10,000	375		
Latin America					$ 8,000	900
		520		1,300		900
3. Very Wealthy						
Pac & EAsia					$20,000	1,100
Soviet Union					20,000	370
Europe			$16,000	550	32,000	570
United States	$15,000	240	28,000	280	50,000	290
		240		830		2,300
Total Wealthy		**1,700**		**2,500**		**10,000**

Most of the other growth rates were set at what seemed to me fairly conservative or plausible estimates. Overall the assumed growth rates, when they are combined, lead to an average growth rate for the world as a whole that is much slower than the growth the world has experienced during the last thirty years. This conservative result applies to both the whole group of advanced countries, and to the whole group of not-yet wealthy countries.

Naturally there is much greater basis for confidence in the average growth rate for the world, or for the group of not yet wealthy countries as a whole, than for any individual country.

The best overview probably comes from a look at the changes in the geographic distribution of wealth and people as shown in Tables 22 and 23.

Table 24 is a summary showing the growth of the wealthy world, looking at regions instead of at individual countries.

Here are The Nine Biggest Countries for 1984, 2024, and 2064. It shows the estimate for each country in millions, and as a fraction of the world population in the year of the projection.

TABLE 25
The Nine Biggest Countries (Population)

1984	(mil.)	frac. of world	2024	(mil.)	frac. of world	2064	(mil.)	frac. of world
China	1000	.21	China	1500	.19	China	1600	.16
India	750	.16	India	1250	.16	India	1600	.16
Soviet Union	275	.06	Soviet Union	340	.04	Nigeria	500	.05
United States	240	.05	Indonesia	300	.04	Soviet Union	400	.04
Indonesia	160	.03	Nigeria	290	.04	Indonesia	350	.04
Brazil	130	.03	United States	280	.04	Pakistan	350	.04
Japan	120	.03	Brazil	240	.03	Bangladesh	300	.03
Bangladesh	100	.02	Pakistan	200	.03	Brazil	300	.03
Nigeria	100	.02	Bangladesh	200	.03	United States	300	.03
9 Biggest	2,900	.62	9 Biggest	4,600	.58	9 Biggest	5,700	.57

Next comes The Eight Richest Big Countries for the same years. It shows the estimates of the changing GNP per capita for each of the countries, based on the growth rates given in Table 29 at the end of the Appendix—which are the same for each of the two forty year periods.

TABLE 26
The Eight Richest Big Countries (GNP per capita)

1984		2024		2064	
United States	$15,000	Japan	$28,000	Japan	$75,000
Germany (W.)	11,000	United States	28,000	Korea	60,000
Japan	10,000	Germany	21,000	United States	50,000
France	10,000	France	20,000	Germany	45,000
United Kingdom	9,000	United Kingdom	16,000	France	45,000
Italy	6,000	Italy	16,000	Italy	40,000
Soviet Union	5,000	Soviet Union	10,000	United Kingdom	30,000
Spain	4,400	Korea	9,000	Soviet Union	20,000

When you put wealth and size of population together you get the list of the biggest economies of the world, as shown in

TABLE 27
The Seven Biggest Economies (GNP)

1984	tril. $	frac. of world	2024	tril. $	frac. of world	2064	tril. $	frac. of world
United States	3.6	.27	United States	8.0	.22	United States	14.0	.16
Soviet Union	1.4	.10	Japan	4.0	.11	Japan	10.0	.11
Japan	1.3	.10	Soviet Union	3.0	.08	Soviet Union	8.0	.09
Germany	.8	.06	China	2.0	.06	Korea	7.0	.08
China	.7	.05	Germany	1.5	.04	China	5.0	.06
France	.5	.04	India	1.5	.04	India	5.0	.06
United Kingdom	5	.04	France	1.2	.03	Germany	3.5	.04
Top Seven	8.0	.62	Top Seven	20.0	.58	Top Seven	50.0	.55

You'll notice that in 1984 the list of biggest economies included only two of the six countries with the largest populations. The "giants" only get enough wealth to have major economies in 2024—when India and China join the list. Europe goes from three countries on the list in 1984, to two in 2024, and to only one, Germany, barely holding on in 2064.

Table 28 provides a list of all the countries that are on one or more of the lists of top countries—and those countries that almost made it onto the lists. There is a fairly wide spread between these eighteen countries and the next largest. (But of course there are many small countries whose GNP per capita is more than high enough to put them on the list of richest countries, if that list were not restricted to countries that also have a fairly sizeable population.

TABLE 28
Ranks in 2064

	Biggest	Richest	Biggest Economies
On all three lists:			
United States	9	3	1
Soviet Union	4	8	3
On two lists:			
Japan	(15)—	1	2
Korea	(10)—	2	4
China	1	—	5
India	1	—	5
Germany	(30)—	4	7
On one list:			
Brazil	8	—	(9)—
France	(31)—	5	(8)—
Italy	(37)—	6	(10)—
United Kingdom	(34)—	7	(13)—
Nigeria	3	—	(14)—
Indonesia	5	—	(12)—
Pakistan	6	—	(15)—
Bangladesh	7	—	(21)—
Contenders			
South Africa		(9)—	
Argentina		(10)—	
Mexico		(11)—	

Appendix B:
Is the Passage to a Human World History or Futurology?
(Continuity and Discontinuity in History)

Can The Future Be History?

This is not a question about free will but about the scope of history. History is the description of the past. But, maybe, if the full understanding of the past strongly enough implies something about the future, then that future is also part of history.

Before considering this idea we must deal with two possibly decisive objections. First, no implication about the future can be absolute. Even cosmology's recently gained understanding of the history of the universe since the first fraction of a second, billions of years ago, which strongly implies the future direction of the material of the universe (at least for a few years), does not tell us about the future with absolute confidence—even if we assume that its history is correct.

The implication about the future paths of the Earth and stars from cosmological history is not absolute because it can be prevented by a new explosion like the previous "Big Bang." No one knows where that came from, so no one can say for sure that it will not happen again—and if it did happen again it would put into a cocked hat all the implications of the future that come from cosmological history.

But why must we say that the future is not implied just because it is not implied absolutely? We do not use such a high standard anywhere else. Most of our knowledge of the past has some degree, and often a large degree, of uncertainty. And in our normal affairs we pay a good deal of attention to expectations about the future that are much less than absolute.

The other potentially decisive reason not to accept the suggestion that the future can ever be part of the subject of history—outside physical realms like geology and cosmology—is that it will be too tempting to be allowed to speak about the future while purporting to speak as an historian. If that were to become an accepted mode, undoubtedly the great majority of predictions that would masquerade as history would turn out to be wrong, to be examples instead of a failure to understand either the past or the complexity and unpredictability of human life.

But let's for a moment put aside the possibility that prudence requires that we accept as a convention that history cannot imply the future. Let's consider whether there might be some cases that could justify the idea that, in human as well as in physical matters, the past might to a significant degree imply the future.

The first example is the human enterprise of science—the creation of human knowledge and understanding of our universe. It seems to me that because of what we know from our experience—that is, the history of science— we can say with a good deal of confidence that science will continue to expand. That is, the history of science implies that in the future more will be known and understood—science will have advanced. And it is in the nature of science that it will advance. To assimilate the opposite possibility—of science not advancing—we would have to change some fundamental aspects of our understanding of science.

I don't know whether this example is significant or valid or not. I put it forward as an existence theorem to show that in some examples of human affairs a full understanding of what has happened (is happening) implies something about what will happen in the future. So much so that there are statements about the future that can reasonably be called a part of the description of the past—of history.

Of course, the case we are interested in in this book is the history of increased human productivity and economic growth during the last several centuries. I believe that a solid understanding of what has happened in this realm implies that economic growth will continue (rate unspecified) at least until the great majority of people live in countries that are wealthy by historic standards.

Another way of putting this proposition is: A debate about whether wealth will spread in the future can profitably be conducted as a debate about the nature of the process by which it has spread in the past. The argument "If you truly understand the spread of wealth in the past you will agree that wealth will continue to spread", can only be adequately answered with an argument about what has been happening in the past—a reason why history is consistant with an abrupt end to the spread of wealth. It is not an adequate answer to say that the future is a different subject than the past. Nor is it adequate to say—although it is true—that we can never be sure about the future.

Of course there is plenty of room for disagreement about the scope of what the past implies about the future, or about the degree of confidence. But that does not justify excluding from a discussion of the past (that is, of history) what it implies about the future.

I would even suggest that in some cases the question of implications for the future is a powerful tool for thinking about the past. Trying to think through what might be implied about the future may force one to try to gain a richer more dynamic understanding of the past. Or it may suggest useful ways to test propositions about the past.

Isn't it fair to say that one of the best tests of a proposition about the past or the present is its predictive power? Or that if there are two conflicting views about the past, one good way to determine which is better history is to see what each view implies about the future, and then to see which prediction is borne out by events? If this is accepted, doesn't it give some support to the hypothesis that history can deal with the future and still be history?

Really, I'm Not One of Those

Enthusiasts are always finding ways to fix the world. "Things are going to be different" is a theme heard over and over again. Those of us with what we like to think of as a mature and realistic appreciation of history's lessons, have learned to be skeptical of this claim.

Often we can see what mistake the enthusiast is making—what he is failing to take into account when he says that the world will be different in the future. Usually we don't waste our time with people who ignore history.

Occasionally everything the latest enthusiast says seems plausible; we can't see what he has wrong. But we are sure there is something. We will no more accept the idea of "stepping out of history" than a scientist will accept the idea of a perpetual motion machine—even if he can't figure out why it won't work. We have much more confidence in our sense of the limits of the human experience than we do in our ability to think through any particular idea.

In the most basic ways human history is consistent. Most wisdom learned in the first century is still wisdom in the twentieth. Nevertheless I believe that to understand what is happening in the world today it is necessary to be able to accept the idea that in some areas of life there are fundamental and unique changes taking place. We skeptics must learn to adjust our understanding of how the eternal verities are expressed, to take into account these changes.

In other words, I am writing as an anti-enthusiast who has a limited enthusiasm. I do not believe that technological advance is necessarily progress in the broadest sense. Nor do I believe that progress is inevitable. I do not believe that wealthier is necessarily better. I do not believe that all critical problems must eventually be solved; I don't even believe that all solvable problems will necessarily be solved.

It is quite common for people to see themselves as being in a time of transition and of rapid change. And there are always visionaries and revolutionaries with ideas of how they can change the world and make life better. Mostly time deals harshly with such people's predictions. History's continuities assert themselves. What seemed like transition looks in hindsight like mere fluctuation, and most revolutions fail or merely lead to counter-revolution. Human character, and the unformulatable laws of complex societies, are extraordinarily resistant to reform.

Generally someone is either an "optimist" or a "skeptic." I want to sign up with the skeptics. The confidence—or lack of skepticism—expressed in this book is a limited confidence, about special features of the world, and is entirely consistant with a determined skepticism, and with great respect for the continuities of history.

The completion of the process described in this book doesn't depend upon human performance—social, political, etc.—that is better than what we have done during the last century, which has scarcely been a triumph of peace or a monument to human wisdom. It does not even depend on the United States avoiding economic collapse. None of the main challenges that have been put forward against the perspective presented here have any substantial basis; they can be shown not to parse. (Of course, the weakness of critics is a standard pitfall for policy analysts. One is not right just because one's critics are wrong.)

Not only has most of the future described in this book already happened, but even though I sometimes use absolute language, I do not really mean to say that even the intellectually modest things predicted here are guaranteed to happen. Not only could they be prevented by a natural calamity, they also could be prevented by some extreme human folly—although I think it takes folly that is more powerful than any in history. So I believe that this book predicts only what even sceptics should assume to be the range of probable outcomes. A contrary result would be very surprising.

A Discontinuity in History

Despite my profound respect for the continuities of history, this book should be seen as having put forward the proposition that we are now in the midst of the greatest—and certainly the quickest—discontinuity in human history, a discontinuity that is having and will have profound and unpredictable effects on almost all aspects of human life.

The discontinuity is between the natural worlds of poverty and the human worlds of wealth. The process that is producing this discontinuity is sustained economic growth resulting from continually increasing human productivity.

Human worlds are not developing because we are trying to make a new world. We are each just trying to live a little better. Scientists are just having fun answering questions, not making a new world. But the result is fundamental changes. Nevertheless much stays the same. Fundamental forces of character, of the dynamics of social processes, of the reality of history, continue. Our wisdom about these fundamentals is still valid, but it must be adjusted to take into account new economic and physical factors.

But, I insist, this book describes something new in history: mass wealth, power, freedom, and knowledge. These have been produced by something else that is new in history: sustained economic growth. None of these ever appeared before the nineteenth century—ever, anywhere.

That these things are factually new in history is uncontroversial. The question is whether they really are different; or are they just interesting wrinkles, like all the differences between renaissance Italy and Periclean Greece?

Is life in a wealthy world sufficiently different from life in all the different natural worlds of the past so that we have to re-examine everything we learned before? I think so. Many lessons will survive this re-examination, but many will have to be at least modified, or adjusted.

Although I deny that this book is based on optimism, I have to admit that it is based on a kind of economic determinism. It assumes that when people multiply their income by ten times it is sure to make fundamental differences in their lives.

In other words, this book says that we are seeing something new and powerful in history, and that we are living in a world that is fundamentally different than all of human history. (Currently the old and new are coexisting because we are still in the period of transition from the natural world to the wealthy human worlds of the future.)

Let me emphasize again that I'm not recommending those worlds. They may be terrible. But I do not see how one can doubt that they are coming, and that they will be profoundly different than the worlds of the past. There will be more differences between any society of the future and any society of the past than between any two societies of the past. (Apart perhaps from a few quibbles.)

Since This Book Is Basically History It Can Not Be Optimistic

When someone says a book is "optimistic," it is usually taken to mean that there is a good chance that the book's predictions will not come true. But I feel that the basic message of this book—including its general view of the future—is essentially history.

The key point of the book is that there is very little chance that the prediction it makes—that we are in the middle of a passage to a human world—will not come true. In fact it isn't really a prediction at all; it is an observation of what is implied by what has already happened. That is, it is history.

Of course I don't think that the numbers in Appendix A—or other specific estimates—are history. The only thing that is history is the basic conclusion that economic growth will continue until most people live in countries that are wealthy by historic standards.

It may be several hundred years before that happens. The process of development in many countries may slow, or stop, or even reverse, for many years. But sooner or later most countries will become productive enough to be wealthy. And it seems quite likely this will happen within a timespan that is short compared to human history—compared to all the millennia during which human beings were poor and dominated by nature.

So I feel that anyone who says that this book is "optimistic" has missed the point. Since the argument of the book is that the future spread of wealth is part of history, a claim that this is an optimistic prediction denies the basic argument.

Part of the problem is the ambiguity of the word "optimistic." At the time that Columbus sailed, many people thought that the world was flat and that he would fall off the edge. Therefore those of his sailors who thought that the Earth was round were optimists. My view is that this book is not quite as optimistic as Columbus's sailors were when they said that the Earth is round.*

* Columbus's sailors were more optimistic than I because, although my "history" may be less certain than the roundness of the Earth, it was quite certain that a round Earth would be better for Columbus's sailors than a flat Earth, but it is not quite so clear that the human world that is coming will be better for people than the natural world was.

Appendix C:
The Idea of "Extraction" from the Earth—Some Suggestions for New Definitions
(Appendix to Chapter 6:)

IN THE TEXT WE SAID THAT raw materials are the things we get from nature. That simple statement is roughly right, but, overlooks a number of messy practical and theoretical questions. These questions almost certainly don't affect the conclusions we are concerned with in this book; but they are interesting.

Here is the line of thought we are following. What nature has given us is finite and fixed, so we want to ask: Will it be enough? But first we have to ask: What in fact do we get from nature? Let's use the word "extraction" to refer to that which we take out of nature's supply so that it is no longer there. This definition has the advantage of being aimed directly at the question we are interested in.

Before we start let me just give one example of the problem. When we look at a lovely piece of scenery we take out or use something from nature. But that is not extraction because our use doesn't reduce what is left for others. (On the other hand, when we cut a big strip mine into a beautiful mountain, although what we take out and use is only coal, the beauty is also taken—unless there is sufficient restoration—so we have to say that the mine extracts both coal and beauty.)* Extraction is both a matter of how much we reduce what exists in nature and how we use what we get from nature.

Economists and statisticians define "raw materials" in a number of ways, based on two different roots of the concept of "raw material." One idea is that a raw material is what you start with when you make something, which has the problem that you can keep pushing further and further back. The other root of the concept of raw material is essentially the idea of extraction as defined here. Raw materials are what we get from nature, other things are what we make ourselves out of the raw materials. The reason for the distinction is that some questions about what we get from nature may be different from questions about what we make ourselves.

Partly because people don't distinguish between the two aspects of the concept of raw materials, and partly because of practical difficulties, the phrase "raw material" usually is not rigorously defined by the idea of extracting from nature. In any event, most studies list the categories of things that they call raw materials.

There are only a few important items which might or might not be included as raw materials. The most important is livestock, especially cattle. Both the US Census Bureau's long term study of *Raw Materials in the US Economy*

* In the first case we used but didn't extract; in the second we extracted but didn't use the beauty.

and the seminal and most important study, by Barnett & Morse in the early '60s for Resources For the Future (*Scarcity and Growth, The Economics of Natural Resource Availability*) included livestock as a raw material. In the most recent years of the Census Bureau study livestock costs amounted to one third of total raw materials costs.

But for the modern production of meat it is much more meaningful to think of grain as the basic raw material and the cow as a semi-finished product. When we slaughter a cow we don't reduce nature's ability to produce cows in the future (except perhaps for a few years, and usually not at all). In terms of how much nature's supply is reduced by our use of a something, slaughtering a cow is more like looking at scenery than it is like mining and burning coal.

While cows cannot be produced without other cows, neither can factories be produced without other factories. Obviously nature did not give us only a fixed supply of beef cattle. People, not nature, determine how many beef cattle there will be. We can have as many as we want, nature only determines the *rate* at which we can increase the herd. And cattle don't necessarily use more land than do factories. They can be, and often are, raised without any pasture. (Despite those reasons my tables of raw material consumption include livestock.)

The difficult questions about what really should be included in extraction concern the distinction between extraction and the use of renewable resources. Renewable resources are produced by the reaping of wild products and by cultivation.

Obviously, when we reap the view of a beautiful scene by looking at it we are not extracting anything. There is no problem of measuring or defining how much extraction there is because our enjoyment of the view is merely the use of a renewable resource. But when we spoil a view we have lots of measurement problems. How can we decide how much the view has been damaged? Some people would think that putting a farm into a scene improves it, others that it hurts it. We also have to decide whether the cost of ruining a view depends on how many people see it.

Even if we postpone the question of "psychological" extractions or uses of nature, there are important difficulties. Many things in nature, like forests or fish populations, have a natural tendency to replace small losses. And sunlight is even better, however much we use today there is just as much tomorrow. For natural wild products like fish or trees there is almost always some rate at which they can be taken or harvested without noticeably reducing the supply. It certainly doesn't make sense to use the word "extraction" for a harvest that will be automatically replenished by nature. We will call such harvesting of renewable wild resources "reaping," which we will define as "any harvesting of a wild product at a rate which is naturally replenished."

Incidentally, an important class of reaping is using the capacity of streams or other environmental units as pollution absorbers or decontaminants. For example, most rivers have the ability to harmlessly decompose some amount of biological contaminants. Only if the capacity of the stream is exceeded does it become polluted. Using the stream to dispose of as much waste as it can handle without becoming polluted is, in effect, "reaping" the disposal capacity of the stream. Similarly, air basins can absorb and dissipate some quantities of air pollutants without becoming polluted. In some areas quite a large amount of pollutants have to be released before there is any real reduction in air quality.

In order to decide whether a particular reaping of a wild product is an extraction or not we have to decide how long a replenishment cycle to allow. Clearly a year is alright. When we harvest wild berries that will grow back next year, it is clear that there has been no extraction. But when we harvest all the trees of a forest so that it takes fifty or five hundred years to grow back, it would seem that we have made at least a partial "extraction," even though the wood we removed will be naturally "replenished" within a very long cycle.

That brings us to the concept of "cultivation," of which the raising of grain and cereal products is the most important example. Cultivation is different than manufacturing or construction because cultivation is based on a biological growth process (seeds, development, etc.). Cultivation is different than reaping of wild products, although many wild products are also based on biological growth processes, because the farmer has to plant the grain; nobody has to plant herring in the ocean.

When a farmer grows a crop of grain he may either increase or decrease his land's ability to grow another crop next year (or next cycle). Whether growing the crop "extracts" any valuable quality from the land depends on the land, the crop, and, most importantly, the techniques practiced by the farmer.

Where a farmer grows a crop of grain in such a way that the land's fertility is in no way reduced, or is even increased, it is hard to see why it is useful to consider that grain as an "extractive product." It is like using the rain that falls from the sky to water the field. Next year the rain will come again. Using it doesn't prevent grandchildren to the nth generation from making the same use.

While the centers of these three ideas, manufacturing (or construction), cultivation, and reaping (of wild products), are clearly distinct from each other,*

* *Review of Definitions*
    Manufacturing—non-biological production of moveable items
    Construction—non-biological production of immoveable items
    Cultivation—production with biological processes started by man
            (necessarily renewable)
    Wild Products—renewable products not planted by man
            both: biological products like fish or tress, and
                non-biological products like sunlight and pollution
              absorption capacity
    Harvesting—taking wild products whether or not they are replenished
    Reaping—harvesting where the product is replenished
        (Both reaping and cultivation are renewable-non-extractive-forms of production, although they may be done in a way that involves some extraction.)

if you push on the definitions you will find increasingly large grey areas where there seems to be little point to the distinction. However we don't care whether or not there is much real distinction between manufacturing, cultivation, and reaping. None of them are extraction; what we are interested in is the distinction between extraction and all other forms of production.

EXTRACTION IS THE KIND OF PRODUCTION that takes something out of nature so that it isn't there any more, and therefore raises the question of whether eventually there might not be enough left to take.

Now I begin to diverge from the best professional analysis of these issues. I believe that agriculture is much less extractive than is generally assumed. All of the value of agriculture is usually assumed to be extractive. This leads to the conclusion that extraction was formerly a very large share of economic activity and has been a declining share for many years.

For the reasons I will state immediately, I believe: that only a small share of agriculture is extractive, that easily available statistics do not tell us what that share is now or what it has been in the past, and that therefore we do not know whether the long term trend is toward increasing extraction or the opposite.

Also, today the overwhelming share of American extraction is the taking and burning of fossil fuels, and this now takes more than twice as large a share of our GNP as it did when this century began. Because I think we know the technology that can limit energy cost below a dangerous level, without fossil fuels, I do not find this historical fact troubling. But those who prefer to rely only on historical arguments need to deal with this view of the historical relation of extraction to the rest of the economy.

With my definition of "extraction," the extraction of raw materials has never been a large part of the economy of any important society. Most economies of the past were mostly agricultural, and if agriculture didn't require much extraction, extraction couldn't have been a big share of their economy. Now our economy is mostly service and white collar work, and even for most physical goods the extracted raw materials used are a fairly small share of the cost.

While extracted raw materials are now and always have been a small share of economies, it is clear that with two important exceptions they are getting even smaller. One exception is fuels, the other important exception is what I define below as "by-product extraction."

Cultivation produces raw materials—wheat, cotton, etc.—but it is not generally extraction because to a first approximation there is as much left in nature after the harvest as there was before planting. But sometimes there is an element of extraction in cultivation. If there is a reduction in the quality or value of the land as a result of cultivation, that reduction is an extraction. It is quite clear that any reduction in the quality of American farmland is a small fraction of the value of the crops produced.* This is true even if one accepts the claims of those who shout about how much we are eroding and converting our farmland.

Often an investment of work on land can improve its agricultural quality. If later the cultivation of a crop on that land reduces its quality by wiping out the benefits of the work invested, perhaps that quality loss from the cultivation isn't an "extraction" but a use of capital or an operating expense. (While farmland is certainly capital for some purposes, we are making a special distinction. We want to distinguish the capital which is the output of human work from the capital that we have received from nature. Farmland is usually a combination of both.)

For particular pieces of land it may be possible to make a meaningful distinction between an extraction of agricultural quality and the use of a prior investment. For example, one may improve land by fencing and draining it, and reduce its quality by using nutrients in growing crops. In this case the same field has simultaneously an improvement and a degradation which are physically separate. But economically the improvement and the degradation merge together; the land has either a net increase or decrease in its value. If you talk about the country or the world as a whole then it is not possible to separate capital disinvestment in land quality from extraction of natural quality. All you know is that each year there is investment in land improvement and there is cultivation which harms land; at the end of the year some land is better than at the beginning of the year and some is worse. The farmland all together is either better or worse than it was at the beginning of the year.

There is another, much smaller adjustment in conventional thinking about extraction that should be made if we wish to have more precise analysis. We can distinguish between the various things that happen to materials after we extract them from nature.

Most of the material extracted, like fuels, we burn or otherwise destroy. Much of it, however we keep around, like the copper in telephone wires or pots, or like the iron in cars either driving or sitting in junk piles. Some of this material is easier to get from the place in which we have put it than it would be to get out of the ground. Such material—e.g., copper in phone wires—

---

* In 1979 the value of US farm output was about $150 billion and the value of all farm land was about $540 billion. Even if farming in 1979 was done so badly that 10% of the value of the farmland was lost, the extraction would have been only a third of the value of the output. But the value of the farmland was not reduced by anything like 10%, if it was reduced at all.

Much of the value of the land is speculative and not influenced by small changes in its agricultural quality. The value of farmland increased by 15% between 1979 and 1980, but it has decreased a great deal since then. The declining value of farmland in the United States does not result from extraction from the land when it is farmed; it results from lower prices for crops because more of the world is able to produce grain efficiently (and other economic factors).

clearly hasn't been extracted, because the amount available hasn't been reduced. The copper in the wires is more available than it was when it was in the ground. You can think of it as being stored temporarily in the wires until it is needed for some better purpose. Sending Aunt Minnie's voice through the copper while it is stored doesn't hurt it. (Whenever we want to use the copper we can put in an aluminum wire—or optical fibers—to replace the copper wire.)

In other cases, when we take something like iron out of the ground and sometime later put it into a junkyard, we have made the iron harder to get than it was before. Such an extraction of iron doesn't destroy the iron, or reduce the amount of iron available. In effect it "buries some iron deeper." This can be thought of as a partial extraction. It may not be as much an extraction as burning would be, but it does reduce the resource value, and may reduce it so much that none is left, although later events can restore the value of the buried iron, since it is still there.

IT IS SOMETIMES DIFFICULT to distinguish between, on one hand, reaping of wild products (which means there must be natural replenishment), and on the other hand, extraction through the use of a wild product or natural value in a way that destroys it. In other words, sometimes it is difficult to apply the concept of a "renewable resource."

Wild products like trees or fish or sunlight can be harvested in ways that either enhance, decrease or leave unaffected the original level of production.

Even though by definition no money is spent planting wild products or on putting them where they are found, a wild product can be expensive, because the cost of harvesting it may be high. In fact the expenses necessary to harvest a wild product may be much larger than the value that is supplied free by nature in creating the product. (Also, the fact that a product comes free from nature doesn't mean that it is free to whoever harvests it; she may have to pay the owner for the right to harvest.)

In order to be able to keep on harvesting a wild product we may spend money to protect the natural replenishment process. All kinds of measures are taken in protecting forests or deer herds, and other wild products. But as we do more and more to help nature to continue to supply the wild product, the reaping component of the value of that product becomes smaller and smaller. In the end it becomes more like cultivation in that most of the value of what we take out comes from what we put in. And, as with some woods, it becomes more economical to plant the trees, which means switching from reaping to cultivation, and which may be a pretty fine line.

HARVESTING WILD PRODUCTS can involve extraction in several different ways:

a) Temporary reduction of natural supply

If the original levels of supply restore themselves without human effort, as many woods or fisheries do, the extraction is the cumulative supply loss before replenishment is complete.

If the reduction in supply level will continue unless human action is taken to restore the original supply level, and it is possible to do so, then the value of the extraction is the cost of restoring supply and the loss of supply in the meantime.

Incidentally I am, of course, including aesthetic and other environmental values as part of wild supply. When it is difficult to measure or to reach agreement about the value of something, it is a mistake to think or act as if it had no value. (It is also a mistake to act as if it had infinite value).

We have noted before that most people define pollution in human terms. That is, most people would say that a piece of desert has been improved, not polluted, when a citrus grove has been planted on it. Similarly, when we talk about the value of the wild supply of something—wood, or fish, or scenery—we mean the value to people. Therefore if a temporary loss of supply of a wild product is a supply that wouldn't have been used anyway, it is not an extraction. (This eliminates much of what seems to be extraction.)

b.) Permanent reduction of wild supply

When people do something that permanently reduces the wild supply of something—like the beauty of a scene or the fish in a lake—they have made an extraction. The value of the extraction is the capitalized value of the reduction in annual wild supply, beginning from whenever the reduced supply would have had value, perhaps immediately.

c). More complete occupation of the Earth

As we increasingly occupy and use the world we bring closer the time when many kinds of wild supply, that originally were of little or no value, would have become useful. Lost future products, which will not be needed until so far in the future that they are now virtually valueless—even with a low discount rate—will become more valuable. Thus the cost of destroying such future products will become greater. This effect may be one of the most important economic effects of occupying the world more fully.

As noted before, often there is extraction without any harvest, as when a forest is destroyed to use the land for something else and the wood is not used. Or, when environmental values of some kind are destroyed as a side effect of some activity.

It may be noticed that this dry analysis in some ways parallels the emotional complaints of environmentalists that we are reducing the value of our natural heritage. It is possible that the formulations suggested here may be a useful way to approach a quantitative expression of environmental concerns. It seems likely that this kind of calculation, if it could be made in a meaningful way, would help us to be conservationist in different, more efficient, ways. Overall I do not know whether such calculations would lead us in the direction of being more conservationist or less. But it seems to me possible that this is the real area where the question of extraction ought to be pursued. It is much more likely that these costs could become significantly larger than that we will not have enough food or raw materials or energy.

I do not say that this analysis is alarming. In many ways our activities up to now have had the effect of increasing the value of the Earth to people, including many of its aesthetic and other psychological values. But I think this may be a good form of analysis to try.

Summary

Generally agriculture is not extraction.
        (although it may involve an element of extraction)

The following are the different kinds of extraction:
    a) Destructive extraction
        The removal from nature of a material and its destruction. For example fuels.
    b) Partial extraction by making materials less accessible
        For example when rich iron ore is turned into junk cars.
    c) By-product extraction
        This is the kind of extraction which happens when a continuing natural value, or the level of supply of a naturally renewable wild product, is reduced by some activity. (e.g., overfishing extracts fish, and strip mining may extract beauty.)
        This is probably the most important kind of extraction.
    d) Extraction by the more complete occupation of the Earth
        This formulation is my invention, and my or may not be useful. It is explained above.

Appendix D: The Rise in Oil Prices Does Not Justify a Scarcity Perspective.

IN 1973-74, THE INTERNATIONAL OIL PRICE roughly quadrupled in a few months. Five years later international oil prices doubled again, in only a few months.

After 1973, people became used to the idea that oil is scarce. Some Americans had the unusual experience of not being able to buy gasoline for their cars, even though they were willing to pay extra.*

We frequently have the experience of not being able to buy something because we don't have enough money. But in the United States it is so unusual as to be shocking when people can't buy something ordinary like gasoline, even when they have the money. In fact the experience of gasoline lines was so shocking that it altered many people's basic view of the world. The brief local shortages, combined with years of rising oil prices, led many people who had not been influenced by the intellectual "limits to growth" and "spaceship Earth" movements to accept the basic idea of scarcity.**

Of course the popular instinct that understands that "if something is getting more expensive it must be scarce" is correct, but that concept must be applied with some care. Appearances can be misleading. And in the case of oil prices they were.

One key fact is that most of the rise in oil prices after 1973 was not the result of the increases in the cost of producing oil (although there had been some cost increases). This is one of the reasons for believing that the oil price rise is not an early sign that we are beginning to run out of oil. (Although we probably will run out of it eventually, maybe in a few generations.) A realistic description of what did happen to energy prices and costs in the last fifteen years—which has nothing to do with approaching shortages—is summarized in the Annex.

The reason for including the Annex to this Appendix even though its topic is very different than the rest of the book, is that I want to show at least

---

* It was not realized at the time, but the shortages that produced the gasoline lines were the result of the government's allocation system. At all times there was enough gasoline available in the United States. (This is not to say that there can never be shortages so great as to require an allocation system; it is just that the gasoline allocation programs of the '70s were unnecessary and produced local shortages.)

** In a talk I gave for Hudson Institute in May 1973 I said that oil prices would probably rise substantially, and that one of the biggest costs to the world of the coming higher oil prices would be the way they would teach a wrong lesson about scarcity. (Of course I didn't realize then how far oil prices would rise and how much the world would be affected.)

one explanation for the recent rapid rise in oil prices that doesn't have any relation to the exhaustion of oil. I think the explanation given in the Annex is correct, but I don't have to depend on it. Some people think it is more accurate to blame the oil price rise on the cartel action of OPEC—which also does not depend on the approaching exhaustion of oil or fossil fuels. Other people have other views about what happened, and these other explanations also don't have any relation to the long-run scarcity of oil.

In brief, there are plenty of things that could have produced our oil price experience apart from approaching long-term exhaustion of oil resources. And, of course, the fact that oil prices have been cut by more than one half now, and seem likely to stay down for some time, supports this view (although I first wrote it long before they fell).

In summary, although before too long we will have to find energy sources to replace conventional oil, the dramatic recent experience with oil prices does not imply or indicate in any way that a scarcity perspective is correct; it illustrates that there are lots of things that can go wrong with the world economy without any basic shortages of raw materials.

Annex to Appendix D: A Theory About What Happened with International Oil Prices

So far the world has taken out of the ground about 10% of the conventional oil that most experts expect will be found and recovered. Before 1973 oil was sold very cheaply on the international market (despite the fact that the "seven sister" oil companies supplied a large share of the market). International prices for oil were well below the cost of many other competing sources of energy, including US oil (although they were high compared to the cost of production in the Middle East).

As a result of low oil prices, oil sales were increasing 7% per year until 1973 and taking a larger and larger share of the energy market. Oil production facilities didn't expand fast enough to keep up with the extremely fast growth in oil consumption. Production facilities would have had to double every ten years to keep up with consumption. The result was that in 1973 almost all the oil that could be produced with existing equipment was being sold.

The fact that a high percent of the oil that the companies were able to produce (not all the oil available in the ground) was being sold, combined with the low price of oil compared to substitutes, and with the fact that the cost of oil was a small share of the cost of most uses of oil (transportation, housing), caused the fourfold increase in oil prices in 1973-74.

Because of the same factors a very large increase in prices was required before there was much reduction in the amount of oil bought, and before non-OPEC sources of oil production could grow enough to make a difference. Oil has the largest sales of any single commodity in the world. It takes a long time to make a significant change in the production or the consumption of oil.

In the five years after the first multiplication of oil prices the official price of oil rose less than the rate of inflation. So the real price of oil on the international market declined from 1974-1978. In the United States, where consumers were initially largely shielded by the government from most of the price increase of international oil, real retail prices rose slowly but continued to be artificially held below the real costs of producing the last barrel of oil that is used.

Real coal prices rose rapidly because oil no longer exerted as much downward pressure, because of a general rise in engineering and construction costs, and because of new safety regulations. (These safety regulations did not accelerate the long-term declining trend in the number of workers killed per ton of coal mined, although they did reduce the number killed per hour worked.) Gas production was able to expand only slowly because of a very complicated regulatory situation in which gas prices had been kept very low for so many years that the level of drilling had been cut way back.

During this time OPEC's sales, which had been growing rapidly, began to fall. By the summer of 1978 the amount of oil in the inventories of oil buyers was low because of the season and because buyers expected the price to continue gradually going down. Relatively suddenly the Iranian revolution knocked out the second largest supplier, which had been producing almost 10% of the world's oil. Most oil buyers responded by increasing their purchases of oil to add to their inventory because they feared shortages and higher prices.

In the year after Iran's oil shipments were almost eliminated, the world produced more oil than it consumed—and the amount of oil in people's inventories *increased*. But as a result of the panic, of the fact that production capacity without Iran was again not much more than sales, and because of market manipulation by the Saudis, international oil prices doubled. (The Saudi oil authorities now regret their action, which they now believe will very substantially reduce the total value of their oil income in the long-run. Their policy during the 1978-1979 oil crisis was very costly to them and to the world.)

In much of the world the doubling of international oil prices in 1978-1979 was harder to adjust to than the quadrupling in price that had taken place in 1973-1974. It meant a bigger increase in the total amount of money spent on oil. Also the price of oil had already risen to a more appropriate range, compared to energy costs in general.

The effect of the second big price increase, combined with cumulative effects of the first one, has been dramatic. OPEC sales are down by more than a third. Even with shipments from the second and third largest producers, Iran and Iraq, greatly reduced because they are fighting each other, there is ample excess oil production capacity. As a result there was a gradual decline in real international oil prices from 1980 to 1986, and then a big drop, to about the 1974 level (in constant dollars) in 1986.

It would be hard (but not impossible) for the panic of 1978-1979 to be repeated. Inventories are much larger. Some lessons were probably learned, and arrangements made to prevent that mistake from being repeated. Today there is no oil exporter that produces as big a share of world energy as Iran did in 1978, although Saudi Arabia is fairly close. (But no three other exporters together have as much capacity as Saudi Arabia.)

One frightening lesson is the power of the "slosh" effect on oil markets whenever there is a general move to increase or decrease oil inventories. Understanding this requires distinguishing between "instantaneous demand" and "ultimate demand"—although this is rarely done. Ultimate demand is the same as consumption, and it can change only slowly. Instantaneous demand is the amount that people are trying to buy at any one moment—which is what directly affects prices. "Slosh" is what happens when instantaneous demand moves quickly up and down, getting far away from ultimate demand for weeks or even months at a time.

Although the slosh effect sounds complicated, and is not generally understood, it is basically fairly straightforward. Increasingly oil prices are determined by what is in effect an auction market. When there are more buyers than sellers the price goes up, and vice versa. In the long run the number of buyers depends on how much oil is being consumed in homes, factories, cars, etc. But in the short run the number of buyers is determined by whether oil is being put into or taken out of inventory. (That is, on whether oil is sloshing into or out of inventories.) For example, if fifty million barrels of oil a day are being consumed, the amount being bought can be anything from thirty million barrels to seventy million barrels, and it can slosh almost from one extreme to another within weeks.

Whether oil is being put into inventories or taken out usually depends on whether the oil industry expects prices to be going down or going up. Why buy oil today if prices are going to be lower next month? It makes more sense to use the oil in inventory first, and buy later. On the other hand, if prices are going up, perhaps very far, or there is a danger of shortages, then the prudent consumer of oil increases his inventory, buying oil today to use later so he doesn't have to buy so much when the prices are higher.

In this way the fear of rising prices can make the demand for oil shoot up. This increase in demand raises the price, which increases the fear of further price rises, and further increases demand. So we can get—as we did in 1978—the strange phenomenon of higher prices increasing rather than reducing demand (until the inventories and pipelines are filled). (The same kind of thing can also happen on the down side.)

It is unlikely, but not impossible, that oil will again become as much a sellers market during the rest of the 1980s. The same can be said, but with less confidence, for most of the 1990s.

In summary, I believe it is a reasonable assessment to say that average real energy prices in 1973 were somewhat too low, compared to their value to users and to long term average production costs. Also oil prices were clearly low in relation to other energy prices. Now, on the other hand, real (inflation-adjusted) average energy costs, worldwide, have about doubled and are probably reasonably close to a sound level. International oil prices rose much faster than other energy costs for awhile, making up for the fact that they had been much lower before 1973. But now oil prices have fallen to a more or less reasonable relationship to other energy prices. However oil may continue to get a smaller and smaller share of the market for energy because people are afraid to again become so dependent on oil suppliers.

I should emphasize that the judgements in this Appendix—unlike most of those in the rest of Part II of the book—are all controversial and uncertain. They also are very approximate. I would not even suggest that they are accurate to better than plus or minus 50%.

Appendix E: Policy-Making Concerning Subtle Environmental Risks

Concept of Risk Efficiency

Public policy can be thought of as involving two different kinds of considerations which are intermingled in almost every practical issue. One consideration can be called "the game against nature." It involves asking what is good for the country as a whole. For example it is clearly good for the country as a whole to avoid inflation, and recession, and unemployment. It is good for the country as a whole to have peace and for our national interests to be protected against foreign competitors or enemies. It is good for the country as a whole for our farming to be done in a way that doesn't ruin our soil resources or excessively damage our environment. In general we have a national interest in producing what we want with minimum total costs in market resources, environmental harm, human misfortune, long-term risks, and other costs that are not reflected in the accounting system. Most important, although almost always overlooked because we have been so successful at dealing with it, we have a very strong, common interest in preserving our country and its government, so that it can maintain order within, protect our national interests against foreign dangers, and hold our allegiance.

The other major consideration in public policy is balancing conflicting interests. As individuals, and as members of groups and categories, our interests are different and usually at least partly conflicting. Rich, middle-class, and poor, young and old, manufacturers and consumers, regulators and doers, East and West, the current generation and future generations, thousands of other groups, and each individual, all have particular interests that conflict with other particular interests.

Sometimes the government transfers money or something else from one group to another. More often the government works on a common problem, part of the national game against nature, in a way that is better for some interests than for other interests. "You don't get something for nothing" applies to the country as well as to individuals. The prices that need to be paid to accomplish national ends cannot be divided evenly (as if that were a meaningful concept), and anyhow most people's preference is not that sacrifices be distributed equally but that justice be done by having the costs borne by someone else.

Public policy disputes involve two things: efforts by various interests to get more for themselves, and disagreement about the best strategy and tactics to use in playing the game against nature, that is, the best methods to use to achieve common goals. There are always disagreements about the best way to do anything, but in principle some answers are clearly better, and one answer may be best. Disagreement can come from differences in ideology, in experience, in the quantity and quality of the thinking behind alternative approaches, in personality, and in many other factors. Also, as everybody knows, differences in opinion often flow in one way or another from differences of interest. So arguments about methods are always, at least partly, arguments about who gets and who pays.

In the game of conflicting interests among ourselves there is no correct answer. (Within a particular value system some answers are better than others. Sometimes also, perhaps especially in poor countries, some divisions of resources within the community are more efficient for the nation as a whole.)

Politics is the process by which we decide about dividing up things among ourselves—to the extent that the government has the authority to do so. While we can arrange procedures to try to make sure that national decisions in the game against nature are made from the point of view of the overall national interest, those procedures are usually fairly weak. Politics is also the process we use ultimately to decide among conflicting views about the best way to achieve our common interests. The fact that politics must decide both processes makes it impossible to reliably separate the competition of conflicting interests from decisions about the common interest.

Apart from abstract values of justice, etc., politics can fail in two ways. It can produce results that are so unsatisfactory to so many and so powerful of the citizens that the system fails to hold together. More commonly politics fails when the process of conflict among internal interests produces decisions that get too far away from the correct policy in the game against nature. That is, one can say that politics fails if the only way that Group X and Group Y can agree to divide things between them is a way which reduces their common welfare. (For example, the trucking industry can get approval for such heavy trucks that the resulting cost of road repair is billions of dollars more than the truckers' savings—and even more out of proportion with truckers' increased profits from using very heavy trucks.)

How inefficient politics can afford to be depends on the nation's situation. A country that is rich and safe can afford great inefficiency. A country that is poor or challenged may need to come reasonably close to maximizing its possibilities if it is not to be badly hurt.

Risk decisions clearly involve both the game against nature and the conflict among ourselves. The interested parties are entitled to pursue their own interests in reducing their own risks or costs, rather than someone else's. The political process is the only way in which these interests can be balanced. Thus politics must and should enter into risk decisions. But we fail if politics takes us too far away from an approximation of one of the better decisions that would be made if dealing with the risk were solely a game against nature.

"Risk efficiency" is the concept which embodies most of the game against nature in the area of public policy about subtle environmental risks. The risk efficiency problem is trying to make decisions about risks that save the most lives and other values with the amount of resources that the nation decides to put into the effort. We want to use the efforts and resources that are devoted to improving health and life expectancy as effectively as possible. We want to avoid as much death and ill health as we can, without wasting money or other resources.

Almost all of the work on these kinds of risk questions done by people who are trying to be rational, that is relatively unbiased and analytical, has focused on the fairly narrow part of the subtle risk problem which is here called "risk efficiency." (There has also been a fair amount of effort devoted to describing people's perceptions about risk and the psychology of risk-avoiding behavior.) Such a discussion of risk efficiency ignores as much or more of the real problem as it addresses. In particular, it ignores questions about who bears the risks and who bears the costs, and about what special considerations flow from the relationships of different groups of people to the risk and cost (such as workers, bystanders, customers, volunteers, etc.) All deaths are not equal. More important, the risk efficiency discussion almost always leaves out of account psychological and social impacts of risks and of efforts to avoid them.

Psychological and Social Impacts of the Risk Problem

Here is a cursory list of a few factors:

1. It is clear that various publics perceive risks inaccurately. (At least this is true for those risks we know—like auto accidents; we assume that people are not more accurate for subtle risks where the correct answer is unknowable.) These inaccurate public perceptions are relevant to policy and to the impact that risks have on people.

2. People care differently about different kinds of deaths—and therefore risks (apart from preferring far ones to near ones). For example, large numbers at one time are particularly avoided. Some kinds of particularly painful, frightening, or otherwise horrible forms of death are especially feared. And greater efforts will be made to avoid risks to children, or other especially innocent or sympathetic victims.

3. Choices and control in relation to risk also influence its acceptability. Freedom of choice is a value. People's relationship to the risk influence is a value.

4. Also society's connection to the risk matter. For example, people find it especially annoying to be killed by their own government's failure to take precautions. Official behavior may be held to higher standards—at least in some circumstance. The moral or other message delivered by some kinds of death or risk sometimes has important values.

In brief, a variety of spiritual and psychological effects of risks and harms, of risk-avoiding programs, and of the debate about risk policy, are important.

327

5. Finally, a major aspect of risk policy is the process of developing public understanding of subtle risk issues and concepts. ("Public" of course means many interwoven levels of publics.) There are a number of reasons why it is hard for most people to understand—intellectually and emotionally—the fundamental ideas and to have the perspectives necessary to think well about the range of subtle risk issues that enter the public discussion. While the problem of public understanding can be dealt with at the level of utility theory, perception studies, etc., the emphasis should be on practical effects of ideas, slogans, and ways of thinking. People will learn to live with the fact that they cannot know how safe or dangerous the products they use and their environments are; just as they cannot know their financial safety or their political dangers. As is true for other risks, study, wisdom, and luck can improve outcomes, and everybody has to decide for themself who to trust and where to use their decision-making resources. Policy makers and communicators need to know how to talk to the public about subtle risks as the degree and nature of understandings change.

How Should Risk Decisions Be Made?

There is no formula for deciding these subtle risk questions. All the studies and research projects will not find an "answer." Even apart from the uncertainty problem there are too many different kinds of considerations for there to be a formula which permits reasonably clearcut decision making. The best that can be done for each decision is to lay out for each alternative* the advantages and disadvantages as clearly as possible, so that the decision maker can weigh the incommensurable in his head as best he can. That is the correct way, I believe, to make a rational, fair-minded decision in the public interest. Some of the complexities that lie behind these simplicities will be discussed below.

Where decisions involve both the game against nature and conflicts among ourselves, our long-term task is to arrange decision making procedures so that the facts and issues are made reasonably clear, and the official decision maker is required to state the basis of his decision. This increases the chance that all interested parties will have a fair crack at being able to advance their interests, and that the overall interest in a not-too-inefficient decision also has a chance of being protected.

This is a very simple and obvious idea that is endorsed by many groups, but it is very hard to implement. It is a goal that we can keep striving toward; but we can only attain partial success. All interested parties, including the decision maker—who is interested in enhancing his political position in some way, such as by appearing in some contexts to be fair and disinterested—are well advised to try to cover their positions in a cloak of concern for the general

---

* Often the most important part of the decision is finding a better alternative, because often the choices that evolve from the normal procedure are all inferior.

interest and an attempt to find the most efficient solution. To the extent that any group's interest is given any special weight, that group and those who favor its interest need to follow a strategy of trying to conceal the special weight. The tactics for pursuing this strategy include avoiding or eliminating evidence for arguments against their position.

Suppose, to take a not very realistic example, that OSHA has to decide whether to allow something that would reduce the risk to the users of a product at the cost of an increased risk to the workers who make the product. Since OSHA is in the Department of Labor it must be especially responsive to the political representatives of organized labor. Therefore the political requirement for the Administrator of OSHA and his supervisors in the Department of Labor is to give special weight to the interests of workers to limit the risks that they face (even beyond the special consideration that a disinterested person might find appropriate for workers because of their continuous exposure, smaller numbers, or whatever). But you can be sure that the formal decision of the Administrator of OSHA will not say that it is better to avoid risks to workers because they are organized and can effectively influence her future and that of her agency more than can the consumers of the product, most of whom will not even know about the additional risk being imposed upon them. Instead she is likely to reach the same result by finding facts that require shifting the risk to the consumer.

In effect, by establishing procedures that (1) put pressure on decision makers to seem to decide on risk-efficiency considerations, (2) give them more ability to do so, and (3) provide facts and analysis so that their decision can be evaluated, we constrain political forces so that it is harder for them to produce decisions that are too far from the socially efficient.*

---

* As emphasized before, it is impossible to know what is a "socially efficient decision" about the typical subtle risk policy question. One can only try to figure out what the socially efficient decision is. We will treat that best-we-can decision as if it were the socially efficient decision.

There is no need to worry, either from a social or a selfish point of view, that a decision maker will be so constrained to pretend to decide on pure risk-efficiency criteria that there will be inadequate room for politics. Rational decisions will have sufficient uncertainty to allow quite adequate play for political forces, even if they are constrained to conceal themselves.

Appendix F: Note on Sources of Information

THE FACT THAT THIS BOOK is written for the ordinary citizen, rather than for scholars does not mean that it is less advanced or less reliable than a book addressed to experts. Although I do not pretend to be a scholar, I am familiar enough with the professional literature and debate on these issues to be confident that the statements and conclusions contained here have no difficulty standing up to professional scrutiny, and I would not hesitate to defend the conclusions of the book before any audience of scholars and experts in the relevant fields.

Writing for the non-expert is not a license to use low quality information or to pass on unsound ideas—it is an obligation to speak in ordinary language and to try to keep the presentation interesting. Most important it means concentrating on the main points, not being diverted by those technical controversies that don't affect the central issues.

The point of this note is not to convince scholars of my familiarity with the professional and academic literature, but to help the ordinary person who may want to read more on the subject or to check to make sure there is evidence to support the conclusions presented here.

The key thing when you are looking for numbers is to start by thinking about what you want to know. So let's go through the main points of the book and consider what numbers are needed to evaluate them and where these numbers can be found.

The first point was that the world is a lot wealthier than it ever has been before. Chapter 1 says that in any year before the last century about $250 of goods and services were produced per person, in the world as a whole. This year people produced about $2,500 per person. Neither of these numbers is precise. Even if everything were counted exactly, and calculated perfectly, these kinds of numbers don't have any real meaning that is more accurate than plus or minus at least 25% or 50%. (See the discussion in Endnote 4 about comparing the GNP of two different countries or of the same country at two different times.)

All that you can be sure of is that we are producing much more per person now than was produced before 1800. Whether it is five times as much, or eight times, or twelve, or twenty times as much, can't be said simply and with complete confidence.

The current GNP numbers used in the book come from the World Bank, which publishes a *World Development Report* every year. (Published for the Bank by the Oxford University Press, and beginning with the 1978 edition.) This is a reasonably neutral and competent source. It is in the nature of such numbers that they are not precise. Nothing said in this book turns on the kinds

331

of disagreements about these numbers that other expert sources might have. There is no alternative source of information about national incomes that has significantly different information or opinions.

In any event, you can see for yourself the basic fact about increasing wealth. Not only do you have the experience of your own lifetime—if you are even thirty years old. But you know something of how people lived when this country was created, and how people lived here during the last century.

Similarly for life expectancy information. Table 1 says that it has gone from thirty years to sixty years in the last two hundred years. (Actually two hundred years ago it was probably below thirty and it is well over sixty now.) But the real point is not statistics but that people are living much longer now than they used to live. If you want to find out about the increase in how long people live, you don't need to go to insurance tables or medical studies. You can go to any cemetery and look at grave stones, or ask any family to see how old the people of previous generations were when they died, and how many children were born that did not grow up.

Again, the numbers used here come from the *World Development Report*. They shouldn't be thought of as at all precise or reliable, especially the ones for the poorer countries. But there is little doubt or controversy about the general pattern or the direction of change.

On population projections I used the *World Development Report*, but the projections of the Population Reference Bureau in Washington, and of the United Nations, are essentially the same. Each organization has different estimates for particular countries, but there are no large systematic differences among them. They are pretty much in agreement that there will be about ten billion people when the current period of population growth comes to an end.*

The next major point is about how much we are spending for raw materials. The numbers here are from standard statistical sources, such as the Bureau of Mines' *Mineral Facts and Problems* or *Mineral Commodity Summaries*, or *Minerals Yearbook*, and much of the information is in the *Statistical Abstract of the United States*.

At the beginning of the *Mineral Commodity Summary* the Bureau of Mines

---

* Of course Paul Demeny of the Population Council will make scathing criticisms of the standard estimates, but he has never said that he believes that a range of 10 billion to 20 billion is too small. Personally I am skeptical about the standard view that population will "level off"—if that is taken to mean constant world population. I don't see why each country should come to exactly the level of fertility necessary to keep population constant. I believe that some countries will have growing populations and others declining populations, and that many will fluctuate above and below net replacement rate (over periods of generations or centuries). Nor do I see why countries with declining populations should exactly balance those with rising populations. So in the long run world population may rise or decline from the level at which it reaches when the current burst of growth ends. The current burst comes from the transition from poverty to wealth. We can see why that burst will end; what we can't see is the longterm impact of continued wealth, or of widespread great wealth (i.e., US levels of income or higher).

has a block diagram called the "The Role of Nonfuel Minerals in the U.S. Economy" which shows how domestic mines, scrap, imported ore, and imported processed minerals relate to the total economy. It shows (for 1982) $20 billion of US ores, $4 billion of scrap, and $4 billion of imported ores, (total $28 billion) being used to produce a total of $202 billion of processed minerals (for example steel bars) that we used in our total economy of $3,060 billion.*

Dividing the Bureau's totals by 232 million (which is the Census Bureau's estimate of the population in 1982) they are saying that $100 per person of mineral raw material led to $800 per person of all the processed minerals needed for an economy of over $13,000 per person. This is essentially the same as the $60 of metals plus $40 of other minerals shown in Chapters 6 and 10.

The problem with numbers for raw materials is to decide what stage of the process from ore to refined product to count. Each metal or mineral is different. Some are converted from ore to a pure form in mills near the mines. Others are shipped almost as they are taken from the ground. Some are priced on the basis of the amount of the metal in the ore, others are priced per ton of some intermediate form of ore or product. In general I tried to get the price at the point that is closest to the point that the mineral comes out of the ground that it is possible to buy it.

I was only able to put all the metals into a single table because I didn't worry too much about being exactly comparable, or exactly right. (I didn't worry about that for two reasons. First, the prices of many of the commodities jump up and down from year to year. Second, the quantities used also fluctuate widely. So any attempt to show a "typical year" can not be precise.

There is no point in being precise when the conclusion would be the same whether we were spending $60 or $120 or $180 per year for the metals we need. Since there is no doubt or controversy about the overall pattern I described, there is no point in trying to be refined about the calculations.

Because of the "energy crisis" the fuel numbers are very easy to get. You can use the *Statistical Abstract* or the informational pamphlets that several oil companies put out every few years, or the reports of the many study groups issued in recent years. There is no substantial disagreement about the basic facts of the past and the present, only about the future.

Until a few years ago almost everybody said that oil (and therefore energy) prices were going to keep on going up.* In 1985 and 1986 crude oil

---

* In addition we imported $6 billion more of processed minerals than we exported ($25 billion compared to $19 billion).

* I and others at Hudson Institute, and a few others, said that prices were more likely to go down than up. (For example, William Brown said so in an article in *Fortune* in May 1980, and he and I did in an article in the *Wall Street Journal* on February 8, 1980.) But most of the industry experts, almost all of the companies, the U.S. government, the World Bank and other international institutions, and most academics, projected constantly rising fuel prices—although there were a few who stood against the crowd.

prices fell by about 50%. (In fact they fell further, but then they rose and seem to have stabilized in the range of 50% of the levels of the early 80s.) Now the academic/industry/government consensus is again that prices will rise. First it was said that this would happen in the 1990s — now some are saying in the late 1990s, and some are saying after the year 2,000. I don't think the current consensus about higher prices in the future has a better basis than the former consensus which turned out to be expensively wrong. However, nobody can be sure; this time the majority of experts might be correct.

At any rate, Chapter 6 says that in 1980 we spent over five times as much on fuels as we did on all other raw materials except food. You can see how stable my conclusions are from the fact that even though the world crude oil price has been cut in half since 1984—when oil was taking two thirds of the fuel bill—the overall pattern I talked about stayed the same: the total bill for raw materials is small compared to the economy, and it is still dominated by fuels.

Fluctuations in the real world are much more important than uncertainties in my information, or arguments about the calculations presented. For example, the oil bill shown in Table 6 declining by some $300 per person, a change which is much bigger than the whole of any other item except food.

On energy, I only relied on three numbers: the broad estimate that crude energy costs are about 10% to 15% of total world GNP, the statement of how much solar energy reaches the Earth, and the estimate that after a century of development the cost of getting our energy from the sun—if we had no better source and had to rely increasingly on solar energy—would not be more than four or six times higher, per unit, than the cost of current sources.* The first two numbers come from the data in all the studies and reports on energy; they are not controversial numbers.

But there is no good source for the third number—the estimated upper bound on the longterm cost of solar energy.

It is the answer to a question that no one is asking. And our experience does not produce much direct evidence. Most people in the energy business don't think we will have to rely on solar energy; they think that for most of our needs there will be better sources of energy for the foreseeable future. (I do not disagree.) So nobody has reason to work hard to bring large-scale solar energy costs down to twice what we are now paying for the average unit of energy we buy today—and we can't observe the result of such an effort when it has not been made. If any one were to do a big study of whether there is any danger of serious harm from long term resource scarcity, a major share

---

* I also relied on the judgement that, if energy costs more than doubled, people would find ways to get what they wanted with a reduced use of energy. I gave the conservative estimate that a quadrupling of energy prices would lead eventually to a halving of energy consumption. Experience suggests that the long term decline in consumption of energy would more nearly match the increase in energy prices— rather than being only half as great.

of the effort should be devoted to evaluating this number—the upper bound on longterm solar energy costs.

On the other hand, a more substantial professional study would devote more attention to other alternative sources of energy—and might well come to the conclusion that solar energy costs are not critical because there are other good options. I chose to focus on solar energy for two reasons. The first is that it simplified the book. Why make complicated arguments to show three or four solutions to our need for energy when we only need one? But the main reason is that it seemed to me to be more convincing to present a single solution—even one with uncertainties involved—than it would be to say: Here are four possibilities, each of them is likely to work, so we can be sure that at least one of them will work.

Logically one should feel more confident with several possibilities—but psychologically the presentation of alternatives creates doubt: After all, if one can fail, why can't they all fail?

Some of the detailed numbers on subtle environmental risks are discussed in the references to Chapter 13, but the numbers that justify the basic conclusion—that technology is a friend and not an enemy, and that such risks to life have been declining—are the life expectancy numbers. So long as we keep on living longer, we can be sure that the net of all risks to life is not growing (except possibly the risk of future immense disasters.)

As discussed in End-Table 8, the numbers on low national morale among university-oriented Americans come essentially out of my head. They are there to express an hypothesis, not to provide evidence. I ask you: does your experience confirm that there is segment of our community that looks at things differently than the large majority of Americans and doesn't know how different it is from the rest of the country? Is the behavior of UOA's that you observe consistant with the suggestion that that group has low national morale? Does the metaphor of low national morale make it easier to understand what you hear being said?

There are many points made in passing in the course of the book that are expressed by numbers—not all of which have been supported by references. None of these points is central to the argument of the book. Generally I have tried to limit myself to points that can be made on the basis of the facts that all parties agree are true—and so do not require using truly controversial numbers. But it would be too tedious to demonstrate that for each of the issues where I succeeded in observing this limitation—and doubtless there are some cases where I did not.

Further Reading

Concerning resources and population the far and away best general book is Julian Simon's *The Ultimate Resource*, published by Princeton University Press in 1981. Simon covers the issues discussed in Part II of this book in much greater detail, and provides much more evidence and discussion of the scientific literature. And he combines scholarly evidence with practical observations and common sense. (His earlier book, *The Economics of Population Growth*, also published by Princeton University Press (in 1977), covers much of this material with even more technical detail and analysis.)* And in 1984 Simon and Herman Kahn edited a book by a number of leading experts called *The Resourceful Earth: A Response to Global 2000* (Basil Blackwell, Oxford & N.Y.). *The Resourceful Earth* provides chapters on specific resources like food, water, climate, forests, etc.

The fascinating story of forests in the United States can be found briefly told in "America's forests in the long sweep of history," *Science*, vol. 204, 1168-74.

In the field of economic development Peter Bauer of the London School of Economics has played a role similar to that of Julian Simon in the area of population and resources, but Bauer is probably ten years further along the path to grudging acceptance by the main stream of professionals in the field. He has two advantages in winning acceptance. First Margaret Thatcher made him a lord and he is getting old, second the evidence for what he has been saying about the ways governments and foreign aid hold back economic growth has been so visible and unambiguous that it is almost impossible to ignore. If you want to read more on these issues his books, such as *Dissent on Development* (Weidenfeld & Nicholson, London, 1976, rev.ed.) and *Equality, the Third World, and Economic Delusion* (Harvard University Press, Cambridge, Mass., 1981), and *Reality and Rhetoric* make the issues very clear and provide plenty of evidence of all kinds.

Theodore W. Schultz' book *Investment in People* provides a professional economic discussion of the increasing economic importance of people as we move into a more human world by increasing productivity and accumulating wealth. His earlier book *Transforming Traditional Agriculture* (Yale University Press, New Haven, 1964) discusses the economics of the process of increasing productivity in the agricultural sector. A recent economic analysis of *How the West Grew Rich* was written by N. Rosenberg and L.E. Birdzell, Jr. (Basic Books, N.Y., 1986). George Gilder's book, *Wealth and Poverty* (Basic Books, N.Y., 1981) is a bolder more imaginative discussion of similar issues.

The basic economic description of the passage to a human world is given with a great deal of detail, and interesting discussions of many related issues, in Herman Kahn's *World Economic Development* (Morrow, N.Y. 1979). And a

---

* Some of the professionals whose gospel Simon has punctured with solid data and analysis, and who have been forced to retreat because it was not possible to refute his conclusions, have managed to pin the label of "extremist" or "mere publicist" on Simon—although no professional forum has rejected any of Simon's substantial positions. My advice is that if you want to read more on this subject his book is the best and most thorough and careful one that has been written. He enters the debate with gusto—although the other side has often been nasty and irresponsible—and occasionally he words his points in ways that I think could be improved, but never in my experience in a way intended to mislead or to cover a weakness in his argument.

broader early look at the future, with a good discussion of how it is possible to talk usefully about the future is found in *The Year 2000* which Kahn wrote with Anthony Wiener (MacMillan, N.Y., 1967).

Recently many people have been puncturing the balloon of excessive concern about environmental risks and pollution—at every level from pure scholarship to popular diatribe. Some examples are: *Toxic Terror,* by Elizabeth Whelan (Jameson Books, Ottawa, 1984); *The Apocalyptics—Cancer and the Big Lie,* by Edith Efron (1984); and *The Coercive Utopians: Social Deception by America's Power Players,* by Rael and Jean Isaac (Regnery Gateway, Chicago, 1983). Bernard L. Cohen does a thorough job of presenting the issues relating to nuclear energy in his book *Before It's Too Late* (Plenum, N.Y., 1983).

Mary Douglas and Aaron Wildavsky provide a thorough and imaginative discussion of how societies feel and think about risks of different kinds in *Risk and Culture* (U. of Cal., Berkeley, 1982) and Wildavsky goes on to discuss strategies for dealing with subtle risks in his forthcoming book *Searching for Safety* (Transaction, Rutgers, N.J., 1987) (This is the book referred to in Chapter 13, which in an earlier draft had the title *No Risk Is the Highest Risk of All.*)

There are two very good books that relate to the discussion here about the difference between University-Oriented Americans and the rest of the population: Frank Armbruster's *The Forgotten Americans: A Survey of Values, Believes, and Concerns of the Majority* (Arlington House, New Rochelle, N.,Y., 1972) and Benjamin Wattenberg's *The Real America; A Surprising Examination of the State of the Union* (Doubleday, Garden City, N.Y., 1974). More recently Wattenberg wrote *The Good News Is that the Bad News Is Wrong* (Simon & Schuster, New York, 1985), which reports on many of the facts discussed here, and which also describes how the American public is beginning to rebound from some of the diversions of the 1960s. Related to this is Herbert I. London's book *Why Are They Lying to Our Children* (Stein & Day, N.Y., 1984) which describes the way many of the points discussed in this book are mistaught in our schools—and misreported in text books.

Here are some examples of the scarcity view of the future, including some of the most prominent: Erik P. Eckholm, *Losing Ground: Environmental Stress and World Food Prospects,* Norton, N.Y., 1976; Paul R. Ehrlich, *The Population Bomb,* Ballantine, N.Y., 1968; *The Global 2000 Report to the President: Entering the Twenty-First Century,* a report prepared by the Department of Environmental Quality and the Department of State under the direction of Gerald O. Barney, Penquin, N.Y., 1980; Donella H. and Dennis L. Meadows, et. al., *The Limits to Growth, A Report to the Club of Rome's Project on the Predicament of Mankind,* Universe Books, N.Y., 1972.

E N D N O T E S

1. No, this isn't a typo; I meant "she." Since there are people who are distressed when a masculine pronoun is used to refer to someone who might be either a man or a woman (as above), in this book when it is convenient to use a pronoun that has gender, and the person referred to may be either male or female, I will sometimes use masculine pronouns and sometimes feminine. If someone finds out which is used more often, please let me know.

2. Some unfortunate consequences of this diversion, and especially of the *Global 2,000 Report* published by the US government in 1980, are discussed in my article "The Myth of Scarcity" in *The Washington Quarterly* for Autumn, 1981.

3. *Pyramids of Sacrifice*, by Peter Berger, is one of the most thoughtful and widely respected discussions of the human costs of economic development. At the beginning of the book Professor Berger presented 26 "theses" about economic growth. These were written some years ago; so I offered the following alternative set of theses to Professor Berger; they are probably more in accord with his current views.

1. Wealth is necessary for many good things.
2. Wealth requires increased productivity.
3. Increased productivity requires change.
4. Change requires pain. (Maybe faster growth requires more pain—but Japan?)
5. As a practical matter it is unthinkable that a nation not modernize eventually. (Therefore change and pain are inevitable.)

6. Modernization and wealth bring their own forms of pain and problems (even apart from that required to achieve wealth).

7. Slower growth means more poverty and danger.

8. Poverty and danger are pain or bring pain.

9. Capitalism is usually more efficient for producing economic growth (increasing productivity).

10. There is no pure capitalism—the question is the degree of private and market (non-political) decision-making about production.

11. Socialism has some tendency toward totalitarianism or at least toward government power that is excessive from a social/political point of view.

12. Socialism is not necessarily (and maybe not on the average) more egalitarian than capitalism—or more successful in delivering any other human-social virtue.

13. Until now people have found it easier to make attractive socialist slogans and claims. (These provide important psychological benefits to some people.)

14. Welfare protection is compatible with capitalism.

15. Slow growth—to reduce the pain of change—is compatible with capitalism. (But the price for slower growth must be increased pain from poverty.) This assumes that part of economic growth can be sacrificed (paid) for either or both: inefficiency or welfare benefits. The less wealth is sacrificed for stupidity (unintended inefficiency) the more is available for mercy and generosity.

16. Violent social revolution has almost always failed to help anyone.

17. Democracy is good. (But not absolutely.)

18. Totalitarianism is bad. (But not absolutely.)

4. A Necessary Aside about the Meaning of "GNP"

No three letters can so quickly bring a glaze to the eyes of most people as "GNP," the familiar acronym for Gross National Product. (GWP, for Gross *World* Product, adds unfamiliarity and pretentiousness to the offense caused by GNP.) Every time I say "GNP" to anyone except an economist I wince. The fact that I do say it, and that I feel required to write this aside, is evidence of how hard it is to get away from the initials GNP—evidence of how useful they are.

Used loosely, as it will be in this book, GNP is just a handy short name for the total output of a country (or GWP for the whole world). It is a statistic that is supposed to sum up all the goods and services produced and sold in a year. So it is a crude measure of the size of a country's economy, or of its annual income. Similarly the increase in GNP is a measure of economic growth, and the rate of increase of GNP is a measure of how fast a country is growing.

Obviously if you divide a country's GNP by the number of people in the country you get the familiar measure of how rich a country is, GNP per capita (or GWP/cap. for the whole world). And the rate of growth of GNP per capita is the standard measure of how fast a country is developing or growing richer.

You, of course, realize that governments spend a lot of money, so that the whole GNP of a country is not spread among the people of that country. And in all countries the rich get much more than an equal share of the income that is left for individuals to spend or save. Therefore most people's spendable income is much less than the GNP per capita of their country. For example, in the U.S. in 1980 the GNP per capita was $13,000, but the median spendable income was $4,000 (median family disposable income of $14,000, divided by the median family size of 3.5 persons).

When you use the word GNP in talking to economists you get a different problem than eyes glazing over. They know that everyone who has looked at the details of how GNP is calculated agrees that it is a terrible statistic which doesn't mean much of anything in the real world. One example, that is often cited to show how arbitrary a measure of output it is, is that if a man marries his housekeeper the GNP goes down, because she no longer gets wages for cooking and cleaning, although there is no real reduction in the country's output—assuming that she continues to do as much cooking and cleaning. (Of course if the couple spends the saved housekeeping wages for something else, that will "restore" the GNP.)

There are also more significant problems with GNP. It is not decreased if the air gets dirtier or the scenery less beautiful (nor increased if pollution is reduced). Nor is the GNP increased if people have more choice of books or gadgets to buy, or of music to listen to. The number of broken marriages or disturbed children is not counted in GNP. It is clear that GNP is not a good measure of national well-being. Neither is GNP per capita a good measure of individual happiness or quality of life.

On the other hand some of these problems with GNP may not make nearly as much difference in practice as they do theoretically. Economists have tried to make estimates of how much GNP would be changed if it took into account physical factors that affect quality of life, such as pollution. The first attempts to do this seem to indicate that the new calculation doesn't change GNP very much from the regular calculation, and that GNP has been growing faster if you take into account the normally ignored factors that are usually cited as affecting quality of life. But these are very slippery calculations that are dominated by assumptions about which there would be much disagreement.

The fundamental meaninglessness of GNP can be seen when you try to compare the GNP's of two countries to each other, say the GNP of the United States in 1981 with that of France in the same year, or the GNP of the United States in 1981 with that of the United States in 1971. The GNP is meant to be the sum of all the TV sets, tennis lessons, and everything else produced.

But since you can't add tennis lessons and TV sets you have to measure both of them by the amount of money they are sold for, and then add up all the money. But which money? US dollars or French francs? US dollars of 1981 or of 1971? The prices are different for each.

So if you think of our GNP as measuring the great big pile of stuff produced by the United States last year, you find something very peculiar. The size of the pile changes by 50% or 100% depending on how you measure it. Unfortunately going from francs to dollars is not like going from celsius to fahrenheit; adding up TV sets and tennis lessons in dollars is not like adding up ounces, pounds, tons and kilograms.*

The best that can be said for GNP as a measure is that it is "the only game in town." There is no other convenient way to express the size of a country's economy, or to measure whether a country is growing economically, or to compare one country's output with that of another.

For crude contrasts there is no problem. Anyone can describe life in poor societies and life in wealthy societies, and for most countries there is no

* The way in which different price structures affect the measurement of GNP can be seen by the following illustration: Suppose that the United States and France only produce guns and butter. In France butter costs 600 francs/ton and guns cost 6,000 francs/case. In the United States butter costs $200/ton and guns cost $1,000/case. The following table gives the GNP of France and the United States measured in francs and in dollars.

	U.S.			**France**		
<u>Item</u>	<u>Vol. of Prod</u>	<u>$ val.</u>	<u>Franc val.</u>	<u>Vol. of Prod</u>	<u>$ val.</u>	<u>Franc val.</u>
guns	2,000 cases	$2 mil.	F12 mil.	100 cases	$100 th.	F600 th.
butter	5,000 tons	<u>$1 mil.</u>	<u>F3 mil.</u>	10,000 tons	<u>$2 mil.</u>	<u>F6 mil.</u>
GNP		$3 mil	F15 mil.		$2.1 mil.	F6.6 mil.

If you measure both GNP's in dollars, the US GNP is 1.4 times bigger than France's. If you measure both GNP's in francs the US GNP is 2.3 times as big as France's.

Since the US output is worth either $3 million or 15 million francs, $3 million must be worth the same as 15 million francs; they will both buy the same thing, the total US output. So one dollar is equal to 5 francs.

But the French output is worth either $2.1 or 6.6 million francs. So, by the same reasoning, one dollar is worth 3.14 francs, not 5 francs. Which is correct?

But suppose we compare the two countries using the regular exchange rates between francs and dollars. Suppose the exchange rate is four francs to the dollar (roughly between 3.14 and 5). The US GNP, which we would obviously measure in dollars, is $3 million, which according to the exchange rate is 12 million francs. The French GNP, measured in francs, is 6.6 million francs—which is $1.65 million at the exchange rate. Using this method the US GNP is unambiguously 1.8 times as big as France's, but we don't know what the US GNP "really" is ($3 million or $1.65 million) or what the French GNP "really" is (6.6 million or 12 million francs).

These anomolies come from what is known as the index number problem, and there is no way to avoid it. There is no single answer.

trouble knowing whether they are poor or wealthy according to the definition, although there may be some borderline cases. For much of what we are discussing in this book these crude qualitative comparisons are quite good enough. But there are problems in describing the extent to which wealth has spread around the world so far, or in trying to use past experience to estimate how fast various countries will become wealthy.

The conclusion is that although I will talk about GNPs and GWPs from time to time throughout the book, and especially in this chapter, I know it doesn't mean too much, and you should know it too. I will try to use GNP in a way that doesn't produce false understandings—and sometimes I will succeed.

5.

Summary of the Demographic Transition

	Before	During	After
Population	low	growing	high
Death rate	high	declining (first)	low
Birth rate (and fertility)	high	declining (later)	low
Population growth	none, or very little	rapid	none, or very little

6. Some Data on Fertility Rates in Developing Countries

The following is the best data available about fertility rates for the biggest countries for which reasonable data exists.

Fertility Rates
(Net Reproduction Rate is 2.1)

MEXICO

1973-75: 6.2
1977-78: 5.2
1979: 4.8

The values are uncertain, but the direction is clear.

INDONESIA

Late 1960's: 5.8 - 6.4
1975:   5

There definitely is a decline, but the rate is uncertain.

THAILAND		BRAZIL	
1965-69:	6.5	1950:	5.9
1964-76:	4.5-4.9	1960:	6.1
1978:	3.7	1965:	5.9
There definitely is a decline, but the		1968-70:	5.3
rate uncertain.		1971-73:	4.8
		Late 1970s:	4.4

According to the University of Chicago Community and Family Study Center, a different source than that of the data shown above, India's estimated fertility rate declined from 5.3 in 1971-2 to 4.7 in 1976; and China's declined from 4.2 to 3.2 between 1968 and 1975.

7. Longer Term Possibilities for World Population

I haven't attempted to look seriously at a world with more than thirty billion people, and I have never heard of anybody who has. But I would be surprised if the problems of 100 billion people were disastrous or even very uncomfortable, although they probably would require substantial adjustments. (For example, if there were 100 billion people living in present day arrangements most of them would have to live in cities. Ninety billion people living at Manhattan density would take about two million square miles, and the other ten billion, if they lived at the densities of wealthy American suburbs, would take five million square miles. That would leave more than seven-eighths of the Earth's land area for other things, including perhaps a few billion farm families and others living in rural areas.)

Thus, even though thirty billion people won't cause any great scarcity problems, we can't say there is no long run population problem. If, after world population roughly "levels off" at ten to twenty billion, it continues to increase "just a little," say one tenth of one per cent per year, it wouldn't take much more than 1,000 years to get to thirty billion and "only" 2,300 years to reach 100 billion. So when I claim that this book shows there need be no dangerous scarcity problems ever, or for thousands of years, I am cheating a little. I am assuming that world population really does level off at no more than about three times the currently predicted level.

While I think this book provides pretty good assurance for the raw material problem for ten to thirty billion people, perhaps even fifty billion. You have to go to another book, not written yet, if you want to worry about world populations over fifty billion (ten times today's population). Such populations are possible in hundreds or thousands of years.

Incidently there is no reason to despair about being able to make a good life in a world with hundreds of billions of people. Although I guess I would despair about trying to write a convincing book in 1986 to show why we should be confident of that.

8. Let's look at a few numbers to get some perspective about whether the experiments with overcrowded rats tell us anything about human life on Earth.

It is difficult to compare rat population densities to human population densities. The experiments that produced bad effects from overcrowding among rats used densities of one rat per square foot or twenty-five million rats per square mile. Since people are about 100 times bigger than rats, that would suggest that the equivalent human population density—before adjusting for the possible greater sensitivity of people—is about 100 square feet per person or 250,000 people per square mile.

People may be more sensitive to crowding than rats, but on the other hand people may be able to organize their relationships to each other in crowded conditions a little better than rats. So it isn't clear that the rat experiments show much of a problem, although many people think that they give an important insight.

But while scientists use rats for experiments that are hard to apply to human situations, actual people have lived for many years in a wide variety of living conditions and degrees of crowding. The *World Almanac* will show for example that the population density of Manhattan is now down to about 60,000 people per square mile—1.4 million people and twenty-three square miles. But much of Manhattan is taken up by parks, and by industrial and other non-residential land. The population density in the most expensive residential areas, for example along Park Ave or West End Ave, approaches 250,000 per square mile, or even more. (And the daytime population density in parts of the Wall Street or mid-town areas, would be much higher.)

Of course if you look at bigger areas (e.g., ten miles by ten miles) as is relevant for population studies, then existing population densities are much lower, mostly around 3,000 per square mile and in a few areas over 10,000.

Or you can look at how much indoor space people have to live and work in—200 square feet per person in good office buildings, and 200-400 square feet per person in apartments comfortable enough for families with $100,000 year incomes. These modern standards are at least 4 times as spacious as the dwellings and work places of ordinary people before this century, because wealth generally *reduces* "crowding."

Interestingly, most people in areas where land is cheap usually spread themselves over less than twice as much indoor space as people in city centers. And people in small towns, where land is cheap, don't spread themselves much more than people in suburbs with very expensive land.

9. The fact that the Earth is finite is not a good reason
for concern about long-run scarcity.
Many people have noticed that, while we do not know how much oil or iron or other resources there are, we do know that the quantity is not infinite. Everything we take out of the Earth (apart from renewable resources) exists

in limited amounts. When those amounts are gone we will not be able to get any more.

The problem with this apparently incontrovertible logic is that it doesn't have any basis for telling us when we will run out. If "when?" were only a question of a few hundreds or even a few thousands of years many people would say, "what difference does it make?" But finite amounts of resources can be enough for millions of years.

It is a well known fact that the sun is "burning" itself out. Once the sun's internal fuel is consumed, and probably much before, it will change drastically in a way that would be difficult for us to live with. At any rate, when the sun's fuel supply is gone it will cease providing the Earth with the energy we need to survive. And the sun is consuming its finite energy supply in almost unimaginably vast quantities. It sends out every day more energy than we use in a thousand years. In other words the sun is a perfect example of a finite resource, and it is our most important resource.

There is scientific disagreement about how soon the burning up of the sun will become dangerous to the Earth. But there is no reputable scientist who believes that it will be sooner than 1 billion years from next Thursday, which is well beyond the span of our attention.

The sun's limited lifetime demonstrates both the strength and weakness of the idea that finiteness is relevant to human needs. While few will be so bold as to say that we can do without the sun, no one has a reason for believing that any other essential resource is "more finite" than the sun. That is, there is no logic that says we will run out of any other essential material before the sun's demise makes other shortages back-page events.

While I try to "think big" I am not prepared to be concerned about the problem of running out of resources more than a million years from now. (And a billion years is a thousand times further in the future.) If I did manage to discipline myself to give some thought to the problems of the world in the year 1,001,988, I certainly wouldn't let any conclusions about that rarefied subject influence my judgment about policy questions today. Sufficient until 1,000,000 years from now is the evil thereof.

The idea of finiteness tells us that there is not enough material to last forever. But why should we care about that, we aren't making plans for people to be here forever—the next 100,000 years is enough to worry about for now. Anyhow, we already know that we can't go on here forever because of the sun. (And movements of the plates which compose the Earth's crust tell us that we are going to have to cope with radically different geography long before we have to face the sun's failure.) So finiteness tells us nothing relevant to policy, nothing that is useful in any way.

We have to know more than that all resources are finite and that therefore there isn't enough forever. We have to know whether we have a problem in billions of years or millions or thousands. And for that we have to use better intellectual tools than the crude definition of finiteness that frightens so many people.

In brief, essential resources exist in only finite quantities, but there is no reason why that implies dangerous shortages in less than a million years, or even before the sun ceases to supply us with essential energy a billion or more years from now.

10. See Simon, Julian, in *Science*, June 27, 1980, pps. 1431-7. Also subsequent publications by Jack Caldwell.

11. To calculate the share of the value of farmland that belongs to the work that went into improving it, you might take total land value today, and for each type of cropland ask what it would cost at today's prices to change it from the condition it was found in to the condition it is in today.

If you think it is wrong to use today's prices to evaluate the work that was done many years ago to "make" the farmland we are using today, we can ask the question in other ways. For example, "When the men who made our farmland did the job, which cost them more, the land or the work to make it arable?" On average, it is safe to say that the human contribution cost more than the land.

Why take today's value for the land and yesterday's price for the work of making it? Instead you could say, "suppose that Grandpa, who bought Illinois land at $1 an acre and spent all his cash and labor to fix it up, could have worked on something else and bought money funds with the proceeds, how would today's value of his work, if he stored it over the years in money funds, compare with the today's value of the land he actually put his work into?" The answer, on average, would certainly be that the value of the work today is almost as much or more than the value of the land today.

12. Under President Carter the Dept. of Agriculture's Soil Conservation Service put out a National Agricultural Lands Study (NALS) and distributed tens of thousands of free copies of their booklet called *Where Have the Farmlands Gone?* (John Block, President Reagan's Agriculture Secretary, endorsed the booklet too.) This booklet and the materials on which it is based are the source of much of the popular and media misinformation about loss of farmland in the US.

The NALS is full of internal inconsistencies. It defines agricultural land as including deserts, swamps, and mountain ranges. It asserts that the rate of loss of cropland to urban and other destructive uses sharply increased in 1967, making a clean break with all our historical experience, although there is much evidence to the contrary. The NALS conclusion was reached on the basis of unthinking manipulation of the numbers from a single study which was based on data from only a small sample of areas. A fuller analysis of the unreality of the NALS is presented in Julian Simon's article "Are We Losing Our Farmland?" (*The Public Interest*, Spring, 1982).

13. See following excerpts from recent article in *Science*.

"U.S. Farm Dilemma: The Global Bad News Is Wrong"

SCIENCE, Vol. 230   25 October 1985   By Dennis Avery

Running Out of Farm Science?

The pessimists assumed that the major discoveries which could sharply increase world agriculture output had already been made. Superficially, there was some justification for accepting this premise. Productivity gains in the United States and other developed countries had slowed in the late 1970's. However, progress in agricultural science has always been somewhat erratic. Over the longer term agricultural science has always moved forward in tandem with other areas of research.

Ongoing research throughout the world has produced a host of new developments that raise agricultural potential:

The first genetically engineered vaccines. One prevents a major form of malaria, the other is the first fully safe weapon against foot-and-mouth disease.[17] Both vaccines are made from protein coatings of the disease organism, which triggers the immune reaction without risk of infection.

The first viral insecticide, which attacks only the *Heliothis* genus of insects (corn earworm, tomato hornworm, tobacco budworm, soybean podworm).[18] The spores of the virus remain in the field after the worms have been killed, and attack any succeeding generations.

A weed, *Stylosanthes capitata*, turned into a high-yielding forage legume for the huge acid savannas of Latin America.[19] The plant outyields the best previous forage crops in the region by 25 percent.

Isoacids, a new class of feed additives for dairy cows. They increase bacterial action and protein synthesis in bovine stomachs, raising milk production or reducing feed requirements. The product is already being test-marketed.

Embryo transplant operations to boost the genetic impact of top-quality dairy cows. The cows are given fertility drugs to induce multiple ovulation, and the fertilized eggs are then transplanted into the ovaries of average cows for gestation. The supercow can thus produce dozens of calves per year instead of just one. Thousands of such operations are now being performed each year.

Short-season hybrids that have extended corn production 250 miles nearer the earth's poles in the past decade.[20] The grain is now being grown as far north as central Manitoba. East Germany has developed a corn hybrid and plans to shift its hog feed from imported shelled corn to a domestically produced mix of corn and cobs.[21]

The first practical hybrids for wheat, rice, and cotton. Hybrid alfalfa and rape-seed are at the field test stage. Triticale has recently outyielded the best wheats under difficult conditions, such as cool temperatures and acid soils.[22]

A system of agricultural research institutions for the Third World. The Consultative Group on International Agricultural Research (CGIAR) now has 14 research centers attacking farm production constraints. These centers produced the original dwarf wheat and rice varieties that launched the Green Revolution. The International Crops Research Institute for the Semi-Arid Tropics (ICRI-SAT), in Hyderabad, India, produced sorghum for Africa. The International Institute for Tropical Agricultural (IITA), at Ibadan, Nigeria, has produced a cassava that resists several endemic diseases, and thus outyields current varieties by three to five times. New peanut varieties from ICRISAT under test in India and Africa show yields several times greater than those of current varieties. The International Laboratory for Research on Animal Diseases (ILRAD), in Nairobi, Kenya, plans to launch a new vaccination program against Africa's tick-bourne East Coast cattle fever within the next year. The International Center for Tropical Agriculture (CIAT), in Cali, Colombia, has produced varieties that double bean yields in Latin America. The International Maize and Wheat Center (CIMMYT), in Mexico City, has new white corn varieties that could nearly double yields in Central America and West Africa. The International Board for Plant Genetic Resources (IBPGR), in Rome, is preserving species. IITA is experimenting with alley cropping for African food production. The International Livestock Center for Africa (ILCA), in Ethiopia, is designing new farming systems that could sharply increase food production in Ethiopia's famine-wracked highlands. The latest miracle rice from the International Rice Research Institute (IRRI), in the Philippines, needs only two-thirds as much nitrogen and one-tenth as much pest protection as previous high-yielding varieties.

Biotechnology, which may ultimately add more to farm productivity than any other development. Biotechnology has already produced the foot-and-mouth disease vaccine and high-fructose corn syrup. In the offing are such possibilities as ammonia-producing soil bacteria that farmers can plant to fertilize their crops, the first plant protein that is nutritionally complete for humans, crops with more built-in drought and pest resistance, and animals with better fat-to-lean ratios.

A Systems Break?

With productivity trends now so strongly positive, pessimistic arguments center on the possibility of "systems breaks"—sudden, sharp changes in external variables that affect agricultural success. In fact, however, high-technology farming has demonstrated tremendous capacity to adjust to sharp economic and environmental changes. It successfully overcame the oil crisis and its attendant escalation in fertilizer prices. It has surmounted the banning of the early persistant pesticides and their broad side-effects, such as the buildup of insect resistance.

Irrigation helps to drought-proof India and Bangladesh. Sudan's new sorghum seeds, in a year so dry that local varieties failed completely, yielded more than the local varieties do in a good year. Dams and drainage cut flood risks and convert swamps to cropland where necessary.

Technology can also broaden the range of production possibilities: Florida's most frost-prone citrus groves are going out of production; imports of frozen juice from Brazil now fill the gap when Florida's crop is hit, and the high prices that used to make the frost risk worthwhile no longer occur.

Neither drought in the Corn Belt nor massive crop failure in the Soviet Union nor the most severe drought in Africa's modern history have produced actual shortages of food in the world (although there have been regional shortages, complicated by transportation difficulties). Most significant, high-technology agriculture is producing more food per capita nearly everywhere in the world, despite the most rapid rates of growth in population and food demand in history.

High-technology agriculture could probably even take a significant degree of change in global climate in stride. Farmers already successfully cope with annual and seasonal weather variability that has far more impact on crop production than would even a major global cooling or warming trend. Any climatic change in the foreseeable future is likely to have only a moderate net effect on world cereal production, with some countries being helped and other hurt, but with the world retaining ample productive capability.[23] Moreover, past changes in world climate have come over periods of centuries—ample time for breeding programs to adapt plants and animals to the new conditions. (There is no solid evidence that a global climatic change is taking place. Meteorologists say that, while overgrazing and deforestation play a part in the drought cycle of the Sahel, the broader African drought of 1983 and 1984 was too large to have been produced by human activities on the continent; rather, the drought was caused by severe Southern Oscillation, a periodic global weather phenomenon that has often produced African droughts in the past.)

17. *U.S. Dept. Agric. Newsmakers* (September 1981), p.2.

18. R. Enlow, *Agric. Res.* 32 (No. 5), 12 (January 1984).

19. *CIAT Int.* 3 (No. 1) (June 1984).

20. J. L. Geadelman, personal communication.

21. W. P. Huth, *Grain Feed Annu. Rep. Ger. Democr. Rep.* (11 February 1985), p. 1.

22. "International Maize and Wheat Improvement Center Annual Report, 1984"(CIMMYT, Mexico City, 1985).

23. Research Directorate, "Crop yields and climate change to the year 2000" (National Defense University, Washington, D.C., 1980).

14. An extraordinary fuss has been made about how we are supposedly endangering our future by threatening to destroy a significant fraction of all the living species found on Earth. This overblown concern reflects a misunderstanding about the nature of the biological concept of "species"—see page 186—combined with wild over-estimates of the rate of destruction of forests.

15. Annex to Chapter 10

Lists of Non-Fuel Minerals

In *To Choose a Future* Ridker & Watson of RFF divide the 77 materials with significant commercial value into three groups, as follows. The assessments summarized here were made on the basis of a careful study of how much materials might be used over the next 50 years.

1. Clearly adequate supply.

Supply in the US and in the world is adequate for at least 50 years without further exploration, without technological advance, and without increased price.

Argon	Gem stones	Perlite
Bromine	Graphite	Pumice
Calcium	Gypsum	Quartz crystals
Chlorine	Magnesium	Sand and gravel
Clays	Iodine	Sodium
Corundum and emery	Lithium	Stone
Industrial diamond	Mica	Strontium
Diatomite	Oxygen	Vermiculite
Garnet		

2. Minerals of lesser economic importance.

These minerals (except for the precious metals) are very small parts of the economy. Furthermore they are either very plentiful or easily replaced by something that is very plentiful.

In each case the reasons for regarding the product as not worth discussing are given in *To Choose a Future* or its references.

Asbestos	Flourine
Barium	Talc
Boron	Tantalum
Feldspar	Columbium
Gold and silver	Silicon
Platinum group	

(The precious metals are recyclable and supply is ample.)
Other nonferrous metals:

Arsenic	Radium	Germanium
Radium	Rare earths	Hathium
Bismuth	Scandium	Indium
Cadmium	Selenium	Yttrium
Cesium	Tellurium	Zirconium
Gallium	Thallium	

3. Minerals Which We Need to Look at More Closely

a. Molybdenum, Titanium, Vanadium

Presently known reserves and prospective reserves enough at least until 2100; United States self-sufficient.

b. Chromium, Potash, Phosphate Rock, and Manganese

Presently known reserves and prospective reserves enough at least until 2100; United States must import.

c. Nickel, Copper, and Cobalt

Undersea nodules may be necessary to hold prices at current levels. If nodules are counted, current prospective reserves are enough at least until 2100.

d. Iron and Aluminum

Plenty of sources available for a very long time at or near current prices. Although it is likely that at some point there will be a switch away from bauxite as the raw material for aluminum. These elements make up a large share of the Earth's crust, and convenient forms are very common. They are the key metallic raw materials we can count on for the very long run. Between them they can perform the functions of a large share of all metals now used.

e. Lead

No problem because resources are probably very large although not yet demonstrated, and because good substitutes are available.

f. Sulphur

No problem. Likely to become a glut on the market.

g. Tin

Current judgments about the amount of tin available suggest that the price may rise within the next 50 years because of lack of resources, but good economical substitutes are available, especially aluminum.

Tin is a candidate for becoming the first major mineral to be largely knocked out of major use by rising prices due to exhaustion of cheap resources. (The world now spends about $2-3 billion a year for tin.)

h. Tungsten

Current judgments about the amount of tungsten available suggest that the price may have to guadruple to bring supply and demand into balance.

Currently the world spends well under $1 billion a year for tungsten. If this quadrupled it would cost about a hundredth of 1% of GWP.

i. Zinc

Modest price increases may be necessary to bring supply and demand into balance in the foreseeable future.

Since *To Choose a Future* focused only on the next 50 years the conclusions it reached about particular materials cannot generally be extended to the much longer time we are concerned with in this book. Their listing is shown here only for illustrative purposes and to give a full list of all the currently "significant" non-fuel minerals now being used.

16. Of course one could reasonably argue that deliberate programs have produced much more harm than mistakes—just taking into account such 20th century operatives as Hitler, Stalin, and the Khmer Rouge.

Of course, some people argue that some of Hitler's early successes were partly due to the actions of "anti-war" movements during the 20s and 30s. Churchill proposed calling World War II "the unnecessary war." So one could view that war as partly the result of the unintended (accidental) effects of unsuccessful attempts to do good. (Similarly for the intentional evil done by Stalin and the Khmer Rouge.) Whether or not such a view is correct, it reminds us that harmful unintended by-products may be produced not only by builders and business executives, but also by people pursuing noble goals.

17. A major nuclear war in the 1980's could also, in addition to its other horrors, produce a substantial set-back to the passage to a human world. Later a great increase in the destructiveness of the weapons available might make the harm that a war could do to the world even greater. On the other hand, the evolution of military technology and strategy might reduce the potential and/or the likely destructiveness of available weaponry. (During the last 20 years the total explosive power of all U.S. nuclear weapons was reduced by more than half as the result of the evolution of military technology.)

With the weapons of the 1980's the worst nuclear war that seems physically possible would kill up to one quarter of all the people of the world in a short time, including all the population of the U.S. and the Soviet Union and all the population of cities with over a million people. It might also destroy about one half of all the capital of the world.

Such a war would also have secondary and indirect effects lasting thousands of years. While there is great technical uncertainty about the exact nature and extent of such indirect and secondary effects, there is a good basis for confidence that they would not be as horrible or as harmful as the direct losses within the first month. That is, the death of over a billion people and the destruction of half of the wealth of the world would be much worse than all of the secondary and indirect effects together. (The "nuclear winter hypothesis" looked for a while as if it might make the secondary effects of a nuclear war worse than the immediate losses. But subsequent scientific analysis has cast great doubts on several of the key estimates used in making the original hypothesis. It now appears that if the hypothesis is valid at all it is only in much weakened form—a possible "nuclear cold spell.")

Jonathan Schell and others have asserted that a nuclear war today could destroy all human life or civilization, and they seem to have calculations or evidence to support such an assertion. But in fact—apart from the nuclear winter hypothesis, which came later—no plausible theory consistent with current scientific knowledge has been provided which suggests how such complete destruction would be possible. (Of course it is possible for all human beings to be killed even without nuclear weapons—with knives—as the population of Masada was when faced with enslavement by the Romans in the year 73 C.E. If everybody could be brought together in groups, nuclear weapons would make a Masada-like ending easier than with knives, but not more plausible.)

Unfortunately, the fact that no one has been able to discover a particular way in which a nuclear war is likely to kill everyone or destroy civilization does not constitute proof that it is impossible—but it does mean that destruction on such a scale is very unlikely.

Since straight-forward estimates, without much exaggeration, and without speculative scientific hypotheses, are that a nuclear war could kill about a billion people, almost a quarter of all the people who are alive, it is hard for me to understand why people would want to exaggerate the danger. Avoiding a billion deaths is a big enough goal to give me ample motivation to avoid nuclear war. I can't imagine how anyone could be so extraordinarily lacking in human feeling as to say "only one quarter of the world's population—that's not enough to deter people, we need to up the ante."

In other writings I have presented my views of how our defense strategies, weapon production programs, and arms control policies could be changed in a way that would greatly reduce the number of people likely to be killed in a nuclear war and also reduce the likelihood of such a war starting. (*Beyond Containment*, A. Wildavsky, ed., ICS Press, San Francisco, 1983, p. 169 et. seq.) This is not the place to consider the probability of nuclear war and how to reduce it. But perhaps this discussion of the conventional wisdom about the inevitability of scarcity and pollution will lead readers to think about the possibility that conventional wisdom about what should be done to avoid nuclear war, and about the possibility of reducing damages if there is a nuclear war, also needs to be reexamined.

In the discussion of natural disasters above we have briefly considered the potential effect on the passage to a human world of disasters that destroy half of all wealth without killing any people. That discussion also applies, with some differences, to the effects of possible major nuclear wars—except that in a major nuclear war the principal harm would be the loss of human life.

Strange as it seems, if one is conjecturing about the population or wealth of the world 200 years from now, it is not necessary, or even helpful, to know whether or not there is a major nuclear war in the 1980's. There is no basis for judging whether the largest nuclear war that seems possible in the 1980's would, if it happened, make the population or wealth of the world 200 years later larger or smaller. The decisive question for determining the population and wealth of the world in 200 years is almost certainly the question of what rates of growth of population and of wealth the people of the world choose by their actions. That is, they will almost certainly have the power to choose either much larger or much smaller population and wealth, regardless of whether they have to start from a smaller base because of a major nuclear war. Needless to say, this is not a reason to be willing to have a nuclear war.

These issues are so sensitive that I should emphasize again the fact that a substantial nuclear war would be a horrible tragedy—even though it would not greatly change the time required to complete the passage to a human world.

When I point out that the apocalyptic assertions of Schell and others do not have any basis in current knowledge—or provide a much lower estimate of the worst case effects of a nuclear war—I do not in any way imply that we can afford to risk a nuclear war, much less that we should start one.

In fact, for many years I have argued that the U.S. should move away from the use it has been making of nuclear weapons in its foreign policy since World War II. ("A Non-Utopian, Non-Nuclear Future World" in *Arms Control & Disarmament*, 1968, vol. 1, Pergamon Press, London.) But I believe that we should use the most realistic estimates we can make when we speak of the dangers of nuclear war. And I also believe that the apocalyptic estimates, often used by those who claim to be pursuing peace, increase the likelihood of nuclear war and increase the expected harm if it occurs—in addition to being wrong and incompetent.

18. This analysis helps deal with many questions that standard industrial psychology studies have had trouble with:

In a company, absenteeism, for example, may reflect the morale in the workers' small groups, but what the employees say to people about the company, and whether they buy stock in it or buy its products, may be more influenced by their morale about the whole company. One can go up while the other goes down. (Which kinds of behavior are influenced by the small group morale and which by the overall organizational morale probably depends on exactly the factors you would expect if you look at it carefully, in specific terms, from the point of view of the people concerned, and then try to predict their behavior on the basis of sympathy and respect for them as people.)

So peoples' morale about their particular office depends on that office, and their morale about the larger organization depends on what is happening with the larger organization. And peoples' morale about their particular office affects primarily their behavior in that setting, and their morale about the overall organization affects their thinking and action about the overall organization. And often the two are woven together in all kinds of subtle ways. How else could it be? The individuals have a number of different sets of relationships, with their various smaller groups and with the overall organization, and therefore several different morales, and the two influence each other but each has to be thought about separately as well as together. And each individual in the organization has his own pattern of morales, so neither the organization nor any of its parts have a single morale.

That is only a little complicated, and except when they are trying to be "scientific" people automatically understand that kind of complication and respond consistently.

19. Does it make sense to continue thinking about economic development in terms of the same 125 or 175 countries that exist today? Will the world still be divided into separate nations a century or two from now? Of course we can't predict in detail, but let's see how much of what we need to know is inherent in the situation.

In principle, the basic organization of the world could change in either of two directions. Conceivably there might be fewer countries, even one "world government." But in view of the sticking power of nations during the last century, it seems quite unlikely that a century from now there will be a single world government—that is, one that is not composed of nations with separate economies. Of course nations might also disappear into regional groupings— such as Europe, the Arab world, Sub-Saharan Africa, or Latin America. But this doesn't seem too likely. And even if it happens it wouldn't invalidate much of what is said here. Each of these relatively plausible units is composed of nations that are at similar levels of wealth. The differences within a country like Italy for example, are not much smaller than the differences between the different countries of Europe.

Perhaps a more likely possibliity is for the world to move in the opposite direction—with nations splitting into smaller, more homogeneous, perhaps more manageable units. Certainly lines of division are visible in many if not most countries of the world.*

If a country's size strongly affected its ability to develop, we would have to pay a lot of attention to the possibility of countries changing size (by combining or splitting). But experience has shown that both big countries and little countries can develop at reasonable speeds. Two of the greatest successes— Taiwan and Singapore—are quite small; and Japan, which is a large country, has also been very successful.

What really matters is freedom of trade. A small country can do very well if a good share of the world is open to trade. Changes in trade restrictions— formal and informal—are likely to be more important than changes in the number of countries. The key thing for the prospects of economic development is the size of the markets available to a company that has a new product or a new way of doing things. Where a large market exists economies of scale are possible, and the benefits of new efficiencies are rapidly transmitted to a

---

* Among the countries with obvious lines of possible division are the United Kingdom, Belgium, Spain, Nigeria, India, and the Soviet Union—and many others. On the other hand, Japan and Korea are each unusually homogeneous countries.

large number of consumers. As a practical matter, national boundaries are not the major restrictions on the size of the market available to producers (although they are very important). Cultural, psychological, and traditional factors inhibiting the flow of goods, services, and ideas, are more important than tariffs and trade restrictions. Many of these traditional inhibitions are weakening as countries all over the world increasingly enter the modern business scene. Psychologically, people are increasingly speaking the same language when they think about doing business together—even if they have to use interpreters.

The best bet is that, during the next eighty or hundred years, business will be more affected by changes in trade restrictions, and by changes in cultural patterns that tend to open markets, than it will by changes in the number of countries in the world.

E N D - T A B L E S

End-Table 1. Already Wealthy Countries

Notes for End-Tables 1-4 are at end of End-Table 4.

Country	Pop'n (mil.)	Est'd Stable Pop'n	GNP/ cap.	Growth Rate '84-'65	Life Expec.	Inf. Mort.	GNP (bil.)
A. Very Wealthy Countries							
United Arab Emirates	1	3	$22,000		72	36	$ 20
Kuwait	2	6	$17,000	− .1	72	22	$ 35
Switzerland	6	6	$16,000	1.4	77	8	$ 100
United States	237	288	$15,000	1.7	76	11	$3,600
Norway	4	4	$14,000	3.3	77	8	$ 55
Canada	25	31	$13,000	2.4	76	9	$ 350
Sweden	8	8	$12,000	1.8	77	7	$ 100
Australia	16	22	$12,000	1.7	76	9	$ 190
Denmark	5	5	$11,000	1.8	75	8	$ 55
Germany (West)	61	52	$11,000	2.7	75	10	$ 680
Finland	5	5	$11,000	3.3	75	6	$ 55
Japan	120	129	$10,500	4.7	77	6	$1,300
France	55	64	$10,000	3.0	77	9	$ 550
Netherlands	14	15	$ 9,500	2.1	77	8	$ 150
Austria	8	7	$ 9,000	3.6	73	11	$ 75
Belgium	10	9	$ 8,500	3.0	75	11	$ 100
United Kingdom	56	59	$ 8,500	1.6	74	10	$ 500
New Zealand	3	4	$ 7,500	1.4	74	12	$ 25
Singapore	3	3	$ 7,500	7.8	72	10	$ 20
Germany (East)	17	17	$ 7,000	4.7	71	11	$ 120
Trinidad & Tobago	1	2	$ 7,000	2.6	69	22	$ 7
Italy	57	57	$ 6,500	2.7	77	12	$ 360
Hong Kong	5	7	$ 6,500	6.2	76	10	$ 30
Very Wealthy	**719**	**803**	**$12,000**	**2.7**	**76**	**10**	**$8,400**
Czechoslovakia	16	19	$ 5,800	4.0	70	15	$ 90
Israel	4	8	$ 5,100	2.7	75	14	$ 20
USSR	275	375	$ 5,000	3.8	67	27	$1,400
Ireland	4	6	$ 5,000	2.4	73	10	$ 20
Spain	39	49	$ 4,400	2.7	77	10	$ 170
Bulgaria	9	10	$ 4,100	5.0	71	17	$ 40
Greece	10	12	$ 3,800	3.8	75	16	$ 40
Venezuela	17	39	$ 3,400	.9	69	38	$ 60
Taiwan	19	28	$ 3,100	7.0	72	20	$ 60
Middle Class Wealthy	**393**	**546**	**$ 4,800**	**3.7**	**69**	**24**	**$1,900**
All Wealthy Countries	**1,100**	**1,300**	**$ 9,000**	**3.0**	**74**	**15**	**$10,000**

End–Table 2. Nearly Wealthy Countries

Country	Pop'n (mil.)	Est'd Stable Pop'n	GNP/ cap.	Growth Rate '84-'65	Life Expec.	Inf. Mort.	GNP (bil.)
Nearly Wealthy Countries							
Saudi Arabia	8	40	$14,600	5.9	62	61	$ 120
Libya	4	17	$ 8,500	−1.1	59	91	$ 30
Oman	1	5	$ 6,500	6.1	53	110	$ 7
Iraq	15	71	$ 3,000	5.3	56	78	$ 45
Iran	44	162	$ 2,700	3.0	61	112	$ 120
Yugoslavia	23	29	$ 2,600	5.4	70	33	$ 60
Algeria	21	81	$ 2,400	3.6	60	82	$ 50
Romania	23	29	$ 2,400	7.0	71	25	$ 55
S. Africa	32	94	$ 2,300	1.4	54	79	$ 75
Argentina	30	53	$ 2,200	.3	70	34	$ 65
Hungary	11	11	$ 2,100	6.2	70	19	$ 25
Poland	37	49	$ 2,100	1.5	71	19	$ 80
Korea (South)	40	66	$ 2,100	6.6	68	28	$ 85
Mexico	77	196	$ 2,000	2.9	66	51	$ 150
Malaysia	15	33	$ 2,000	4.5	69	28	$ 30
Panama	2	4	$ 2,000	2.6	71	25	$ 4
Uruguay	3	4	$ 2,000	1.8	73	29	$ 6
Portugal	10	13	$ 2,000	3.5	74	19	$ 20
Brazil	133	293	$ 1,700	4.6	64	68	$ 230
Chile	12	20	$ 1,700	− .1	70	22	$ 20
Syria	10	39	$ 1,600	4.5	63	55	$ 15
Jordan	3	17	$ 1,600	4.8	64	50	$ 5
Total: Nearly Wealthy	**553**	**1326**	**$ 2,300**	**3.7**	**65**	**55**	**$1,300**

End–Table 3. Countries Where Economic Growth Is Well Begun

Country	Pop'n (mil.)	Est'd Stable Pop'n	GNP/ cap.	Growth Rate '65-'84	Life Expec.	Inf. Mort.	GNP (bil.)
Well Begun Countries							
Colombia	28	59	$1,400	3.0	65	48	$ 40
Cuba	10	14	$1,400		75*	16*	$ 15
Lebanon	3	6	$1,350		68	41	$ 4
Korea (North)	20	46	$1,300	3.0	68	28	$ 25
Tunisia	7	18	$1,300	4.4	62	79	9
Paraguay	3	8	$1,200	4.4	66	44	$ 4
Costa Rica	3	5	$1,200	1.6	73	19	$ 4
Guatamala	8	27	$1,200	2.0	60	66	$ 10
Turkey	48	109	$1,200	2.9	64	86	$ 60
Ecuador	9	26	$1,200	3.8	65	67	$ 10
Jamaica	2	4	$1,200	− .4	73	20	$ 3
Congo PR	2	9	$1,100	3.7	57	78	$ 2
Mauritius	1	2	$1,100	2.7	66	26	$ 1
Peru	18	46	$1,000	− .1	59	95	$ 20
Dominican Rep.	6	15	$1,000	3.2	64	71	$ 6
Botswana	1	5	$ 960	8.4	58	72	$ 1
Albania	3	6	$ 950		70	43	$ 3
Mongolia	2	6	$ 950		63	50	$ 2
Nicaragua	3	12	$ 860	−1.5	57	70	$ 3
Thailand	50	101	$ 860	4.2	64	44	$ 45
Cameroon	10	51	$ 800	2.9	54	92	$ 8
Zimbabwe	8	33	$ 760	1.5	57	77	$ 6
Nigeria	96	528	$ 730	2.8	50	110	$ 70
Egypt	46	126	$ 720	4.3	60	94	$ 35
Papua New Guinea	3	11	$ 710	.6	52	69	$ 2
El Salvador	5	16	$ 710	− .6	65	66	$ 3
Honduras	4	15	$ 700	.5	61	77	$ 3
Morocco	21	66	$ 670	2.8	59	91	$ 15
Philippines	53	137	$ 660	2.6	63	49	$ 35
Ivory Coast	10	46	$ 610	.2	52	106	$ 6
Total:							
Well Begun	**482**	**1553**	**$ 910**	**2.8**	**60**	**75**	**$400**

*But for other estimates see N. Eberstadt, "Literacy and Health: The Cuban 'Model,'" *Wall Street Journal*, Dec. 10, 1984.

End–Table 4. Barely Started Countries

Country	Pop'n (mil.)	Est'd Stable Pop'n	GNP/ cap.	Growth Rate '84-'65	Life Expec.	Inf. Mort.	GNP (bil.)
Group A: India and China							
India	750	1700	$260	1.6	56	90	$200
China	1000	1600	$310	4.5	69	36	$300
Group B: Growing Nicely							
Yemen (North)	8	39	$550	5.9	45	155	$ 4
Indonesia	159	361	$540	4.9	55	97	$ 90
Lesotho	2	6	$530	5.9	54	107	$ 1
Pakistan	92	353	$380	2.5	51	116	$ 35
Sri Lanka	16	32	$360	2.9	70	37	$ 6
Kenya	20	111	$310	2.1	54	92	$ 6
Ruanda	6	40	$280	2.3	47	128	$ 2
Uganda	15	84	$230	2.9	51	110	$ 3
Burundi	5	24	$220	1.9	48	120	$ 1
Malawi	7	38	$180	1.7	45	158	$ 1
Burma	36	87	$180	2.3	58	67	$ 6
Total Gps A&B Growing Nicely	**2100**	**4500**	**$320**	**3.1**	**61**	**65**	**$650**

Country	Pop'n (mil.)	Est'd Stable Pop'n	GNP/ cap.	Growth Rate '84-'65	Life Expec.	Inf. Mort.	GNP (bil.)
Group C: Problems							
Yemen (South)	2	7	$550		47	146	$ 1
Bolivia	6	22	$540	.2	53	118	$ 3
Liberia	2	11	$470	.5	50	128	$ 1
Zambia	6	35	$470	−1.3	52	85	$ 3
Angola	9	43	$470		42	144	$ 4
Mauritania	2	8	$450	.3	46	133	$ 1
Senegal	6	30	$380	− .5	46	138	$ 2
Sudan	21	101	$360	1.2	48	113	$ 8
Ghana	12	54	$350	−1.9	53	95	$ 4
Guinea	6	24	$330	1.1	38	176	$ 2
Haiti	5	14	$320	1.0	55	124	$ 2
Sierra Leone	4	17	$310	.6	38	176	$ 1
Benin	4	20	$270	1.0	49	116	$ 1
Central Afr. Rep.	3	12	$260	− .1	49	138	$ 1
Madagascar	10	48	$260	−1.6	52	110	$ 3
Somalia	5	30	$260		46	153	$ 1
Togo	3	16	$250	.5	51	98	$ 1
Tanzania	22	123	$210	.6	52	111	$ 5
Mozambique	13	67	$200		46	125	$ 3
Niger	6	36	$190	−1.3	43	142	$ 1
Vietnam	60	167	$180		65	50	$10
Burkina Faso	7	31	$160	1.2	45	146	$ 1
Nepal	16	74	$160	.2	47	135	$ 3
Afghanistan	15	60	$150		37	200	$ 2
Mali	7	36	$140	1.1	46	176	$ 1
Zaire	30	130	$140	−1.16	51	103	$ 4
Laos	4	17	$140		45	153	$ 1
Kampuchea	7	30	$140		50	75	$ 1
Bangladesh	98	310	$130	.6	50	124	$15
Chad	5	22	$120	−1.8	44	139	$ 1
Ethiopia	42	204	$100		44	172	$ 4
Bhutan	1	4	$ 80	− .1	44	135	$ 0
Total: Problems	**438**	**1803**	**$200**	**.1**	**50**	**120**	**$100**

SUMMARY Barely Started Countries

Group A: India and China

India	750	1700	$300	1.6	56	90	$200
China	1000	1600	$300	4.5	69	36	$300
Gp. B: Growing	400	1200	$400	3.6	54	100	$150
Gp. C: Problems	400	1800	$200	.1	50	120	$100
Total Gp 4:	**2,600**	**6,300**	**$300**	**2.7**	**59**	**75**	**$750**

SUMMARY of Tables 1-4
Sums or Weighted Averages

Very Wealthy	700	800	$11,700	2.7	76	10	$ 8,400
Middle Class Wealth	400	500	$4,800	3.7	69	24	$ 1,900
Nearly Wealthy	600	1300	$2,300	3.6	64	61	$ 1,300
Well Begun	500	1600	$ 900	2.8	60	75	$ 400
India	700	1700	$ 300	1.6	56	90	$ 200
China	1000	1600	$ 300	4.5	69	36	$ 300
Poor But Growing	400	1200	$ 400	3.6	54	100	$ 150
Problems	400	1800	$ 200	.1	50	120	$ 100
World Total	**4700**	**10000**	**$2,700**	**3.0**	**64**		**58 $13,000**
Total Already Wealthy	**1100**	**1300**	**$9,200**	**3.0**	**73**		**15 $10,000**
Total Not Yet Wealthy	**3600**	**9000**	**$ 700**	**2.9**	**61**		**72 $ 2,500**
Total World	**4700**	**10000**	**$2,700**	**3.0**	**64**		**58 $13,000**

Notes for End-Tables 1-4

This information comes from *World Development Report 1986* by the World Bank.

While many of the numbers in the table are controversial or uncertain, and have other problems as well, I don't think the weaknesses of the numbers reduce their validity for the limited purposes they are used for in this book. But the reader is warned again of the false precision of such numbers. Accuracy is uncertain, but often a smaller problem than a lack of meaningfulness of any precision greater than say 25%.

In a few cases I have inserted estimates of my own not included in the World Bank tables; derived by interpolation. For countries that are too small to noticeably affect the totals I haven't bothered to fill in the blanks left by the Bank.

The World Bank report says that these tables include all countries with 1980 population over 1 million. There are thirty-four UN/World Bank members with smaller populations which together total about 12.5 million people (about one-fourth of 1% of the population included in the table).

Explanation of Headings
Estimated Stable Population
This is the number given in Table 17 of the Bank report as the hypothetical size of the stationary population of each country. It says how large the

population of that country will be when it stops growing—if the assumptions used in the Bank's calculations are correct. It is calculated by assuming that the experience of declining death rates and declining fertility rates will continue in each country until that country's population levels off and has zero growth.

How soon a country reaches zero growth depends mostly on the speed with which death and fertility rates decline and on the age structure of the current population.

Table 17 also gives the estimated year that each country will reach its stationary population. For the United States it is 2030, based on reaching a reproduction rate of one in the year 2000. The last country to reach a stationary population, according to the Bank calculation, is Afghanistan in 2160. All the wealthy and nearly wealthy countries are estimated to reach stationary population before 2100. The last big country to reach stationary population, according to the Table, is Bangladesh in 2135. India gets to a stationary population in 2115, and China forty-five years earlier.

In summary, the Bank calculations suggest that world population growth will have declined very drastically, with all the big countries having reached a reproduction rate of one, by about fifty years from now. If this becomes true world population growth will have essentially stopped by about 130 years from now.

While neither the World Bank or anybody else would put any faith at all in these specific numbers, their calculations represent the general thinking of essentially all population experts today. During the last decade or so this expert consensus has been moving to lower and lower estimates of future population growth in response to the new and better data received over this period.

My personal rough judgement is that it is very likely (perhaps three chances out of four) that in the year 2200 world population will be between eight and twenty billion, and that the world population growth rate at that time will be between –.2% and +.6%. (Doubling in a century means a growth rate of .7%.) I think that it is less than even money that in the year 2200 the world population will be below 11 billion and the population growth rate below .001% as indicated by the World Bank table. But there may be no other precise estimate that is more likely than the Bank's.

GNP/cap.
This is 1984 GNP divided by 1984 population for each country.

Growth Rate '65-'84
This is the growth rate of GNP per capita from 1965 to 1984.

Life Expectancy
This is how many years a baby born in 1984 would live, if the rate at which each age group in the country was dying in 1984 were to continue. (In other words, if in 1984 .5% of five-year-old children died, this calculation assumes that .5% of the babies born in 1984 who reach their fifth birthday will die before their sixth birthday, and similarly for each age.)

In fact, since virtually all death rates are declining, the average baby born in 1984 will almost certainly live longer than the life expectancy shown here.

Infant Mortality
This is the estimated number of babies, out of each one thousand live births in 1980, who died before reaching their first birthday.

End-Table 5: World Bank Estimate of Purchasing Power Parities

The technical notes to the World Bank tables give the following estimate of purchasing power parities for 1975.

These numbers give the estimates made by the Bank of how much more (or in a few cases less) each country's money would buy compared to the official rate.

For example, the number 322 listed opposite India below means that 100 Indian rupees will buy 3.22 times as much in India as you could buy in the United States with the dollars that you would get for 100 rupees at the official exchange rates.

Africa

Kenya	195
Malawi	255
Zambia	149

Asia

India	322
Iran	171
Japan	110
S. Korea	254
Malaysia	198
Pakistan	312
Philippines	251
Sri Lanka	365
Syria	250
Thailand	261

Latin America and the Caribbean

Brazil	158
Colombia	283
Jamaica	123
Mexico	170
Uruguay	217

Europe

Austria	100
Belgium	88
Denmark	79
France	91
W. Germany	88
Yugoslavia	156
Hungary	168
Ireland	114
Italy	112
Luxembourg	91
Netherlands	89
Poland	139
Romania	137
Spain	136
United Kingdom	111

End-Table 6: Notes for Text Table 6: Use of Raw Materials in the U.S. (1980)

FOOD   2,000 lbs.   25¢/lb. $500 per person per year

This roughly represents the weight and price of food raw materials (grain, cattle, etc.) as they are sold by farmers or other primary producers. Many crude approximations were used to put the numbers, for the very different kinds of food raw materials, into a common set of units. But these numbers are accurate enough to make meaningful contrasts with other raw materials. (As discussed in the text and Appendix C, food is included in this list of raw materials because it is conventional to do so; there is a good case for listing most food raw materials, and especially animal food products like meat and dairy foods, as semi-finished products, rather than raw materials.)

FUELS   16,000 lbs.   6¢/lb. $950 per person per year
composed of:

OIL   6,000 lbs.   10¢/lb. $600 per person per year

6,000 pounds is about twenty barrels or 800 gallons, and 10¢ a pound is 75¢/gallon or $32/barrel. (Of course the price of oil has come down by about one half since 1984.) The energy value of oil is about six million BTU per barrel or forty million BTU per ton. So this price is equal to $5 per million BTU. The price is the world price (in 1984); most of the oil has a much lower production cost and a moderately lower replacement cost.

COAL   6,000 lbs.   2¢/lb. $120 per person per year

Coal energy values are about twenty-two million BTU per ton. This price is $4/ton or $1.80 per million BTU. It represents a rough average of production costs or prices at the mine head. This is a reasonable way to think of the raw material cost if the mine is not too far from the user.

NATURAL GAS   4,500 lbs.   5¢/lb. $225 per person per year

Gas is usually bought by consumers in units of a thousand cubic feet (KCF)*; 4,500 pounds is 100 KCF. Each KCF produces about one million BTU (1 MBTU) of energy. So this price is equal to $2.25 per million BTU. Partly because of the regulatory history, production costs (and well-head prices) in the United States range from perhaps 20¢ to $6 per KCF. Large quantities of new gas will probably cost near the upper end of that range to find, produce, and deliver to the United States (although there will also continue to be large quantities produced at much lower historical costs.) $2.25/KCF is a guess at what the mean is; it is probably meaningful plus or minus one or two dollars.

DRINKING WATER   2,000 lbs.   1¢/lb.   20¢/cap./year

This is about 240 gallons, or three quarts a day. The price is about 80¢ per thousand gallons, which is about the cost of desalinating sea water. Most cities and other suppliers pay much less to get their water. Water delivered to the home often costs somewhat more, because of delivery and other costs. (Another familiar unit, for irrigation water, is the acre/ft. One hundredth of a cent per pound is equal to $260 per acre/ft. Most farmers pay only a small fraction of that.)

METALS   1,000 lbs.   6¢/lb. $60 per person per year

This is half a ton, at $120 per ton. (If silver and gold were excluded the average cost of metals would be only about $100/ton. In other words, the gold and silver we consume each year costs about 20% as much as all the other metals we consume, and weigh virtually nothing—one-half ounce per person.) Iron, which is 90% by weight of the metals we use, is about $30-$40 per ton. Manganese, which is a major metal, is less than $20 per ton. Copper, which is the most widely used expensive metal, costs about $1,500 per ton. Since we use about thirty pounds of copper per person—at 75¢/lb.—the cost of copper represents about one-third of all we spend on metals. In 1980 copper sold for $1.00/lb., but because of several possibilities—big ore sources and substitutability—the cost of copper can never rise above $5/lb. (1980$) for long, and probably cannot rise that far.

WOOD   2,000 lbs.   2¢/lb. $40 per person per year

Most people know wood by the board/foot or the cord. A board/foot is about five pounds (with wide variations). A cord is about two tons or 4,000 pounds. These prices seem so low because most of the value (cost) of wood is added after the logs are harvested from the forest. This price includes transportation to the mill, which averages about half the cost.

MISC. MINERALS   2,000 lbs.   2¢/lb. $40/cap./year

There are about six major non-metallic minerals included here. Prices range from $20—$100/ton, and per capita use varies from 100—700 pounds per year, or $4-$8 per person per year. They are used primarily as fertilizer, construction materials, and also in the chemical industries. They include lime, phosphate, potash, cement, gypsum, and sulfur.

STONE, SAND, & GRAVEL   20,000 lbs.   1¢/lb. $30/cap.

Of course this is ten tons at about $3/ton. Cost to the user is dominated by transportation cost (distance). These products are almost like dirt (fill) which sometimes you have to pay to take away, and which you can often buy for delivery cost, or less.

---

* This is usually written "MCF," but we are using "M" to stand for "million" and so we will use "K" to stand for "thousand."

End-Table 7: Statistical Annex to Chapter 14

Defining the Category of "university-oriented Americans"

In order to estimate the number of university-oriented Americans (UOAs) we will first estimate the percent of the work force in the category UOA and then assume that an equal percent of the total population are in that category.

To estimate the percent of the work force in category UOA we will use an estimated percent for each of the segments of the work force identified in the *Statistical Abstract*, and then reduce the total of these estimates by an estimate of how many are above 60 years old.

It is impossible to over-emphasize the spuriousness of any precision these numbers may seem to have. Since category UOA is at best a loose concept there is no way that I can meaningfully say, for example, that 10% of farmers and farm managers are part of category UOA.

All that these numbers are meant to illustrate is a possible specific composition of about 10% of the labor force in category UOA, and what it would mean in total numbers if category UOA included, for example, all university faculties, 30% of the lawyers, a small share of the accountants, etc.

The category-UOA groups add up to 12% of the whole work force; approximately 10% of the work force is sixty or over. Therefore UOA's are approximately 10% of the work force or 10% of the total population.

In brief, the category of university-oriented Americans includes about half of professional and technical workers, about a quarter of managers and administrators, 10% of clerical and kindred workers, and a few others, and their families.

U.S. Work Force, 1980*

Occupation	#1 millions of people	#2 % of Occup in Cat. UOA (MS est.)	#3 .millions in Cat. UOA (#1 X #2)
Professional, Technical & Kindred			
accountants	1.05	.05	.05
computer specialists	.58	1.00	.58
electrical engineers	.36	.40	.14
other engineers	1.07	.20	.21
lawyers & judges	.55	.30	.16
librarians, etc	.20	1.00	.20
scientists-physicists, chemists and others	.30	1.00	.30
pers'l & lab. rel.	.45	.20	.09
physicians	.43	.50	.22
other medical & dental	.35	.30	.11
registered nurses	1.30	.30	.39
dieticians, therapists, etc	.27	.30	.08
health technicians	.57	.30	.17
religious workers	.31	.50	.16
social scientists	.28	1.00	.28
social & recreation workers	.50	.40	.20
college & university teachers	.55	1.00	.55
other teachers	3.16	.30	.95
engineering & scientific technicians	1.10	.30	.33
technicians n.e.c.	.21	.20	.04
vocational-educational counselors	.18	.50	.09
athletes, etc.	.11	.00	.00
editors & reporters	.18	1.00	.18
other entertainers	.99	1.00	.99
other research	.18	1.00	.18
professional & technical n.e.c.	.39	.50	.20
Sub-total: Professional & Technical	**15.61**	**.45 (calc'd)**	**6.84**

*Data from: U.S. Stat. Abst. Table #675, Employed Persons, 1980

Occupation	#1 millions of people	#2 % of Occup in Cat. UOA (MS est.)	#3 .millions in Cat. UOA (#1 X #2)
Managers & administrators (non-farm)			
(including)			
bank & financial	.64	.30	.19
buyers (wholesale & retail)	.19	.30	.06
health administrators	.21	1.00	.21
building managers-superintendent	.15	.05	.01
office managers n.e.c.	.45	.10	.05
pub. off'ls & admin	.43	.60	.26
purchasing agents & buyers	.24	.05	.01
restaurant, cafeteria & bar	.67	.05	.03
sales managers	.70	.05	.04
school administrators	.43	1.00	.43
managers & administrators n.e.c.	6.81	.20	1.36
Sub-total: Managers & Administrators	**10.92**	**.24 (calc'd)**	**2.64**
Sub-total: Professional & Technical	15.61	.45 (calc'd)	6.84
Sub-total: Managers & Administrators	10.92	.24 (calc'd)	2.64
Sales workers	6.17	.95	.31
Clerical & kindred workers	18.10	.10	1.82
Craft workers	12.53	.00	.00
Operatives & drivers	13.81	.00	.00
Laborers & farm workers	5.67	.00	.00
Farmers & farm managers	1.48	.10	.15
Health service workers	1.90	.10	.19
Service workers except health	11.06	.00	.00
Total	**97.27**	**.12 (calc'd)**	**11.94**

Category UOA groups total 12% of the whole work force.
Approximately 10% of the work force is 60 or over.
Therefore UOA's are approximately 10% of the work force or 10% of the total population.

End-Table 8

Annex to Chapter 17:
Hypothetical Number Manipulation

For anyone who likes to play with hypothetical numbers here is a quantitative expression of the hypothesis in the chapter.

U.S. Population	1946	1986
UOA's	7 million (5%)	24 million (10%)
% low morale	(30-40%)	(67-75%)
Others	133 million	216 million
% low morale	(15-20%)	(20-30%)
Total	**140 million**	**240 million**
Low-morale population		
UOA's	2-3 million	16-18 million
Others	20-27 million	43-65 million
Total low morale	**22-30 million**	**59-83 million**
% of total population	(16-21%)	(25-35%)
High morale population		
UOA's	4-5 million	6-8 million
Others	106-113 million	151-173 million
Total high morale	**110-118 million**	**157-181 million**
Total Population	140 million	240 million

If this hypothesis is at all realistic it is apparent how important it is to distinguish the two groups. If you don't do so, the only change between 1946 and 1986 is an increase in low morale from about 18% of the population to about 30%—which if it were spread evenly would not be very significant.

But when you divide the population into two groups you see that low morale in the UOA category has changed from a minority to a big majority, which produces a dramatic change in the feelings within that group—because within a group minority morale feelings are usually somewhat hidden.

Before there were only two-to-three- million low morale UOA's and they were almost lost in the total population. Now there are 16-18 million low-morale UOA's, and they can live surrounded by their own kind, and not realize that they are different from most people. There are enough of them to staff all the media and other opinion-making jobs in the country.

End-Table 9
Another Diagnostic Test for Low National Morale
(Especially for the Environmental Protection Community)

Column A	Column B
Doomsday View	**Problems-of-Incomplete-Success View**

1. Things are getting worse: —more scarcity —more pollution —more dangers	Overall things are getting better: —less effort needed to extract the raw materials that we need; —less pollution (although poorer countries may go through a phase of increased pollution); —longer lives and better health; —US park area and protected wilderness has expanded greatly during the last generation; —we can better afford to further improve the protection of health, wildlife, and environmental amenities.
2. Modern technology produces great dangers to health.	On balance, modern technology already has—and can be expected to continue to have in the future—great life and health saving benefits; even though new technology also produces dangers, the harm from which must be limited by intelligent and vigorous actions.

3. Since sooner or later we will run out of resources, it is wrong to use disproportionate or unnecessary amounts of energy or raw material.

Current raw material use does not threaten or deprive anyone—now or in the future. Equity questions are the same for resources as for money. Waste is as wrong as ever, but not because of physical scarcity.

4. *Drastic* action to protect health and the environment is necessary because of the dominance of people and organizations who care only for *profit* and don't care about other values except under compulsion.

If everybody were a saint, the problem of finding appropriate rules and practices for environmental and health protection would still be very difficult because of genuine technical uncertainty and conflicting public interests and values. (Although clearly the problem is complicated by the clash of private and special interests—many of which are not financial.)

End-Table 10
Projection Reference Table

Country	1984 Pop. (mil.)	2024 Pop. (mil.)	2064 Pop. (mil.)	1984 GNP per capita	1984 GNP per capita (adjusted)
Europe					
France	55	62	64	$10,000	$10,000
Germany (united)	78	72	69	10,000	10,000
Italy	57	57	57	6,400	6,400
United Kingdom	56	58	59	8,600	8,600
EUR Small Group #1 (9)	85	90	90	12,000	12,000
EUR Small Group #2 (5)	78	88	96	4,600	4,600
EUR Small Group #3 (6)	107	124	137	2,200	2,200
United States	237	282	288	$15,000	$15,000
USSR	275	340	375	$ 5,000	$ 5,000
Pacific & East Asia					
Indonesia	159	298	361	$ 540	$ 800
Japan	120	125	129	11,000	11,000
Korea (united)	60	98	110	1,600	1,600
Philippines	53	100	130	660	860
Thailand	50	85	101	860	1,000
Vietnam	60	124	162	180	400
PAC Small Group #1 (5)	42	61	69	7,000	7,000
PAC Sm Gp#2 (4)	16	31	55	350	460
China (united)	1048	1500	1600	$ 312	$ 625
South & West Asia					
Afghanistan	15	40	58	$ 150	$ 300
Bangladesh	98	200	300	130	260
Burma	36	65	84	180	360
Iran	44	110	156	2,700	2,700
Iraq	15	44	71	3,000	3,000
Nepal	16	46	73	160	320
Pakistan	92	200	340	380	700
Turkey	48	90	108	1,200	1,200
SWAs Small Group #1 (4)	12	35	54	15,000	15,000
SWAs Small Group #2 (3)	17	40	62	2,400	2,424
SWAs Small Group #3 (6)	31	62	90	520	790

2024 GNP per capita	2064 GNP per capita	Actual Growth Rate 1965-1984	Assumed Growth Rate 1984-2064	1984 GNP (bil.)	2024 GNP (bil.)	2064 GNP (bil.)
$20,000	$40,000	3.0	1.8	$ 550	$1,200	$ 2,600
21,000	45,000	3.2	1.9	800	1,700	3,500
16,000	40,000	2.7	2.3	350	900	2,300
16,000	30,000	1.6	1.6	500	900	1,800
23,000	45,000	2.5	1.7	1,000	2,000	4,000
10,000	22,500	3.4	2.0	350	900	2,200
4,500	9,300	3.8	1.8	250	550	1,300
$28,000	$50,000	1.7	1.5	$3,600	$7,900	$14,400
$10,000	$20,000	3.8	1.7	$1,400	$3,300	$ 7,500
$ 1,900	$ 4,700	4.9	2.2	$ 90	$ 600	$ 1,800
28,000	75,000	4.7	2.5	1,300	3,600	9,700
9,500	55,000	5.4	4.5	100	1,000	6,600
1,800	4,000	2.6	1.9	35	180	500
2,000	4,000	4.2	1.7	40	170	400
900	2,000	(1.5)	2.0	10	112	300
17,000	40,000	3.7	2.2	300	1,000	2,800
900	1,900	.1	1.8	6	30	100
$ 1,400	$ 3,000	4.5	2.0	$ 330	$2,000	$ 4,800
$ 590	$ 1,200	(.1)	1.7	$ 2	$ 25	$ 50
600	1,400	.6	2.1	15	145	600
900	2,000	2.3	2.2	6	60	150
4,000	6,000	3.0	1.0	120	450	900
3,300	3,500	5.3	.2	45	150	250
720	1,600	.2	2.0	3	25	50
1,570	3,500	2.5	2.0	35	350	1,400
2,900	7,000	2.9	2.2	60	250	800
14,000	13,700	4.4	(.1)	180	500	750
6,000	13,800	4.1	2.2	40	250	900
1,750	3,900	3.1	2.0	15	100	350

Country	1984 Pop. (mil.)	2024 Pop. (mil.)	2064 Pop. (mil.)	1984 GNP per capita	1984 GNP per capita (adjusted
India	749	1250	1600	$ 260	$ 520
Africa					
Algeria	21	48	76	$ 2,400	$ 2,400
Egypt	46	95	124	720	900
Ethiopia	42	105	190	100	200
Ghana	12	32	50	350	670
Kenya	20	58	104	310	600
Morocco	21	46	62	670	870
Mozambique	13	36	62	200	400
Nigeria	96	290	500	730	900
S. Africa	32	65	90	2,300	2,300
Sudan	21	58	95	360	690
Tanzania	22	70	120	210	420
Uganda	15	40	76	230	460
Zaire	30	80	124	140	280
AFR Small Group #1 (7)	42	106	173	1,500	1,600
AFR Small Group #2 (4)	20	55	90	255	480
AFR Small Group #3 (8 faster)	41	116	201	290	580
AFR Small Group #4 (8 slower)	42	117	202	290	580
Latin America					
Argentina	30	46	52	$ 2,200	$ 2,200
Brazil	133	240	290	1,700	1,700
Colombia	28	50	58	1,400	1,400
Mexico	77	145	190	2,000	2,000
LA Small Group #1 (5)	35	35	54	2,700	2,700
LA Small Group #2 (7)	49	92	131	1,100	1,100
LA Small Group #3 (6)	32	65	93	840	960

2024 GNP per capita	2064 GNP per capita	Actual Growth Rate 1965-1984	Assumed Growth Rate 1984-2064	1984 GNP (bil.)	2024 GNP (bil.)	2064 GNP (bil.)
$ 1,200	$ 3,000	1.6	2.2	$ 200	$1,600	$ 4,800
$ 4,700	$ 9,000	3.6	1.7	$ 50	$ 250	$ 700
1,600	3,000	4.3	1.5	30	150	400
440	1,000	.4	2.0	4	45	200
1,200	2,200	(1.9)	1.5	4	40	100
1,300	2,800	2.1	1.9	6	80	300
2,100	5,000	2.8	2.2	15	100	300
760	1,400	(.2)	1.6	3	25	100
1,600	3,000	2.8	1.5	70	450	1,500
5,600	13,500	1.4	2.2	75	400	1,300
1,400	2,700	1.2	1.7	8	90	300
870	1,800	.6	1.8	5	60	200
710	1,100	2.9	1.1	3	30	100
620	1,400	(1.6)	2.0	4	60	200
3,500	7,800	2.1	2.0	60	380	1,400
1,100	2,400	2.4	2.0	5	60	200
1,300	2,800	(.1)	2.0	10	150	550
700	900	(.1)	.5	10	80	200
$ 5,300	$13,000	.3	2.2	$ 75	$ 250	$ 700
3,800	8,000	4.6	2.0	250	900	2,300
3,000	6,500	3.0	1.9	40	150	400
5,000	12,000	2.9	2.3	150	700	2,300
6,000	12,500	.8	1.9	90	200	600
2,500	5,400	1.7	2.0	50	220	700
1,900	3,700	.0	1.7	30	125	350

End-Table 11
The Members of the Small Country Groups

	Popul. (mil.)	GNP per capita
Europe Small Country Group #1		
Switzerland	6	$16,300
Norway	4	13,900
Canada	25	13,300
Sweden	8	11,900
Denmark	5	11,200
Finland	5	10,800
Netherlands	14	9,500
Austria	8	9,100
Belgium	10	8,600
Total and average	**85**	**$11,564**
Pacific/East Asia Small Country Group #1		
Australia	16	$11,700
New Zealand	3	7,700
Singapore	3	7,300
Hong Kong	5	6,300
Malaysia	15	2,000
Total and average	**42**	**$6,993**
Europe Small Country Group #2		
Czechoslovakia	16	$5,800
Ireland	4	5,000
Spain	39	4,400
Bulgaria	9	4,100
Greece	10	3,800
Total and average	**78**	**$4,606**
Europe Small Country Group #3		
Portugal	10	$2,000
Yugoslavia	23	2,620
Romania	23	2,400
Hungary	11	2,100
Poland	37	2,100
Albania	3	950
Total and average	**107**	**$2,235**
South & West Asia Small Country Group #1		
Saudi Arabia	8	$14,600
Un. Arab Emira	1	21,900
Kuwait	2	16,700
Oman	1	6,500
Total and average	**12**	**$14,883**

	Popul. (mil.)	1984 GNP per capita
South & West Asia Small Country Group #2		
Syria	10	$1,600
Jordan	3	1,600
Israel	4	5,100
Total and average	17	**$2,424**
Latin America Small Country Group #1		
Venezuela	17	$3,400
Panama	2	2,000
Uruguay	3	2,000
Chile	12	1,700
Trinidad & Tob	1	7,200
Total and average	35	**$2,728**
		GNP/capita bef. adjust.
Latin America Small Country Group #2		
Paraguay	3	$1,200
Costa Rica	3	1,200
Guatemala	8	1,200
Ecuador	9	1,200
Jamaica	2	1,200
Peru	18	1,000
Domin. Repub.	6	1,000
Total and average	49	**$1,103**

	Popul. (mil.)	1984 GNP per capita	Adjusted 1984 GNP per capita
Pacific & East Asia Small Country Group #2			
Papua New Guin	3	$710	$800
Mongolia	2	950	950
Kampuchea	7	140	280
Laos	4	140	280
Total and average	16	**$348**	**$461**
Latin America Small Country Group #3			
El Salvador	5	$710	$800
Honduras	4	700	790
Cuba	10	1,400	1,400
Nicaragua	3	860	860
Bolivia	6	540	810
Haiti	5	310	640
Total and average	32	**$837**	**$962**

	Popul. (mil.)	1984 GNP per capita	Adjusted 1984 GNP per capita
Africa Small Country Group #1			
Tunisia	7	$1,300	$1,300
Botswana	1	960	960
Cameroon	10	800	920
Zimbabwe	8	760	880
Ivory Coast	10	610	850
CongoPR	2	1,100	1,100
Libya	4	8,500	8,500
Total and average	**42**	**$1,499**	**$1,608**
South & West Asia Small Country Group #3			
Lebanon	3	$1,350	$1,350
Mauritius	1	1,090	1,090
Yemen (North)	8	550	810
Sri Lanka	16	360	720
Yemen (South)	2	550	810
Bhutan	1	80	160
Total and average	**31**	**$519**	**$792**
Africa Small Country Group #2			
Lesotho	2	$530	$800
Ruanda	6	280	560
Burundi	5	220	440
Malawi	7	180	360
Total and average	**20**	**$255**	**$484**
Africa Small Country Groups #3 & #4 *			
Liberia	2	$470	$770
Zambia	6	470	770
Mauritania	2	450	750
Senegal	6	380	730
Guinea	6	330	660
Sierra Leone	4	310	620
Benin	4	270	540
Central Afr. R.	3	260	520
Madagascar	10	260	520
Togo	3	250	500
Niger	6	190	380
UpVol (BurFs)	7	160	320
Mali	7	140	280
Chad	5	140	280
Angola	9	470	770
Somalia	5	260	520
Total and average	**83**	**$293**	**$546**

*For the projection this group was divided into two groups, without specifying which countries are in each group, and the assumption was made that one group would grow faster than the other.

I N D E X